CONGRESS

EDITED BY BENJAMIN GINSBERG
AND KATHRYN WAGNER HILL

Congress

THE FIRST BRANCH—COMPANION READINGS

Yale
UNIVERSITY PRESS
NEW HAVEN & LONDON

The list of credits at the back of this book constitutes a continuation
of this copyright page.

Yale University Press books may be purchased in quantity for educational,
business, or promotional use. For information, please e-mail
sales.press@yale.edu (U.S. office) or sales@yaleup.co.uk (U.K. office).

Set in Times Roman type by Integrated Publishing Solutions,
Grand Rapids, Michigan.
Printed in the United States of America.

Library of Congress Control Number: 2019955099
ISBN 978-0-300-22063-6 (paperback : alk. paper)

A catalogue record for this book is available from the British Library.

This paper meets the requirements of ANSI/NISO Z39.48-1992
(Permanence of Paper).

CONTENTS

PREFACE

THE ESSAYS IN THIS VOLUME ARE intended to supplement our core text, *Congress: The First Branch.* Each essay amplifies or illustrates a point made in the text, and each is followed by a set of study questions drawn from the essay; the answers can be found in the text itself.

Many of the essays were written especially for this volume, though some have appeared elsewhere in different form. Two chapters—a selection from *The Federalist Papers,* and "The Letters of Pacificus and Helvidius"—are included because the views of James Madison and Alexander Hamilton continue to inform contemporary political discussions.

We hope these essays and articles will contribute to readers' understanding of Congress and respect for the complexities of democratic government. Government by a representative assembly is complex, cumbersome, and frustrating. But without such an assembly, the phrase "popular government" would have little meaning.

CONGRESS

PART ONE

CONGRESS AND ITS HISTORY

The Federalist No. 62: The Senate

Independent Journal, Wednesday, February 27, 1788

Publius [James Madison]

To the People of the State of New York:

HAVING examined the constitution of the House of Representatives, and answered such of the objections against it as seemed to merit notice, I enter next on the examination of the Senate.

The heads into which this member of the government may be considered are:
I. The qualification of senators;
II. The appointment of them by the State legislatures;
III. The equality of representation in the Senate;
IV. The number of senators, and the term for which they are to be elected;
V. The powers vested in the Senate.

I. The qualifications proposed for senators, as distinguished from those of representatives, consist in a more advanced age and a longer period of citizenship. A senator must be thirty years of age at least; as a representative must be twenty-five. And the former must have been a citizen nine years; as seven years are required for the latter. The propriety of these distinctions is explained by the nature of the senatorial trust, which, requiring greater extent of information and stability of character, requires at the same time that the senator should have reached a period of life most likely to supply these advantages; and which, participating immediately in transactions with foreign nations, ought to be exercised by none who are not thoroughly weaned from the prepossessions and habits incident to foreign birth and education. The term of nine years appears to be a prudent mediocrity between a total exclusion of adopted citizens, whose merits and talents may claim a share in the public confidence, and an indiscriminate and hasty admission of them, which might create a channel for foreign influence on the national councils.

II. It is equally unnecessary to dilate on the appointment of senators by the State legislatures. Among the various modes which might have been devised for constituting this branch of the government, that which has been proposed by the convention is probably the most congenial with the public opinion. It is recommended by the double advantage of favoring a select appointment, and of giving to the State governments such an agency in the formation of the federal government as must secure the authority of the former, and may form a convenient link between the two systems.

III. The equality of representation in the Senate is another point, which, being evidently the result of compromise between the opposite pretensions of the large and the small States, does not call for much discussion. If indeed it be right, that among a people thoroughly incorporated into one nation, every district ought to have a PROPORTIONAL share in the government, and that among independent and sovereign States, bound together by a simple league, the parties, however unequal in size, ought to have an EQUAL share in the common councils, it does not appear to be without some reason that in a compound republic, partaking both of the national and federal character, the government ought to be founded on a mixture of the principles of proportional and equal representation. But it is superfluous to try, by the standard of theory, a part of the Constitution which is allowed on all hands to be the result, not of theory, but "of a spirit of amity, and that mutual deference and concession which the peculiarity of our political situation rendered indispensable." A common government, with powers equal to its objects, is called for by the voice, and still more loudly by the political situation, of America. A government founded on principles more consonant to the wishes of the larger States, is not likely to be obtained from the smaller States. The only option, then, for the former, lies between the proposed government and a government still more objectionable. Under this alternative, the advice of prudence must be to embrace the lesser evil; and, instead of indulging a fruitless anticipation of the possible mischiefs which may ensue, to contemplate rather the advantageous consequences which may qualify the sacrifice.

In this spirit it may be remarked, that the equal vote allowed to each State is at once a constitutional recognition of the portion of sovereignty remaining in the individual States, and an instrument for preserving that residuary sovereignty. So far the equality ought to be no less acceptable to the large than to the small States; since they are not less solicitous to guard, by every possible expedient, against an improper consolidation of the States into one simple republic.

Another advantage accruing from this ingredient in the constitution of the Senate is, the additional impediment it must prove against improper acts of legislation. No law or resolution can now be passed without the concurrence, first, of a majority of the people, and then, of a majority of the States. It must be acknowledged that this complicated check on legislation may in some instances be injurious as well as beneficial; and that the peculiar defense which it involves in favor of the smaller States, would be more rational, if any interests common to them, and distinct from those of the other States, would otherwise be exposed to peculiar danger. But as the larger States will always be able, by their power over the supplies, to defeat unreasonable exertions of this prerogative of the lesser States, and as the facility and excess of law-making seem to be the diseases to which our governments are most liable, it is not impossible that this part of the Constitution may be more convenient in practice than it appears to many in contemplation.

IV. The number of senators, and the duration of their appointment, come next to be considered. In order to form an accurate judgment on both of these points, it will be proper to inquire into the purposes which are to be answered by a senate; and in order to ascertain these, it will be necessary to review the inconveniences which a republic must suffer from the want of such an institution.

First. It is a misfortune incident to republican government, though in a less degree than to other governments, that those who administer it may forget their obligations to their constituents, and prove unfaithful to their important trust. In this point of view, a senate, as a second branch of the legislative assembly, distinct from, and dividing the power with, a first, must be in all cases a salutary check on the government. It doubles the security to the people, by requiring the concurrence of two distinct bodies in schemes of usurpation or perfidy, where the ambition or corruption of one would otherwise be sufficient. This is a precaution founded on such clear principles, and now so well understood in the United States, that it would be more than superfluous to enlarge on it. I will barely remark, that as the improbability of sinister combinations will be in proportion to the dissimilarity in the genius of the two bodies, it must be politic to distinguish them from each other by every circumstance which will consist with a due harmony in all proper measures, and with the genuine principles of republican government.

Secondly. The necessity of a senate is not less indicated by the propensity of all single and numerous assemblies to yield to the impulse of sudden and violent passions, and to be seduced by factious leaders into intemperate and pernicious resolutions. Examples on this subject might be cited without number; and from proceedings within the United States, as well as from the history of other nations. But a position that will not be contradicted, need not be proved. All that need be remarked is, that a body which is to correct this infirmity ought itself to be free from it, and consequently ought to be less numerous. It ought, moreover, to possess great firmness, and consequently ought to hold its authority by a tenure of considerable duration.

Thirdly. Another defect to be supplied by a senate lies in a want of due acquaintance with the objects and principles of legislation. It is not possible that an assembly of men called for the most part from pursuits of a private nature, continued in appointment for a short time, and led by no permanent motive to devote the intervals of public occupation to a study of the laws, the affairs, and the comprehensive interests of their country, should, if left wholly to themselves, escape a variety of important errors in the exercise of their legislative trust. It may be affirmed, on the best grounds, that no small share of the present embarrassments of America is to be charged on the blunders of our governments; and that these have proceeded from the heads rather than the hearts of most of the authors of them. What indeed are all the repealing, explaining, and amending laws, which fill and disgrace our voluminous codes, but so many monuments of deficient wisdom; so many impeachments exhibited by each succeeding against each preceding session; so many admonitions to the people, of the value of those aids which may be expected from a well-constituted senate?

A good government implies two things: first, fidelity to the object of government, which is the happiness of the people; secondly, a knowledge of the means by which that object can be best attained. Some governments are deficient in both these qualities; most governments are deficient in the first. I scruple not to assert, that in American governments too little attention has been paid to the last. The federal Constitution avoids this error; and what merits particular notice, it provides for the last in a mode which increases the security for the first.

Fourthly. The mutability in the public councils arising from a rapid succession of new members, however qualified they may be, points out, in the strongest manner, the necessity of some stable institution in the government. Every new election in the States is found to change one half of the representatives. From this change of men must proceed a change of opinions; and from a change of opinions, a change of measures. But a continual change even of good measures is inconsistent with every rule of prudence and every prospect of success. The remark is verified in private life, and becomes more just, as well as more important, in national transactions.

V. To trace the mischievous effects of a mutable government would fill a volume. I will hint a few only, each of which will be perceived to be a source of innumerable others.

In the first place, it forfeits the respect and confidence of other nations, and all the advantages connected with national character. An individual who is observed to be inconstant to his plans, or perhaps to carry on his affairs without any plan at all, is marked at once, by all prudent people, as a speedy victim to his own unsteadiness and folly. His more friendly neighbors may pity him, but all will decline to connect their fortunes with his; and not a few will seize the opportunity of making their fortunes out of his. One nation is to another what one individual is to another; with this melancholy distinction perhaps, that the former, with fewer of the benevolent emotions than the latter, are under fewer restraints also from taking undue advantage from the indiscretions of each other. Every nation, consequently, whose affairs betray a want of wisdom and stability, may calculate on every loss which can be sustained from the more systematic policy of their wiser neighbors. But the best instruction on this subject is unhappily conveyed to America by the example of her own situation. She finds that she is held in no respect by her friends; that she is the derision of her enemies; and that she is a prey to every nation which has an interest in speculating on her fluctuating councils and embarrassed affairs.

The internal effects of a mutable policy are still more calamitous. It poisons the blessing of liberty itself. It will be of little avail to the people, that the laws are made by men of their own choice, if the laws be so voluminous that they cannot be read, or so incoherent that they cannot be understood; if they be repealed or revised before they are promulgated, or undergo such incessant changes that no man, who knows what the law is to-day, can guess what it will be to-morrow. Law is defined to be a rule of action; but how can that be a rule, which is little known, and less fixed?

Another effect of public instability is the unreasonable advantage it gives to the sagacious, the enterprising, and the moneyed few over the industrious and uniformed mass of the people. Every new regulation concerning commerce or revenue, or in any way affecting the value of the different species of property, presents a new harvest to those who watch the change, and can trace its consequences; a harvest, reared not by themselves, but by the toils and cares of the great body of their fellow-citizens. This is a state of things in which it may be said with some truth that laws are made for the *few,* not for the *many.*

In another point of view, great injury results from an unstable government. The want of confidence in the public councils damps every useful undertaking, the success and profit of which may depend on a continuance of existing arrangements. What prudent merchant will hazard his fortunes in any new branch of commerce when he knows not but that his plans may be rendered unlawful before they can be executed? What farmer or manufacturer will lay himself out for the encouragement given to any particular cultivation or establishment, when he can have no assurance that his preparatory labors and advances will not render him a victim to an inconstant government? In a word, no great improvement or laudable enterprise can go forward which requires the auspices of a steady system of national policy.

But the most deplorable effect of all is that diminution of attachment and reverence which steals into the hearts of the people, towards a political system which betrays so many marks of infirmity, and disappoints so many of their flattering hopes. No government, any more than an individual, will long be respected without being truly respectable; nor be truly respectable, without possessing a certain portion of order and stability.

Publius

Discussion Questions

1. In Madison's view, why is the Senate necessary?
2. What does Madison mean by "mutability in the public councils"? Why might this be a problem?
3. Why does the Senate provide equal representation for each state? Do Madison's arguments have as much force today as they did when the Constitution was adopted?

Staggered Terms for the Senate: Origins and Irony

Daniel Wirls

There could be no new Senate. This was the very same body, constitution-
ally and in point of law, which had assembled on the first day of its
meeting in 1789. It has existed without any intermission from that day
until the present moment, and would continue to exist as long as the
Government should endure. It was emphatically a permanent body.
Senator James Buchanan, 1841[1]

BASED ON THE FACT THAT ONLY one-third of the Senate is up for reelection
every two years, the Senate is said to be, unlike the House, a continuing or permanent body, to the point where scholars and senators have claimed it is the
same Senate that first met in 1789. Staggered terms—any arrangement of terms
of office so that all members of a body are not appointed or elected at the same
time—are one of the constitutional provisions that distinguish the Senate from
the House and are the foundation for the notion of the Senate as a continuing
body. We take staggered Senate terms for granted, but why were they included
in the Constitution? The structure and composition of the Senate was the most
contentious matter debated and resolved at the Constitutional Convention (Swift
1996, 9; Wirls and Wirls 2004). And staggered Senate terms are on any list of the
decisions of 1787 that made the Senate the Senate. Even so, despite the volume
of scholarship on the convention and the creation of the Senate, the origins and
adoption of staggered terms have not been explored in any depth or with any
rigor and are not even mentioned in many cases of relevant scholarship.[2]

Despite or because of the dearth of scholarship, a conventional wisdom has dominated, one that interprets staggered elections as part of the framers' intent to create an insulated, stable, deliberative—and thereby continuing or permanent—Senate. Staggered terms for the Senate have been interpreted in a particular fashion by historians, political scientists, and journalists alike, in a matter-of-fact manner that draws upon assumption more than evidence. For example, the authors of a recent history of the Senate claim that the framers "decided that only one-third of the senators come up for election each two years, further to insulate the Senate from popular enthusiasms or turmoil" (MacNeil and Baker, 2013, 15). Almost ninety years earlier Lindsay Rogers wrote much the same thing, as have many others in between.[3] Robert Caro, in perhaps the best-selling book on the Senate, writes that "the Framers armored the Senate against the people," and on top of state selection and long terms, staggered elections "would be an additional, even stronger, layer of armor" (Caro 2002, 9–10). My work on the creation of the Senate is another example (Wirls and Wirls 2004, 210). In general there is an ahistorical quality to many of the assertions regarding the Constitutional Convention's use of staggered elections, as if they emerged ex nihilo in Philadelphia as "the solution" to the problem of complete turnover of the Senate (for example, Barbash 1987, 135), instead of seeing staggered terms as a familiar practice from state constitutions that might have had a different or more complicated function. In this way, selection by state legislatures, six-year terms, and staggered elections are almost always thought of and portrayed as a harmonious package to create a less democratic upper house. This interpretation has, however, little basis in the origins of and intention behind the Senate's staggered terms.

I draw upon three sources of evidence—the meaning and application of "rotation" in postrevolutionary America, the deliberations and decisions at the Constitutional Convention, and the arguments during ratification—to show that the conventional wisdom requires substantial revision. Staggered terms were (1) in the revolutionary era, a mechanism to ensure "rotation," or democratic turnover; (2) added to the Constitution as part of a compromise to assuage opponents of an insulated Senate and obtain a majority in support of a long term for that body; and (3) portrayed during ratification as a form of rotation that counteracted the perceived dangers of the long term and a Senate aristocracy. Whatever the effects in practice, staggered terms were intended primarily to mitigate the potential dangers of a legislative body with long individual tenure by exposing it to more frequent electoral influence. The irony is that staggered elections, a category of rotation intended to disrupt the accumulation and perpetuation of institutional power, came to be seen as part and parcel of the Senate's conservative purpose and produced the notion of an undying Senate or continuing body. As we will see, my argument is not that these and other similar characterizations are wrong in their implications about the *potential effects* of the combination of long and staggered terms. The historical analysis will show that the conventional wisdom is misleading and inaccurate as far as the primary *intentions and political interests* that led to the addition to the Constitution of staggered terms for the Senate.

The Use and Purpose of Staggered Terms in the Late Eighteenth Century

In the years leading to the Constitutional Convention, including the wave of state constitutions written in the 1770s and 1780s, staggered terms—the phrase was not used in this period—were one of a set of mechanisms used to create what was called "rotation." In discussions of the tenure of any governmental office, the term "rotation" was invoked with some regularity to refer to the frequency with which the membership of an institution would be subject to change in whole or in part. Rotation was about devices that ensured regular turnover in officeholders and encompassed two approaches: (1) provisions that limited reeligibility for office, that is, forms of what we now call term limits; (2) provisions that staggered the terms of membership in legislatures or other governmental bodies by dividing the membership into groups or classes to be selected in different years (Wood 1969; Main 1967; W. P. Adams 1980; Manin 1997).

In his 1776 "Thoughts on Government," John Adams endorsed rotation, in the form of term limits, but annual terms held a higher status, "there not being in the whole circle of the sciences, a maxim more infallible than this, 'Where annual elections end, there slavery begins'" (Adams 1983, 406). Annual elections, the paramount mechanism of democratic accountability in the revolutionary era, were frequently paired with eligibility rotation as a powerful check on governmental power. For example, the Articles of Confederation restricted delegates to Congress to serving no more than three years of any period of six, in addition to annual terms. In combination, short terms and reeligibility restrictions had an additive effect to ensure rotation.

Unlike limits on reeligibility, rotation in the form of staggered elections could be applied only to chambers with terms greater than one year, and even going into the summer of 1787, annual elections were still the norm. In addition to the Congress of the Confederation, every state save one had annual elections for its lower house (South Carolina had two-year terms).

Nevertheless, the revolutionary and founding era saw an attenuation in the vise grip of annual elections. Even many champions of annual elections for the lower house acknowledged the virtue of balancing the kind of electoral check that one-year terms represented with the accumulation of wisdom and experience, and they at least limited insulation from popular pressure. In the colonial era most upper houses were councils—some with indefinite appointments—that combined executive and legislative functions. The new state constitutions created upper houses that were more democratic in their selection, more clearly separated from the executive, and with longer terms than the assembly (Main 1967; W. P. Adams 1980; Kruman 1997). The innovation of legislative senates with longer terms was tied to rotation in every case except Maryland, which also featured a system of electors to pick its senate.

The scholarship on state constitutions does not spend much time on staggered elections for the new senates, but several historians quickly note or imply that upper-chamber rotation was to enforce turnover and electoral accountability (Main 1967; W. P. Adams 1980; Kruman 1997). Perhaps it was self-evident given the context. With the lower house of nearly every state elected for one year, no rotation was required. This implies quite directly that these state constitutions, aside from Maryland's, were trying to combine a longer term in the upper house with turnover and the electoral check. The virtue of a longer term for some positions could be balanced by rotation in the form of staggered elections. The length of term and staggered-term rotation were compensatory rather than additive.

A few state constitutions, including those of Virginia and Pennsylvania, provide contextual evidence for staggered terms as a form of rotation, but Delaware serves as a telling example. Its 1776 constitution created a "legislative council" composed of three councilors elected from each of the three counties that composed Delaware. These nine councilors served three-year terms, but one councilor *from each county* would be rotated out each year (Constitution of Delaware 1776). Given that the lower house, the House of Assembly, was elected to annual terms, and even the executive privy council had two-year terms with rotation and limits on reeligibility, it is difficult to see the rotation in the legislative council as anything but that, especially as it was rotation within each county's group of three councilors. The counties would not forego an annual influence on the nature and direction of their representation in the upper house.

Rotation and the Senate at the Constitutional Convention

Given this backdrop of recently formed and tested state charters, the delegates to the convention were familiar with staggered terms as a form of rotation for offices with longer terms. Its ultimate application to the proposed national Senate, therefore, is not surprising, but neither was it automatic. However, when the delegates added staggered terms, they did so as part of a compromise to balance the longest Senate term attainable with a form of rotation.

The Constitutional Convention opened with consideration of the so-called Virginia Plan, or Randolph Resolutions, which were largely the work of James Madison. Madison was the foremost advocate for an independent and stable Senate, one characterized by experience, knowledge, detachment, and elevated selection. If staggered elections had been part of a plan for augmenting the continuity or detachment of the second branch, it is probable that Madison would have included such a provision in the Virginia Plan, especially given that Virginia's state senate had a four-year term with one-quarter going out every year. Madison was, however, an avowed proponent of the Maryland Senate with its term of five years—the longest of any state—and no rotation.

Only two weeks into the proceedings, the convention delegates first considered the periods of service for both chambers. This took place before the delegates got bogged down in the debates over equal and proportional representation and the interests of small and large states, but it followed the unanimous decision in favor of selection of senators by state legislatures. On June 12 long terms *for both chambers* won decisive initial victories, with three-year terms for the House prevailing 7–4, and seven years for the Senate by 8–1–2, with no mention of any type of rotation.

The first proposal for rotation, of any kind, did not come until several days later, and it was for the House, not the Senate. When the delegates reconsidered the House term, some pushed for a shorter tenure, citing in some cases the annual elections that were still common at the state level. In a clear splitting of the difference, three years was struck by a decisive vote in favor of two years,

Vote #	Date	Motion	PA	DE	VA	NC	CT	MA	MD	NJ	SC	GA	NY	Yes	No	Div.
58	June 12	7 years	Y	Y	Y	Y	N	D	Y	Y	Y	Y	D	8	1	2
89	June 25	strike 7	N	N	N	Y	Y	Y	D	Y	Y	Y	Y	7	3	1
90	June 25	6 years	Y	Y	Y	Y	Y	N	D	N	N	N	N	5	5	1
92	June 25	5 years	Y	Y	Y	Y	Y	N	D	N	N	N	N	5	5	1
94	June 26	9 with rotation	Y	Y	Y	N	N	N	N	N	N	N	N	3	8	
95	June 26	6 with rotation	Y	Y	Y	Y	Y	Y	Y	N	N	N	N	7	4	

The Long Term Coalition   The Balancers   The Short Term Coalition

Fig. 2.1: Votes on Senate term length and rotation at the Constitutional Convention. *Note:* "Div." means a state's vote was divided. *Source:* from the *Congressional Globe*, quoted in Legislative Reference Service (now CRS) 1917, 4–5.

which presumably did not require any rotation but was long enough to be practical given the distances representatives would have to travel (*RFC* 1966, 1:360–62). It bears repeating that the first recorded mention of staggered terms is in a proposal for the lower chamber and in the spirit of the usual meaning and purpose of rotation.

The final decision on Senate terms was more difficult and protracted. Despite the initial agreement by the 8–1–2 vote, many delegates had concerns that seven years was too long. When the delegates returned to the question of Senate terms, a few days after having reduced the House term to two years, a proposal was made by Nathaniel Gorham of Massachusetts for four years instead of seven with "1/4 to be elected every year."[4] This was countered by a proposal for seven years "to go out in fixed proportions." Six years was then suggested as more convenient for rotation. But the delegates did not vote to add staggered terms at this point. They took the first step of striking seven years by a 7–3–1 vote. Long terms continued to do poorly, with six and five years falling short on the same 5–5–1 votes (fig. 2.1) (*RFC* 1966, 1:396, 415–16).

The next day, Gorham, the same delegate who had started things off the day before with the proposal for four years with rotation, tried to end the gridlock by proposing six years but with the additional provision of "one third of the members to go out every second year." Delaware's George Read, who still favored life appointments, countered with nine years and one-third rotation. After some debate, nine years with rotation lost 8–3, but six years with rotation won 7–4 (*RFC* 1966, 1:421–26). Given the earlier opposition to six and even five years, it is clear that rotation helped seal the deal, and rotation was about change, not continuation. It was a way to temper long terms with fresh blood.

A closer examination of the patterns of voting on term length and rotation strongly suggests that rotation alleviated concerns, whether ideological or political, of some delegates about a longer term and made it possible for them to swing the votes of key states. With the states arrayed by the consistency of their support for long or short terms, three groups emerge (see fig. 2.1). Pennsylvania, Delaware, and Virginia equal one another in support for long terms in each of the six votes and form the long-term coalition. On the other end of the spectrum, New Jersey, South Carolina, Georgia, and New York match each other in opposition to longer terms and form the short-term coalition. In the middle are the balancers, with North Carolina and Connecticut all but part of the long-term coalition, and Massachusetts and Maryland providing the crucial swing votes on June 26. Notice that on June 25 North Carolina and Connecticut voted for six- and five-year terms (with rotation having been suggested at different times, but not as yet included in the motions), but Massachusetts (in the negative) and Maryland (divided) failed to support either. Only when six years with rotation was proposed did the two latter states add their support and turn a 5–5–1 deadlock for six years without rotation into a 7–4 victory for six years with staggered terms.

While the records provide extensive debate about the purpose and merits of a long Senate term, only a few comments convey an explicit rationale for rotation. For example, Read, who noted that he would "still prefer 'during good behaviour,' but being little supported in that idea, he was willing to take the longest term that could be obtained," instead proposed nine years with triennial rotation (*RFC* 1966, 1:421). Given that he favored life appointments to the Senate, his inclusion of rotation was a recognition of the political need to offset long terms with refreshment and change. At the other end of the spectrum, Roger Sherman sought the shortest term feasible and argued that "the two objects of this body are permanency and safety to those who are to be governed. A bad government is the worse for being long. Frequent elections give security and even permanency. . . . Four years to the senate is quite sufficient when you add to it the rotation proposed" (*RFC* 1966, 1:431–32). Sherman contrasted the "permanency" of four-year terms (versus his state's annual elections) against the turnover provided by rotation.

Their deliberations and actions show that the framers primarily viewed and used Senate rotation as a tool for fostering electoral accountability rather than institutional autonomy or insulation in the antidemocratic sense. Staggered terms became part of a compromise, a means to an end, a way to balance the merits of long terms against the threat of permanency. In short, one side, the staunch advocates of a republican Senate, got as long a term as possible, and some who feared an entrenched aristocracy or who needed some degree of compensation or political cover, got this form of rotation.

Staggered Terms in the Ratification Debates

The structure and powers of the Senate were significant controversies during ratification, including the six-year term, which many conventioneers and commentators felt was too long. Staggered elections for the Senate were less of a topic, but evidence from the various debates during ratification, treated with appropriate caution, underscores that the main purpose was to offset the concerns that attended long terms.

Annual elections and various forms of rotation were important principles in the critiques of the proposed Constitution. Many opponents of the proposed Constitution thought two years was too long a term for representatives. Some critics still favored the provisions in the Articles of Confederation that combined annual terms for delegates to Congress with the additional restriction of serving no more than three years of any period of six.

Such was anti-federalist fear of a detached Senate aristocracy that staggered elections might not have been assuasive. A delegate to the Massachusetts convention referred to staggered Senate terms as "but a shadow of rotation" (*ED,* 2:48). "Brutus," the premier anti-federalist essayist, referred to the Senate's staggered terms as a form of rotation, but he condemned the absence of eligibility rotation and called for a reduction to a four-year term (*DHRC* 1976, 5:66–67). Indeed, the length of House and Senate terms was among the more frequent criticisms of the proposed Constitution, with anti-federalists often suggesting one-year and four-year terms instead (Main 1961; Maier 2011). Even if some thought it an insufficient form of rotation, anti-federalists neither criticized nor sought to repeal the provision for staggered terms.

In turn, advocates of ratification invoked staggered terms as a powerful check on a permanent or insulated Senate. Many pro-ratification delegates argued against term limits, the other form of rotation, and against recall, but staggered terms for the Senate were a different and necessary type of rotation. A search of the debates at the state conventions produced seventeen such endorsements of staggered terms by a total of eleven proponents of ratification. All the references characterize staggered terms as a safeguard against a "perpetual" Senate, a Senate aristocracy. Subjecting one-third of the Senate to election every two years would keep senators attentive to their states and bring in new sentiments about government and policy.

In Massachusetts, Fisher Ames called Senate rotation a "very effectual check upon the power of the Senate" (*ED,* 2:246). "By constructing the senate upon rotative principles," said Charles Cotesworth Pinckney to his fellow South Carolinians, "we have removed . . . all danger of an aristocratic influence," while allowing the long term of six years to provide the "advantages of an aristocracy," including wisdom and experience (Bailyn 1993, 2:588–89). Finally, Alexander Hamilton endorsed staggered terms at the New York convention, arguing "that safety and permanency in this government are completely reconcilable" (*ED,* 2:318–19). The man who, at the center of his major speech at the convention, proposed life terms for senators likely would not have thought of staggered terms as a way to increase senate "permanency." Instead, as he put it, two equally important principles—the safety of electoral accountability and the detached judgment and experience provided by "permanency"—could be harmonized by balancing long terms with rotation.

Staggered Terms and the Senate

Given the origins of Senate staggered elections, how and when did the idea of staggered elections as a form of rotation dissipate to be replaced by and large with an interpretation that conflated them with Senate insulation and detachment? That remains uncertain. After ratification some famous commentators, including St. George Tucker and Joseph Story, continued to see staggered terms as rotation (Blackstone 1803, bk. 1, 196; Story, n.d., secs. 709–12, 724).

Nevertheless, at some point during the early nineteenth century—the when and how are a bit of a mystery—senators began developing and applying the doctrine of the Senate as a continuing body. As indicated by the opening quotation from Senator Buchanan, this goes back to at least 1841, and such statements imply that the doctrine was by that point a well-developed one. Staggered elections for the Senate, whatever their intended effect, created a continuing body in the literal meaning of the term: a body whose membership is subject to only fractional change at any point in time. "Continuing body" developed into a constitutional self-conception. But the mere fact developed into a constitutional self-conception and set of practices, such that the actions of past senators could and should bind or restrict current members of the body. This turns "continuing body" into constitutional doctrine and practice (Beth 2005, 5; Bruhl 2010). I do not trace the development of the continuing-body doctrine (something that has not been in the literature), but my work suggests the following conjecture about its relationship to the interpretation of staggered terms. Could it be that the Senate began to construct itself as a continuing body, based on the fact of staggered terms, and as the doctrine of a continuing body took hold, the functional purpose of and intent behind staggered terms evolved to harmonize with the construction of the doctrine?

That is, instead of a particular interpretation of staggered terms' founding purpose driving the idea of a continuing body, the appeal and utility of the continuing-body doctrine drove the interpretation of founding intent for this small but important feature of the Constitution. Senators developed a motivated bias for appealing and adhering to what became the conventional wisdom. The Senate's self-conception and definition as a continuing and deliberative body circled back to build and reinforce the conventional wisdom. More generally, as the Constitution was put into practice and concerns about long terms quickly disappeared amid a gradual process of democratization, the most obvious effect of staggered terms was the insulation of two-thirds of the Senate at every national election—rather than the opportunity to refresh one-third with new blood. As the average tenure of representatives and senators quickly converged, the difference in institutional knowledge and stability seemed less important than the difference in electoral cycles. These developments, along with a lack of scholarship on the origins of staggered terms specifically, facilitated the understandable conflation, by senators and scholars alike, of staggered elections with longer terms and selection by state legislatures as part of the founders' conservative intentions.

My purpose in formulating this hypothesis is to suggest the possibility that just as the origins of staggered terms for the Senate are more complex and inter-

esting than the conventional wisdom implies, the relationship between the interpretation of staggered terms and the development of the doctrine of the Senate
as a continuing body has likely been an interdependent and mutually reinforc-
ing discursive process. Regardless of the exact relationship to the continuing-
body doctrine, the result was a conventional interpretation based more on the
consequences of staggered terms in practice and discourse than on their historical origins.

Stretching from the state constitutions through ratification, "rotation" had
one purpose, ensuring the turnover of officeholders, and staggered elections
were viewed as a form of rotation. The general argument that the framers added
staggered terms to further insulate the Senate and further distinguish it from the
democratic House is unsustainable. When joined together, however, long and
staggered terms certainly had multiple effects. Even if the intentions and politics of the convention led to the addition of staggered elections to temper long
terms, the combination produced a body that, in comparison to the House, never
would be subject to the same degree of potential electoral change.

The irony is that staggered elections, a category of rotation intended to prevent the entrenchment or perpetuation of institutional power, produced instead
the notion of an undying Senate or continuing body and are interpreted as a vital
part of the Senate's conservative purpose. Among other things, the continuing-
body doctrine has been the chief reason the Senate does not vote on its rules of
procedure at the start of each Congress, as does the House. Once a Senate tra-
dition, this practice of not voting on the rules was itself turned into one of the
standing rules (Rules of the Senate, V, sec. 2) in 1959. The doctrine of a continuing body is also an important part of the rationale for the higher (two-thirds)
supermajority threshold to cut off debate on proposed changes in Senate rules
of procedure.

Senators and scholars alike will no doubt continue to debate the constitutional and institutional status of the doctrine. This history of the purpose of staggered terms makes the following contribution: staggered terms were for institutional accountability not institutional entrenchment. For the Senate to entrench
its decisions, to make them all but perpetual, is the opposite of the main intention behind staggered terms, even if that original purpose in no way affects
senators' right or ability to develop and apply their self-conception as a continuing body. In fact, such practices take the Senate beyond the worst fears of
rotation's advocates insofar as the continuing-body doctrine entrenches not sim-

ply the power of current members but the decisions of those who are no longer in office, a majority that no longer exists. This leaves the result that the new majority—something that rotation was intended to produce—has been effectively anchored to the past.[5]

More generally, seeing staggered terms as a form of electoral accountability, as a form of rotation, reminds us of the complexity of the Senate's creation. The Senate was of course the object of the Great Compromise that tried to blend Madison's Senate of farsighted statesmen with equal and direct representation of states. Placed at the intersection of several constitutional vectors or tensions—responsiveness and deliberation, legislative and executive powers, states and nation—the Senate reflected the multiple forces and goals at work in its construction. The central elements of the Senate's composition—selection by state legislatures, six-year terms, and staggered elections—are a package that embodies the various ideas and interests. By contrast, the common understanding of Senate staggered terms tends to see and portray the Senate as a neater, more coherent package than it actually was: the founders intended the Senate to be the less democratic chamber, therefore the features of its composition, including staggered terms, all contributed to that goal. The Senate was certainly intended to be the more conservative or undemocratic of the legislative chambers, but not every aspect of its construction fit that mold. The combination of long terms and staggered elections evince the framers' efforts, with both abstract principles and political necessity in the mix, to balance stability with responsiveness in the design of republican institutions.

Notes

The author thanks Richard Beth, Matthew Green, Gregory Koger, Frances Lee, Paul Quirk, and Donald Wolfensberger for their comments and suggestions.

1. Sen. James Buchanan, 1841, from the *Congressional Globe,* quoted in Legislative Reference Service 1917, 4–5.
2. This claim is based on an extensive bibliographic search, a complete accounting of which is available from the author.
3. According to Rogers (1926, 15), "the terms of the major branches . . . are so arranged as to raise effective shields against gusts of popular passion. . . . Senators serve for six years . . . and one-third of the membership is renewed every two years."
4. Robert Yates's notes record Gorham as proposing "that the senators be classed, and to remain 4 years in office; otherwise great inconveniences may arise if a dissolution should

take place at once." (*RFC* 1966, 1:415). "Inconveniences" without more context is ambiguous. But it is worth remembering that Gorham's Massachusetts held annual elections for every level of its state government, including its senate.

5. The 113th Senate, with its historic alteration of the rules in 2013, severed one of those moorings by a vote of 52–48. Whether the change made by this contentious and controversial use of the "constitutional" or "nuclear option" will endure depends in part on the outcome of future Senate elections, structured, as they are, by staggered terms.

References

Adams, John. 1983. "Thoughts on Government" (1776). In *American Political Writing During the Founding Era, 1760–1805,* ed. Charles S. Hyneman and Donald S. Lutz. Indianapolis: Liberty Press, 402–9.

Adams, Willi Paul. 1980. *The First American Constitutions: Republican Ideology and the Making of the State Constitutions in the Revolutionary Era.* Chapel Hill: University of North Carolina Press.

Bailyn, Bernard, ed. 1993. *The Debate on the Constitution: Federalist and Antifederalist Speeches, Articles, and Letters During the Struggle over Ratification.* 2 vols. New York: Library of America.

Barbash, Fred. 1987. *The Founding: A Dramatic Account of the Writing of the Constitution.* New York: Simon & Schuster.

Beth, Richard S. 2005. "'Entrenchment' of Senate Procedures and the 'Nuclear Option' for Change: Possible Proceedings and Their Implications." Washington, DC: Congressional Research Service.

Blackstone, William. 1803. *Blackstone's Commentaries with Notes of Reference to the Constitution and Laws of the Federal Government of the United States and of the Commonwealth Of Virginia, by St. George Tucker.* Philadelphia: William Young Birch and Abraham Small.

Bruhl, Aaron-Andrew P. 2010. "Burying the 'Continuing Body' Theory of the Senate." *Iowa Law Review* 95 (5): 1401–65.

Caro, Robert A. 2002. *The Master of the Senate.* New York: Vintage Books.

Constitution of Delaware, 1776. http://avalon.law.yale.edu/18th_century/de02.asp.

DHRC [*The Documentary History of the Ratification of the Constitution*]. 1976. Ed. Merrill Jensen. 22 vols. Madison: Wisconsin Historical Society Press.

ED [*Elliot's Debates: The Debates in the Several State Conventions on the Adoption of the Federal Constitution*]. Ed. Jonathan Elliot. 4 vols. http://memory.loc.gov/ammem/amlaw /lwed.html.

HJM [Hamilton, Alexander; John Jay; and James Madison]. 1982. *The Federalist.* Ed. Jacob Ernest Cooke. Middletown, CT: Wesleyan University Press.

Kernell, Samuel, and Gary C. Jacobson. 2000. *The Logic of American Politics.* Washington, DC: CQ Press.

Kruman, Marc W. 1997. *Between Authority & Liberty: State Constitution Making in Revolutionary America.* Chapel Hill: University of North Carolina Press.

Legislative Reference Service, Library of Congress. 1917. *The Senate as a Continuing Body.* Washington, DC: Government Printing Office.

Lowi, Theodore J., and Benjamin Ginsberg. 1990. *American Government: Freedom and Power.* New York: W. W. Norton.

MacNeil, Neil, and Richard A. Baker. 2013. *The American Senate: An Insider's History.* Oxford: Oxford University Press.

Maier, Pauline. 2011. *Ratification: The People Debate the Constitution, 1787–1788.* New York: Simon & Schuster.

Main, Jackson Turner. 1961. *The Anti-federalists: Critics of the Constitution, 1781–1788.* New York: W. W. Norton.

———. 1967. *The Upper House in Revolutionary America, 1763–1788.* Madison: University of Wisconsin Press.

Manin, Bernard. 1997. *The Principles of Representative Government.* New York: Cambridge University Press.

RFC [*The Records of the Federal Convention of 1787*]. 1966. Edited by Max Farrand. 3 vols. New Haven, CT: Yale University Press.

Rogers, Lindsay. 1926. *The American Senate.* New York: Alfred A. Knopf.

Stewart, Charles, III. 1992. "Responsiveness in the Upper Chamber: The Constitution and the Institutional Development of the Senate." In *The Constitution and American Political Development,* ed. Peter F. Nardulli. Chicago: University of Illinois Press, 63–96.

Story, Joseph. n.d. *Commentaries on the Constitution of the United States.* http://archive.org/details/commentariesonco01storuoft.

Swift, Elaine K. 1996. *The Making of an American Senate: Reconstitutive Change in Congress, 1787–1841.* Ann Arbor: University of Michigan Press.

Wirls, Daniel, and Stephen Wirls. 2004. *The Invention of the United States Senate.* Baltimore: Johns Hopkins University Press.

Wood, Gordon. 1969. *The Creation of the American Republic: 1776–1787.* Chapel Hill, NC: University of North Carolina Press.

Discussion Questions

1. Staggered terms were seen as a form of "rotation" of officeholders. Why was rotation valued as a feature of constitutional government? For example, what did it allegedly guard against?

2. In what way are staggered terms evidence that the design of the Senate was the result of compromise or balancing of different interests?

3. What is the relationship between staggered terms and the Senate's description of itself as a "continuing body"?

PART TWO

CONGRESS AND REPRESENTATION:
ELECTIONS, PARTIES, AND LOBBYING

Super PACs in Federal Elections: Overview and Issues for Congress

R. Sam Garrett

Introduction and Highlights of Key Findings

The development of super PACs (political action committees) is one of the most recent components of the debate over money and speech in elections. Some perceive the creation of super PACs as a positive consequence of deregulatory court decisions in *Citizens United* and the related case *SpeechNow*. For those who advocate for super PACs, these new political committees provide an important outlet for political speech advocating independent calls for election or defeat of federal candidates. Others contend that they are the latest outlet for unlimited money in politics, which, while legally independent, are functional extensions of one or more campaigns.

This report does not attempt to settle that debate, but it does provide context for understanding what super PACs might mean for federal campaign finance policy and federal elections. The report does so through a question-and-answer format with attention to super PAC activities in 2010 and 2012 and what those findings might mean looking ahead.

Selected findings and observations include the following points:

- Super PACs potentially have major policy and electoral consequences. A variety of issues related to the state of law and regulation affecting super PACs, disclosure, agency administration, and other topics might be relevant as Congress considers whether to pursue oversight or legislation.

- Additional regulation of super PACs might be attractive to those who believe that these organizations are thinly veiled extensions of individual campaigns. Those who believe super PACs are independent speakers might counter that super PACs' spending is not coordinated with campaigns and, therefore, should be subject to fewer disclosure requirements or other obligations than entities that can contribute to candidates.
- Most super PACs are financially modest, but a few raise and spend substantial sums. Ten super PACs accounted for almost 75 percent of all super PAC spending in 2010. A similar but less dramatic distinction emerged during the 2012 cycle, when ten super PACs accounted for approximately 65 percent of total spending.
- For the 2012 cycle, super PACs raised a total of $826.6 million and spent a total of $799.2 million.
- In 2010 and 2012, 70–80 percent of super PAC spending directly supported or opposed federal candidates through independent expenditures (IEs). Super PACs spent $620.9 million on IEs supporting and opposing House, Senate, and presidential candidates in 2012—almost ten times the approximately $65 million spent in 2010.
- Super PAC IEs in 2012 House and Senate races were more likely to favor Democrats than in 2010. Most super PAC IEs at the presidential level favored Republicans.
- Large contributions are permissible but, for some, raise concerns because of the way in which they are disclosed, or because they would be impermissible if given directly to candidate campaigns, or both. The original source of super PAC contributions need not necessarily be reported to the Federal Election Commission (FEC) if the contributions are routed through entities such as some 501(c) organizations.

Organization and Scope of the Report

Questions and answers about selected super PAC topics organize the following discussion in this chapter. In particular:

- "Brief Answer" sections provide short summary information responding to each question.

- The "Discussion" following each brief answer expands on the analysis. These discussions include bullet points designed to help the reader navigate the text.
- Tables and figures throughout the report summarize selected fundraising and spending data discussed in the text.

Before proceeding, readers should be aware of this report's scope and purpose. This report is intended to provide an overview of the developing role of super PACs in American elections, with an emphasis on summaries of available spending data and major policy issues that may face Congress.[1] The report discusses selected litigation to demonstrate how those events have changed the campaign finance landscape and affected the policy issues that may confront Congress; it is not, however, a constitutional or legal analysis.

The report is also not intended to be a political analysis of strategic advantages or disadvantages surrounding the choice to form a super PAC or of super PACs' effects on individual candidates. Fully addressing how super PACs have affected individual races and candidates would require political analysis beyond the scope of this report. Nonetheless, understanding aggregate spending patterns in individual races (as opposed to campaigns) may assist Congress in its consideration of potential legislative, regulatory, or oversight responses.

Given the rapid development and frequently changing nature of super PACs, the report is not intended to address every organization or policy issue that may be relevant. It reflects current understanding of super PACs based on the analysis described throughout the report. Importantly, however, because federal election law and regulation have not been amended to address the role of super PACs, the findings presented here may be subject to alternative interpretations or future developments. Campaign finance data discussed in the report were collected and analyzed as noted in the text and discussed in the appendix at the end of this chapter.

Finally, a note on terminology may be useful. The term "independent expenditures" (IEs) appears throughout the report. IEs refer to purchases, often for political advertising, that explicitly call for election or defeat of a clearly identified federal candidate (for example, "vote for Smith," "vote against Jones"). The campaign finance lexicon typically refers to "making IEs," which is synonymous with the act of spending funds for the purchase of calling for the election or defeat of a federal candidate. Parties, PACs, individuals, and now, super PACs, may make IEs. IEs are not considered campaign contributions and cannot be coordinated with the referenced candidate.[2]

What Are Super PACs?

Brief Answer

Super PACs first emerged in 2010 following two major court rulings that invalidated previous limits on contributions to traditional PACs. As a result of the rulings, in *Citizens United* and *SpeechNow,* new kinds of PACs devoted solely to making independent expenditures emerged.[3] These groups are popularly known as "super PACs"; they are also known as "independent expenditure-only committees" (IEOCs). Independent expenditures (IEs) are frequently used to purchase political advertising or fund related services (such as voter canvassing). IEs include explicit calls for election or defeat of federal candidates but are not considered campaign contributions.

IEs must be made independently of parties and candidates. In campaign finance parlance, this means IEs cannot be *coordinated* with candidates or parties. Determining whether an expenditure is coordinated can be highly complex and depends on individual circumstances.[4] In essence, however, barring those making IEs from coordinating with candidates means that the entity making the IE and the affected candidate may not communicate about certain strategic information or timing surrounding the IE. The goal here is to ensure that an IE is truly independent and does not provide a method for circumventing contribution limits simply because an entity other than the campaign is paying for an item or providing a service that could benefit the campaign.

Table 3.1 provides an overview of how super PACs compare with other political committees and politically active organizations. In brief, super PACs are both similar to and different from traditional PACs. Super PACs have the same reporting requirements as traditional PACs, and both entities are regulated primarily by the federal election law and the FEC as political committees. Unlike traditional PACs, super PACs cannot make contributions to candidate campaigns. Super PACs' abilities to accept unlimited contributions make them similar to organizations known as 527s and some 501(c) organizations that often engage in political activity.[5] However, while these groups are governed primarily by the Internal Revenue Code (IRC), super PACs are regulated primarily by federal election law and the FEC.

Discussion

Super PACs originated from a combination of legal and regulatory developments. Most notably, in January 2010 the Supreme Court issued a decision in *Citizens United v. Federal Election Commission.*[6] *Citizens United* did not directly address the topic of super PACs, but it set the stage for a later ruling that affected their development, as I will discuss.

CITIZENS UNITED AND SPEECHNOW As a consequence of *Citizens United,* corporations and unions are now free to use their treasury funds to make expenditures (such as for airing political advertisements) explicitly calling for election or defeat of federal or state candidates (independent expenditures, or IEs), or for advertisements that refer to those candidates during preelection periods, but do not necessarily call explicitly for their election or defeat (electioneering communications). Previously, such advertising would generally have had to be financed through voluntary contributions raised by traditional PACs (those affiliated with unions or corporations, nonconnected committees, or both).

A second case paved the way for what would become super PACs. Following *Citizens United,* on March 26, 2010, the U.S. Court of Appeals for the District of Columbia held in *SpeechNow.org v. Federal Election Commission*[7] that contributions to PACs that make only IEs—but not contributions themselves—could not be constitutionally limited.

Also known as "independent-expenditure-only committees" (IEOCs), the media and other observers called these new political committees simply *super PACs.* The term signifies their structure: akin to traditional PACs but without the contribution limits that bind traditional PACs. As discussed in the next section, after *Citizens United* and *SpeechNow,* the FEC issued advisory opinions that offered additional guidance on super PAC activities.

As the data that follow show, the most obvious effects from super PACs are likely to be on the nation's electoral campaigns. By definition, super PACs are devoted to engaging in independent activities. They cannot[8] make direct contributions to campaigns or coordinate their activities with campaigns. Nonetheless, super PACs could dramatically shape the environment affecting campaigns, particularly if they choose to engage in express advocacy that explicitly calls

Table 3.1. Basic Structure of Super PACs versus Other Political Committees and Organizations
(Refers to federal elections only)

	Is the entity typically considered a political committee by the FEC?	Must certain contributors be disclosed to the FEC?	Can the entity make contributions to federal candidates?	Are there limits on the amount the entity can contribute to federal candidates?	Can federal candidates raise funds the entity plans to contribute in federal elections?	Are there limits on contributions the entity may receive for use in federal elections?
Super PACs	Yes	Yes	No	Not permitted to make federal contributions	Yes, within FECA limits	No
"Traditional" PACs[a]	Yes	Yes	Yes	$5,000 per candidate, per election	Yes, within FECA limits	$5,000 annually from individuals; other limits established in FECA[b]
National Party Committees	Yes	Yes	Yes	$5,000 per candidate, per election	Yes, within FECA limits	$32,400 from individuals (2014 cycle); other limits established in FECA
Candidate Committees	Yes	Yes	Yes	$2,000 per candidate, per election	Yes, within FECA limits	$2,600 per candidate, per election from individuals (2014 cycle); other limits established in FECA
527s[c]	No	No, unless independent expenditures or electioneering communications[d]	No	Not permitted to make federal contributions	N/A	No

| 501(c)(4)s, (5)s, (6)s[e] | No | No, unless independent expenditures or electioneering communications[f] | No | Not permitted to make federal contributions | N/A | No |

Source: CRS adaptation from Table 1 in CRS Report R41542, *The State of Campaign Finance Policy: Recent Developments and Issues for Congress*, by R. Sam Garrett; and Federal Election Commission, "Contribution Limits 2013–2014," http://www.fec.gov/ans/answers_general.shtml, accessed September 16, 2016.

Notes: National party committees may accept individual contributions up to the $100,200 amount shown in the table for separate accounts for (1) presidential nominating conventions (headquarters committees (e.g., DNC; RNC) only); (2) recounts and other legal compliance activities; and (3) party buildings. For additional discussion, see *CRS Report R43825, Increased Campaign Contributions Limits in the FY20-15 Omnibus Appropriations Law: Frequently Asked Questions*, by R. Sam Garrett.

[a]This report uses the term "traditional PACs" to refer to PACs that are not super PACs. Here, the term includes separate segregated funds, nonconnected committees, and leadership PACs. The table assumes these PACs would be *multicandidate committees*. Multicandidate committees are those that have been registered with the FEC (or, for Senate committees, the secretary of the Senate) for at least six months; have received federal contributions from more than fifty people; and (except for state parties) have made contributions to at least five federal candidates. See 11 C.F.R. § 100.5(e)(3). In practice, most PACs attain multicandidate status automatically over time.

[b]As noted later in this report, nonconnected PACs utilizing an exemption per the *Carey* case may raise unlimited amounts for independent expenditures if those amounts are kept in a separate bank account and not used for contributions.

[c]As the term is commonly used, 527 refers to groups registered with the Internal Revenue Service (IRS) as Section 527 political organizations that seemingly intend to influence federal elections in ways that place them outside the FECA definition of a political committee. By contrast, political committees (which include candidate committees, party committees, and political action committees) are regulated by the FEC and federal election law. There is a debate regarding which 527s are required to register with the FEC as political committees. FEC contributor disclosure for these organizations applies only to those who designate their contributions for use in independent expenditures or electioneering communications. This table does not address general reporting obligations established in tax law or IRS regulations. For additional discussion, see CRS Report RS22895, *527 Groups and Campaign Activity: Analysis Under Campaign Finance and Tax Laws*, by L. Paige Whitaker and Erika K. Lunder.

[d]Federal tax law requires that 527s periodically disclose to the IRS information about donors who have given at least $200 during the year. See 26 U.S.C. § 527(j). This information is publicly available. See 26 U.S.C. § 6104.

[e]For additional discussion of these groups, see CRS Report RL33377, *Tax-Exempt Organizations: Political Activity Restrictions and Disclosure Requirements*, by Erika K. Lunder, and CRS Report R40183, *501(c)(4) Organizations and Campaign Activity: Analysis Under Tax and Campaign Finance Laws*, by Erika K. Lunder and L. Paige Whitaker.

[f]Federal tax law requires that these groups disclose information to the IRS about donors who have given at least $5,000 annually. See 26 U.S.C. § 6033. Unlike information on donors to political committees and 527s, however, this information is confidential and not made public. See 26 U.S.C. § 6104.

for election or defeat of particular candidates. In addition, despite prohibitions on coordination of super PAC activities with campaigns, some observers have raised concerns that super PACs might not be independent of candidate campaigns in practice.[9] Super PACs are treated as political committees and are regulated primarily by the Federal Election Campaign Act (FECA) and FEC regulations, unlike some other "outside" spenders, such as organizations regulated primarily under Sections 527 and 501(c) of the Internal Revenue Code (IRC).

Why Might Super PACs Matter to Congress?

Brief Answer

The development of super PACs is one of the most recent chapters in the long-running debate over political spending and political speech. Super PACs potentially have major regulatory and electoral consequences. As data in this report show, super PACs have emerged quickly and have become a powerful spending force in federal elections. Nonetheless, as of this writing, federal election law and regulation have not been amended to formally recognize and clarify the role of super PACs. Congress may wish to consider the issue through legislation or oversight.

Discussion

Several policy issues and questions surrounding super PACs may be relevant as Congress considers how or whether to pursue legislation or oversight. These topics appear to fall into three broad categories:

- the state of law and regulation affecting super PACs
- transparency surrounding super PACs
- how super PACs shape the campaign environment

For those advocating their use, super PACs represent newfound (or restored) freedom for individuals, corporations, and unions to contribute as much as they wish for independent expenditures that advocate election or defeat of federal candidates. Opponents of super PACs contend that they represent a threat to the spirit of modern limits on campaign contributions designed to minimize potential corruption.

Additional discussion of these subjects appears throughout this report.

How Have Super PACs Been Regulated?

Brief Answer

Thus far, Congress has not enacted legislation specifically addressing super PACs. Existing regulation and law governing traditional PACs apply to super PACs in some cases. The FEC has issued advisory opinions on the topic but has not approved new regulations on super PACs.

Discussion

The FEC is responsible for administering civil enforcement of the FECA and related federal election law. The commission began considering a notice of proposed rulemaking (NPRM) expected to address various *Citizens United* issues shortly after the Supreme Court's January 2010 decision.[10] After disagreement throughout 2011 and two previous deadlocked[11] votes, in December 2011 commissioners approved a notice of proposed rulemaking (NPRM) posing questions about some aspects of what form post–*Citizens United* rules should take.[12] Among other points, the agency essentially asks how broadly new rules should define permissible corporate and union independent expenditures and electioneering communications. It is unclear to what extent final rules, if adopted, will address super PACs.

Despite the lack of amendments to federal law or campaign finance regulation, the FEC has issued advisory opinions (AOs) that provided guidance on some super PAC questions.[13] These AOs responded to questions posed by members of the "regulated community," as those governed by campaign finance law are sometimes known, seeking clarification about how the commission believed campaign finance regulation and law applied to specific situations involving super PACs. Six AOs are particularly relevant for understanding how the FEC has interpreted the *Citizens United* and *SpeechNow* decisions with respect to super PACs, as briefly summarized here:

- In July 2010, the FEC approved two related AOs in response to questions from the Club for Growth (AO 2010-09) and Commonsense Ten (AO 2010-11).[14] In light of *Citizens United* and *SpeechNow,* both organizations sought to form PACs that could solicit unlimited contributions to make independent expenditures (that is, form super PACs). The commission determined that the organizations could do so. In both AOs, the commission advised that while post–*Citizens United* rules were being drafted, political committees intending to operate as super PACs could supplement their statements of organization (FEC form 1) with letters indicating their status.[15] The major policy consequence of the Club for Growth and Commonsense Ten AOs was to permit, based on *Citizens United* and *SpeechNow,* super PACs to raise unlimited contributions supporting independent expenditures.[16]

• In June 2011, the commission approved an AO affecting super PAC fundraising. In the Majority PAC and House Majority PAC AO (AO 2011-12), the commission determined that federal candidates and party officials could solicit contributions for super PACs within limits.[17] Specifically, the commission advised that contributions solicited by federal candidates and national party officials must be within the PAC contribution limits established in the FECA (for example, $5,000 annually for individual contributions).[18] It is possible, however, that federal candidates could attend fundraising events—but not solicit funds themselves—at which unlimited amounts were solicited by other people.

• In AO 2011-11, the commission responded to questions from comedian Stephen Colbert. Colbert's celebrity status generated national media attention surrounding the request, which also raised substantive policy questions. The Colbert request asked whether the comedian could promote his super PAC on his nightly television program, *The Colbert Report.*[19] In particular, Colbert asked whether discussing the super PAC on his show would constitute in-kind contributions from *Colbert Report* distributor Viacom and related companies. An affirmative answer would trigger FEC reporting requirements in which the value of the airtime and production services would be disclosed as contributions from Viacom to the super PAC. Colbert also asked whether these contributions would be covered by the FEC's "press exemption," thereby avoiding reporting requirements.[20] In brief, the commission determined that coverage of the super PAC and its activities aired on *The Colbert Report* would fall under the press exemption and need not be reported to the FEC. If Viacom provided services (for example, producing commercials) referencing the super PAC for air in other settings, however, the commission determined that those communications would be reportable in-kind contributions.[21] Viacom would also need to report costs incurred to administer the super PAC.[22]

- On December 1, 2011, the FEC considered a request from super PAC American Crossroads. In AO 2011-23, Crossroads sought permission to air broadcast ads featuring candidates discussing policy issues. American Crossroads volunteered that the planned ads would be "fully coordinated" with federal candidates ahead of the 2012 elections but also noted that they would not contain express advocacy calling for election or defeat of the candidates.[23] In brief, the key question in the AO was whether Crossroads could fund and air such advertisements without running afoul of *coordination* restrictions designed to ensure that goods or services of financial value are not provided to campaigns in excess of federal contribution limits.[24] (As a super PAC, Crossroads is prohibited from making campaign contributions; coordinated expenditures would be considered in-kind contributions.) Ultimately, the FEC was unable to reach a resolution to the AO request. In brief, at the open meeting at which the AO was considered, independent commissioner Steven Walther and Democrats Cynthia Bauerly and Ellen Weintraub disagreed with their Republican counterparts, Caroline Hunter, Donald McGahn, and Matthew Petersen, about how FEC regulations and the FECA should apply to the request.[25] As a result of the 3–3 deadlocked vote, the question of super PAC sponsorship of "issue ads" featuring candidates appears to be unsettled. Although deadlocked votes are often interpreted as not granting permission for a planned campaign activity, some might also regard the deadlock as a failure to prohibit the activity. As a practical matter, if the FEC is unable to reach agreement on approving or prohibiting the conduct, it might also be unable to reach agreement on an enforcement action against a super PAC that pursued the kind of advertising Crossroads proposed.

- Also at its December 1, 2011, meeting, the FEC considered AO request 2011-21, submitted by the Constitutional Conservatives Fund (CCF) PAC. CCF is a leadership PAC[26] affiliated with Senator Mike Lee. CCF and other leadership PACs are not super PACs, although the CCF AO request is arguably relevant for super PACs. Specifically, in AO request 2011-21, CCF sought permission to raise unlimited funds for use in independent expenditures, as super PACs do. The FEC held, in a 6–0 vote, that because CCF is affiliated with a federal candidate, the PAC could not solicit unlimited contributions. To the extent that the CCF request is relevant for super PACs, it suggests that leadership PACs or other committees affiliated with federal candidates may not behave as super PACs.

To summarize, although the FEC has not yet issued rules regulating super PACs, AOs have provided guidance relevant for some circumstances. Perhaps most notably, through the Club for Growth (2010-09) and Commonsense Ten (2010-11) AOs, the commission confirmed that super PACs could accept unlimited contributions and use those funds to make independent expenditures. In AO 2011-12 (Majority PAC and House Majority PAC), the commission granted permission for federal officeholders and party officials to solicit super PAC funds within the limits established in the FECA. The Colbert AO (2011-11) applies to the relatively unique situation of a media personality discussing his super PAC on his television program. The Colbert AO may, nonetheless, have broad implications in the future by presenting a model for other media personalities and organizations to voice their support for or opposition to political candidates, for media corporations to have greater latitude to support personalities who do so, or both. The FEC was unable to reach a consensus on American Crossroads' request (AO 2011-23) to air "issue ads" featuring candidates. Finally, in AO 2011-21, the commission determined that leadership PACs could not engage in unlimited fundraising for independent expenditures, as super PACs do.

What Information Must Super PACs Disclose?

Brief Answer

Super PACs must follow the same reporting requirements as traditional PACs. This includes filing statements of organization[27] and regular financial reports detailing most contributions and expenditures.

Discussion

In the Commonsense Ten AO, the FEC advised super PACs to meet the same reporting obligations as PACs known as "nonconnected committees" (for example, independent organizations that are not affiliated with a corporation or labor union). These reports are filed with the FEC[28] and are made available for public inspection in person or on the commission's website.

Super PACs and other political committees must regularly[29] file reports with the FEC[30] summarizing, among other things,

- total receipts and disbursements;
- the name, address, occupation, and employer[31] of those who make more than $200 in unique or aggregate contributions per year;
- the name and address of the recipient of disbursements exceeding $200;[32] and
- the purpose of the disbursement.[33]

Reporting timetables for traditional PACs, which appear to apply to super PACs, depend on whether the PAC's activity occurs during an election year or non–election year:

- During *election years,* PACs may choose between filing monthly or quarterly reports. They also file pre- and post-general-election reports and year-end reports.[34]
- During *nonelection years,* PACs file FEC reports monthly, or "semi-annually" to cover two six-month periods. The latter includes two periods: (1) "mid-year" reports for January 1–June 30; and (2) "year-end" reports for July 1–December 31.[35]

Super PACs also have to report their IEs.[36] IEs are reported separately from the regular financial reports discussed earlier. Among other requirements,

- independent expenditures aggregating at least $10,000 must be reported to the FEC within 48 hours; 24-hour reports for independent expenditures of at least $1,000 must be made during periods immediately preceding elections;[37] and
- independent expenditure reports must include the name of the candidate in question and whether the expenditure supported or opposed the candidate.[38]

The name, address, occupation, and employer for those who contributed more than $200 to the super PAC for IEs would be included in the regular financial reports discussed here, but donor information is not contained in the IE reports themselves. In addition, as the "Is Super PAC Activity Sufficiently Transparent?" section discusses later in this report, the original source of some contributions to super PACs can be concealed (either intentionally or coincidentally) by routing the funds through an intermediary.

Overall, What Did Super PACs Raise and Spend in the 2010 and 2012 Federal Elections?

Brief Answer

Super PAC activity increased substantially between 2010 and 2012, in terms of both the number of super PACs that were active in the elections and their financial activity. Approximately 80 organizations quickly formed in response to the 2010 *Citizens United* and *SpeechNow* rulings. These first super PACs spent a total of approximately $90.4 million, more than $60 million of which was spent on IEs advocating for or against candidates.[39] Just 10 super PACs accounted for almost 75 percent of all super PAC spending in 2010.[40] In 2012, although more than 800 super PACs registered with the FEC, only somewhat more than half of those groups reported raising or spending funds.[41] For the 2012 cycle, super PACs reported raising a total of $826.6 million and spending a total of $799.2 million.[42]

Discussion

To assess where and how super PACs became involved in federal elections, the Congressional Research Service (CRS) analyzed super PAC reports filed with the FEC for the 2010 and 2012 cycles. The appendix provides additional information about the methodology used to gather the data and conduct the analysis.

During the 2010 election cycle, 79 groups registered as super PACs spent a total of approximately $90.4 million. This sum is perhaps notable not only for its size but also because most of these organizations did not operate until the summer of 2010.[43] Super PAC resources in 2010 were highly skewed, meaning that a relatively small number of groups accounted for a large amount of finan-

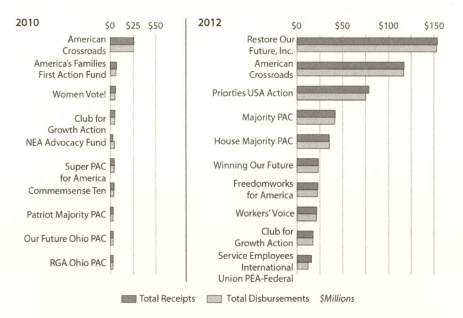

Fig. 3.1: Top ten super PACs by total receipts and disbursements, 2010 and 2012. *Note:* Amounts in the figure refer to total receipts and disbursements as reported to the FEC, not just independent expenditures. *Source:* CRS figure and analysis of super PAC data in the FEC Committee Summary File.

cial activity—both individually and as a proportion of all super PAC activity (fig. 3.1).

In 2012, super PAC financial activity remained skewed, but overall fundraising and spending increased sharply. For example, although all super PACs spent less than $100 million in 2010, two Republican super PACs alone—Restore Our Future and American Crossroads—each spent more than $100 million in 2012. These two groups were the only super PACs that raised or spent more than $100 million in 2012. The most financially active Democratic super PAC, Priorities USA Action, spent approximately $75 million. All other super PACs individually raised and spent less than $50 million.

Even though the number of super PACs grew sharply—from 80 to more than 800 between 2010 and 2012—many were not actively involved in fundraising or spending. In fact, only about 450 super PACs reported raising or spending any money during the 2012 cycle.[44] Most that did so exhibited relatively modest activity; these super PACs raised a median of approximately $53,000 and spent a median of approximately $57,000.[45]

**Table 3.2. The Ten Super PACs Reporting the Most Receipts
and Disbursements for the 2012 Election Cycle**

Committee Name	Total Receipts	Total Disbursements
RESTORE OUR FUTURE, INC.	$153,741,731	$153,316,373
AMERICAN CROSSROADS	$117,472,407	$117,044,325
PRIORITIES USA ACTION	$79,050,419	$75,333,806
MAJORITY PAC	$42,121,541	$42,117,050
HOUSE MAJORITY PAC	$35,844,951	$35,689,886
WINNING OUR FUTURE	$23,921,705	$23,861,421
FREEDOMWORKS FOR AMERICA	$23,453,198	$22,621,967
WORKERS' VOICE	$21,855,151	$21,687,667
CLUB FOR GROWTH ACTION	$18,253,913	$17,931,937
SERVICE EMPLOYEES INTER- NATIONAL UNION PEA-FEDERAL	$16,264,036	$13,079,983

Source: CRS analysis of super PAC data in the FEC Committee Summary File.

Notes: Committee names appear as listed in the FEC data accessed March 2013. All figures are
rounded compared with the original data. These figures could be affected by future amended filings.
Total disbursements include all expenditures, not only independent expenditures. The table relies on
combined receipt and disbursement data. Separate analyses of disbursement and spending data could
yield different results.

Nonetheless, dozens of super PACs raised or spent millions of dollars. Specifically, 75 super PACs reported raising or spending a total of at least $1 mil-
lion; 27 raised or spent at least $5 million.[46] Just 16 super PACs reported raising
or spending at least $10 million during the 2012 cycle. A small number of super
PACs also dominated fundraising and spending in 2012, albeit to a slightly
smaller degree than in 2010. Whereas 10 super PACs accounted for about 75
percent of super PAC fundraising and spending in 2010, 10 super PACs in 2012
collectively raised approximately $531.8 million and spent approximately
$522.7 million, representing about 65 percent of all super PAC spending.

Table 3.2 summarizes financial activity of the 10 super PACs reporting the
largest receipts and expenditures for 2012. The table reports total disbursements rather than only IEs. Therefore, it is important to note that although these
entities raised and spent the most overall, other super PACs might have more
direct impact on the election through higher spending on IEs that call for election or defeat of particular candidates.

What Did Super PACs Spend Supporting or Opposing Federal Candidates in 2010 and 2012?

Brief Answer

Super PACs spent approximately $65.8 million on IEs directly supporting or opposing federal candidates in 2010. That amount increased almost tenfold in 2012, when super PACs spent $620.9 million in IEs supporting and opposing House, Senate, and presidential candidates.[47] Most of that spending was far more likely to oppose candidates than to support candidates. Some of the increase in spending would be expected during a presidential election year, but the rapid growth in super PAC activity during just two election cycles suggests that the groups are solidifying their presence in American elections. As the data will show, super PACs were active across federal elections.

Discussion

As noted earlier, super PACs spent approximately $90.4 million in 2010 overall and almost $800 million overall in 2012. Their independent expenditures—those expenses devoted to calling explicitly for election or defeat of a federal candidate and perhaps the best indicator of super PACs' influence in elections—accounted for 70–80 percent of their spending during both election cycles. Table 3.3 shows how super PACs chose to prioritize their spending on House, Senate, and presidential contests in 2012.

When considering super PAC spending on IEs in 2010 and 2012, readers might find percentages more illustrative than raw spending totals.[48] Regarding the percentage of IE spending favoring and opposing candidates across various types of races in 2010 and 2012,[49] there are both similarities and differences between super PAC IE spending in those years across chambers and parties (fig. 3.2).

Although overall spending increased sharply, as discussed previously, the ratio of support and opposition spending in House-contest IEs among super PACs was roughly consistent between 2010 and 2012. A large plurality of the spending—approximately 46 percent of IE spending in 2010 and 42 percent of IE spending in 2012—opposed Republican candidates, compared with about 30–26 percent of IEs that opposed Democrats. In Senate contests, a greater proportion of spending favored Democrats in 2012 than in 2010. Specifically, less

Table 3.3. Overview of 2012 Super PAC Independent Expenditures by Type of Race and Party

Chamber	Party	Support or Oppose	Total IE Spending
HOUSE	DEMOCRATIC	OPPOSE	$26,473,473
		SUPPORT	$16,693,098
	REPUBLICAN	OPPOSE	$42,988,145
		SUPPORT	$16,875,654
SENATE	DEMOCRATIC	OPPOSE	$34,313,099
		SUPPORT	$12,188,177
	REPUBLICAN	OPPOSE	$63,514,924
		SUPPORT	$24,033,595
PRESIDENTIAL	DEMOCRATIC	OPPOSE	$189,330,326
		SUPPORT	$18,086,773
	REPUBLICAN	OPPOSE	$118,289,181
		SUPPORT	$58,064,074

Source: CRS analysis of 2012 Federal Election Commission independent expenditure reports.

Notes: Information in the table is as reported in FEC independent expenditure reports. CRS calculated the information in the "Total IE Spending" column. The table excludes third-party and independent candidates.

than one-third of super PAC IE spending in 2010 Senate contests favored Democrats by either opposing Republicans (28.1 percent) or supporting Democrats (3.1 percent). In 2012, however, more than half of super PAC IE spending favored Democrats by opposing Republicans (47.4 percent) or supporting Democrats (9.1 percent). At the presidential level, almost two-thirds of 2012 super PAC IEs favored Republicans by either supporting Republicans (15.1 percent) or opposing Democrats (49.3 percent). (Super PACs did not exist in the 2008 presidential cycle.)

Most Super PAC IE Spending Targeted Relatively Few Races

As the preceding section shows, most 2012 super PAC spending occurred in the presidential race. Examining activity in House and Senate races may be especially relevant for Congress. As with other data discussed throughout this report, super PACs spent more on IEs affecting House and Senate races in 2012 than in 2010. That spending also affected more races. Super PACs spent

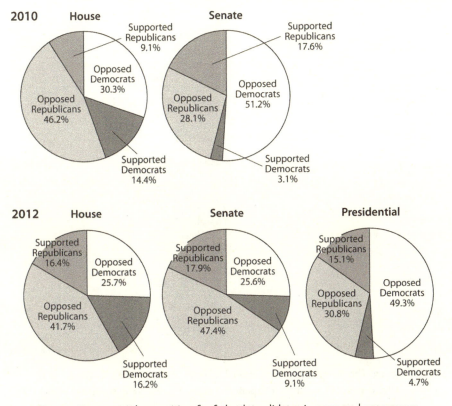

Fig. 3.2: Support and opposition for federal candidates in 2010 and 2012 super PAC independent expenditures. *Notes:* Support and opposition labels are taken from independent expenditure reports. Percentages are based on dollar amounts spent, not number of expenditures. The figure excludes IEs made supporting and opposing independent and third-party candidates. *Source:* CRS figure and analysis of Federal Election Commission independent expenditure reports.

the most on IEs in twenty-five House and Senate races from 2010 and 2012 (fig. 3.3).

Total super PAC IE spending in 2010 races ranged from just $1,100 (in a Kentucky House race) to more than $10 million in the Colorado Senate contest. In 2012, super PAC spending ranged from less than $1,000 in a few House races to $14.5 million in the Wisconsin Senate race.[50] The scope of spending also increased, from 111 House and Senate races in 2010 to 203 in 2012.

Not surprisingly, when super PACs chose to make IEs, they targeted their efforts carefully. In fact, the $10.1 million super PACs spent on IEs in just one Senate race—in Colorado—accounted for 16.5 percent of all super PAC IE

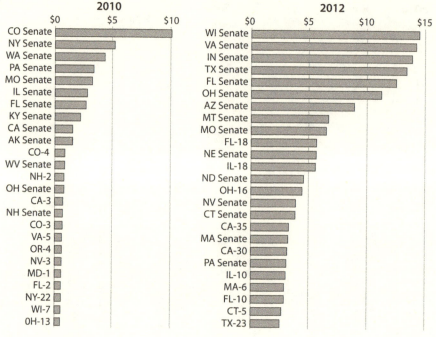

Fig. 3.3: The twenty-five congressional races in 2010 and 2012 in which super PACs spent the most on independent expenditures. *Note:* Numbers after some states are congressional districts. *Source:* CRS figure and analysis of Federal Election Commission independent expenditure reports.

spending in 2010. Of the approximately $60 million super PACs spent in IEs overall in 2010, about 60 percent ($37.4 million) were in the ten Senate contests in which super PACs invested most heavily.[51] In 2012, despite spending in more races, most spending was again targeted to a relative few. Almost 70 percent of super PAC IE spending occurred in twenty-five races (see right side of fig. 3.3).

What Major Super PAC Issues Might Be on the Horizon?

Brief Answer

Because super PACs are new players in elections and because federal law and regulation have not been amended to reflect their presence, Congress might wish to conduct oversight or pursue legislative activity to clarify these new groups' place in federal campaigns. Super PAC activity might also be relevant for congressional oversight of the FEC as that agency continues to consider post–*Citizens United* rulemakings and reporting requirements. Looking ahead, questions about super PAC relationships with other organizations (particularly the issues of coordination and contribution limits), transparency, and their effect on future elections may be of particular interest.

Discussion

Super PACs address some of the most prominent and divisive issues in campaign finance policy. Most attention to super PACs is likely to emphasize their financial influence in elections, as is typically the case when new forces emerge on the campaign finance scene. Underlying that financial activity is law, regulation, or situational guidance (for example, advisory opinions)—or the lack thereof—that shapes how super PACs operate and are understood.

POLICY APPROACHES As noted previously, despite *Citizens United* and *Speech-Now,* federal election law and FEC regulations have not, as of this writing, been amended to reflect the rise of super PACs. If Congress considers it important to recognize the role of super PACs in some way, it could amend the FECA to do so. As it has generally done with other forms of PACs, Congress could also leave the matter to the FEC's regulatory discretion.[52] The following points may be particularly relevant as Congress considers how or whether to proceed:

- Because advisory opinions do not have the force of regulation or law, the status of super PACs is arguably unsettled. Additional legislative or regulatory action to implement super PAC components of *Citizens United* and *SpeechNow* might provide additional clarity to those wishing to organize or contribute to super PACs.
- If Congress believes additional clarity would be beneficial, it could choose to enact legislation. This approach might be favored if Congress wishes to specify particular requirements surrounding super PACs, either by amending the FECA or by directing the FEC to draft rules on particular topics. Legislation has a potential advantage of allowing Congress to specify its preferences on its timetable. It has the potential disadvantage of falling short of sponsors' wishes if sufficient agreement cannot be found to enact the legislation. No legislation introduced in the 112th

or 113th Congresses focuses specifically on super PACs, but some bills contain relevant provisions. In the 113th Congress, H.R. 270 (Price, NC) would bar super PAC fundraising by federal candidates and officeholders. The 2013 version of the DISCLOSE Act—H.R. 148 (Van Hollen, MD)—proposes new disclaimer requirements that would apply to ads funded by super PACs and other entities.

- As an alternative to legislation, Congress could choose to defer to the FEC or perhaps other agencies, such as the Internal Revenue Service (IRS) or the Securities and Exchange Commission (SEC), with respect to new or amended rules affecting super PACs. This approach has the potential advantage of delegating a relatively technical issue to an agency (or agencies) most familiar with the topic, in addition to freeing Congress to pursue other agenda items. It has the potential disadvantage of producing results to which Congress might object, particularly if the six-member FEC deadlocks, as it has done on certain high-profile issues in recent years. The result could resemble the status quo, in which there are few definitive answers about how super PACs are regulated. If Congress were to choose the rulemaking approach, providing as explicit instructions as possible about the topics to be addressed and the scope of regulations could increase the chances of the rules reflecting congressional intent. Doing so might also increase the chances that consensus could be achieved during the implementation process.

Potential Policy Questions and Issues for Consideration

Despite some high-profile activity in 2010 and 2012, much about super PACs remains unknown. This lack of knowledge is due to both the status of these entities as new players in elections and the unsettled state of law and regulation surrounding the entities. The following points may warrant consideration as the super PAC issue continues to emerge.

What is the Relationship Between Super PACs and Other Political Committees or Organizations?

As noted previously, the FEC considers super PACs to be political committees subject to the requirements and restrictions contained in FECA and FEC regulations. As such, super PACs are prohibited from coordinating their activities with campaigns or other political committees (for example, parties).[53] Particularly during the 2012 election cycle, some observers raised questions about whether super PACs were really operating independently or whether their activities might violate the spirit of limits on contributions or coordination regulations. The following points may be relevant as Congress assesses where super PACs fit in the campaign environment:

- Concerns about super PAC independence appear to be motivated at least in part by the reported migration of some candidate-campaign staff members to super PACs that have stated their support for these candidates.[54]
- A second source of concern may be that legally separate organizations (for example, 501(c) tax-exempt political organizations, which are generally not regulated by the FEC or federal election law) operate alongside some super PACs.[55] Media reports (and, it appears, popular sentiment) sometimes characterize these entities, despite their status as unique political committees or politically active organizations, as a single group. Questions also emerged during the 2012 cycle about whether some large contributions—which would be prohibited if they went to candidate campaigns—were essentially routed through super PACs as IEs. Donors who wish to do so may now contribute to candidate campaigns in limited amounts, and in unlimited amounts to super PACs supporting or opposing these or other candidates.
- As noted previously, super PACs must identify donors who contributed at least $200. This requirement sheds light on contributions that go directly to super PACs, but not necessarily those that go indirectly to super PACs. In particular, the original source of contributions to trade associations or other organizations that later fund IEs through super PACs could go unreported. For example, assume Company A made a contribution to Trade Association B, and placed no restrictions on how the contribution could be used. Trade Association B then used Company A's funds to contribute to a super PAC. Trade Association B—not Company A—would be reported as the donor on FEC reports. An essential element in this relationship in this series of events is whether the original contribution was "made for the purpose of furthering" an independent expenditure (fig. 3.4). In practice, this means that those who do not wish their identities to be reported to the FEC could make an unrestricted donation to an

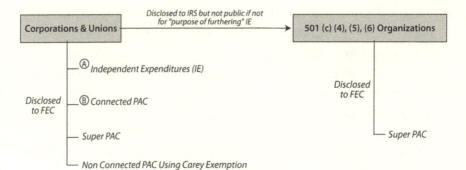

Fig. 3.4: Sample disclosure for corporations and unions using direct spending versus contributions to other entities. *Notes:* An individual could also spend funds as described on the left side of the figure (e.g., as could a corporation or union). The 501(c) groups on the right side of the figure refer to social welfare organizations [(c)(4)s], unions [(c)(5)s], and trade associations [(c)(6)s]. *Source:* CRS figure based on analysis of current disclosure requirements discussed throughout this chapter.

intermediary organization, which then funnels the money to a super PAC. By contrast, if a corporation, union, or individual chooses to contribute directly to a super PAC, or to make IEs itself, the entity's identity would have to be disclosed to the FEC.

a. Reporting obligations would also apply to electioneering communications (ECs), if applicable, although such a scenario appears unlikely for super PACs.

b. A corporation or union could provide administrative support to a connected PAC, but contributions must come from voluntary donations raised subject to FECA limits.

- Because super PACs are prohibited from coordinating their activities with campaigns, Congress might or might not feel that gathering additional information about super PACs' independence is warranted. Whether or not super PACs are sufficiently independent and whether their activities are tantamount to contributions could be subject to substantial debate and would likely depend on individual circumstances.

- Concerns about the potential for allegedly improper coordination between super PACs and the candidates they favor are a prominent aspect of the debate thus far, but some might contend that more coordination would benefit super PACs and candidates by permitting them to have a unified agenda and message. Candidate frustration with "outside" spending is not unique to super PACs. Indeed, uncoordinated activities by traditional PACs, parties, and interest groups are a common occurrence in federal elections, although some contend that super PACs make concerns about outside messages increasingly urgent.[56] Some observers contend that the ability to coordinate should, therefore, be increased. Others, however, warn that permitting more communication between outside groups and campaigns would facilitate circumventing limits on campaign contributions. If Congress wished to limit potential coordination between super PACs and candidates or parties, it could amend the FECA to supersede the existing coordination standard, which is currently housed in FEC regulations and has long been complex and controversial.[57]

- It remains to be seen whether super PACs will compete with or complement other institutional actors in elections, particularly other entities that engage in independent expenditures, such as political parties. It is also unclear whether, over time, super PACs will primarily focus on multiple candidates or single candidates. Thus far, developments suggest that, as with other nonparty groups, super PACs could both complement and threaten traditional parties. After the 2012 elections, for example, some observers blamed super PACs for exacerbating alleged divisions among Republicans, while others saw them as a resource to eliminate primary candidates whom some political professionals viewed as insufficiently mainstream to win general elections.[58]

- Over time, some "traditional" PACs—not operating as super PACs— might be able to adapt some super PAC organizational characteristics. Specifically, in October 2011 the FEC announced that in response to an agreement reached in a recent court case (*Carey v. FEC*),[59] the agency would permit *nonconnected* PACs—those that are unaffiliated with corporations or unions—to accept unlimited contributions for use in independent expenditures. The agency directed PACs choosing to do so to keep the IE contributions in a separate bank account from the one used to make contributions to federal candidates.[60] As such, nonconnected PACs that want to raise unlimited sums for IEs are now able to create a separate bank account and meet additional reporting obligations rather than form a separate super PAC. It remains to be seen how widely this practice will be adopted. Even if widespread, super PACs could continue to serve as an avenue for those other than nonconnected PACs (for example, PACs connected to labor organizations or corporations, or groups of individuals) to engage in unlimited fundraising and spending on IEs.

Is Super PAC Activity Sufficiently Transparent?

In addition to the organizational questions noted earlier—which may involve transparency concerns—Congress may be faced with examining whether enough information about super PACs is publicly available to meet the FECA goal of preventing real or apparent corruption.[61] The following points may be particularly relevant as Congress considers transparency surrounding super PACs:

- In the absence of additional reporting requirements, or perhaps amendments clarifying the FEC's coordination[62] rules, determining the professional networks that drive super PACs will likely be left to the media or self-reporting. In particular, relationships between super PACs and possibly related entities, such as 527 and 501(c) organizations, generally cannot be widely or reliably established based on current reporting requirements.[63]
- As the appendix notes, and as is the case with most political committees, assessing super PAC financial activities generally requires using multiple kinds of reports filed with the FEC. Depending on when those reports are filed, it can be difficult to summarize all super PAC spending affecting federal elections. Due to amended filings, data can change frequently. Reconciling IE reports with other reports (for example, those filed after an election) can also be challenging and can require technical expertise. Streamlining reporting for super PACs might have benefits of making data more available for regulators and researchers. On the other hand, some may argue that because super PAC activities are independent, their reporting obligations should be fewer than for political committees making or receiving contributions.
- Because super PACs (and other PACs) may file semiannual reports during non–election years, information about potentially significant fundraising or spending activity might go publicly unreported for as long as six months. Consequently, some super PACs did not file detailed disclosure reports summarizing their 2011 activity until after the 2012 Iowa caucus and primaries in states such as New Hampshire, Florida, and South Carolina.

- Given the preceding points, a policy question for Congress may be whether the implications of the current reporting requirements represent "loopholes" that should be closed or whether existing requirements are sufficient.[64] If additional information is desired, Congress or the FEC could revisit campaign finance law or regulation to require greater clarity about financial transactions. As with disclosure generally, the decision to revisit specific reporting requirements will likely be affected by how much detail is deemed necessary to prevent corruption or accomplish other goals.

Conclusion

Super PACs are only one element of modern campaigns. Regular media attention to super PACs might give an overstated impression of these organizations' influence in federal elections. Nonetheless—and notwithstanding that much about the organizations remains to be seen—there appears to be no shortage of individuals and organizations eager to form these new political committees that can raise and spend unlimited sums supporting or opposing federal candidates.

Super PACs join other groups in American politics, such as parties and 527 organizations, that are legally separate from the candidates they support or oppose, but that some regard as practically an extension of the campaign. Questions of super PAC independence were particularly relevant in 2012, as super PACs competed to elect or defeat congressional and presidential candidates. As with most campaign finance issues, whether Congress decides to take action on the super PAC issue, and how, will likely depend on the extent to which super PAC activities are viewed as an exercise in free speech by independent organizations versus thinly veiled extensions of individual campaigns.

Appendix: Methodological Notes

The information about super PAC fundraising and spending contained in this report resulted from CRS analysis of FEC data. This appendix briefly discusses the methodology employed and notes caveats that may affect how the data are interpreted or replicated. Alternative approaches would likely yield different results. CRS consulted extensively with FEC staff about data matters.[65]

This report relies primarily on two data sources. Notes in the text, tables, and figures identify the data for each point of analysis. As explained in the text of the report, super PACs file at least two kinds of regular financial reports with the FEC: (1) monthly or semiannual summaries of all fundraising and spending (FEC form 3X and schedule E);[66] and (2) twenty-four- or forty-eight-hour notices of independent expenditures (which may also be filed using schedule E). Because these reports cover different periods and are filed at different times, slight differences in fundraising and spending amounts are common. Reconciling the reports can be particularly challenging and time-consuming, and may be of limited utility because differences between the two are usually small.

For the overall fundraising and spending amounts discussed in the report, the analysis relies on summaries of total fundraising and spending (derived from the 3X filings) provided by the FEC for 2010, or as accessed from the FEC committee summary file for 2012. The analysis of spending that supports or opposes candidates comes from the independent expenditure (IE) reports, which provide the clearest statements of super PAC spending favoring one candidate or another and which are filed in real time. Amended or duplicate filings may change the results if replicated in the future. Amended filings appear not to have been a major factor in the 2010 data. For 2012, CRS analyzed all IE filings and deleted filings that appeared to be superseded by amendments. Nonetheless, variation in campaign finance data is typical depending on the source, when the data were accessed, and how amendments were handled.

In the absence of additional reporting requirements, identifying super PACs currently requires the assumption that a super PAC has notified the FEC of its status by letter. To isolate super PAC spending on IEs, CRS accessed the entire 2010 and 2012 IE data files and selected those made by organizations that had notified the commission of their super PAC status.[67] Some cases of ambiguous organization names (for example, various state-level chapters of a national organization or groups with similar names but different filing obligations) required consultation with FEC staff. It is possible that organizations that were excluded are, in fact, super PACs but filed reports incorrectly or not at all. Similarly, because data throughout the report rely on information reported to the FEC, an organization whose spending was too low to trigger disclosure requirements would not be reflected in the report. Therefore, the data exclude a presumably small amount of super PAC financial activity. Missing data might be exacerbated if a super PAC did not believe its activities required disclosure, or if, for example, it chose not to file until federal election laws or regulations were amended to explicitly address super PACs.

For the analysis of spending on individual races, CRS standardized spellings of candidate names and the indicators for the districts or states in which they sought election. The total spending amounts and total IE amounts listed for the House and Senate races discussed are based on amounts from individual candidate reports contained on the FEC website, which CRS combined to yield totals for the entire race. These totals include primary and general election activity, and are listed as such on the FEC website.

CRS calculated the *favored Democrats* and *favored Republicans* amounts by totaling sums in IE reports listed as supporting or opposing candidates from each major party (for example, *favored Democrats* includes expenditures reported as supporting Democrats or opposing Republicans). The *favored* measure arguably accounts for the overall effect of IE spending by examining both supportive and opposing messages that could benefit one candidate over another. The measure assumes that, for example, a negative message (reported as *opposed*) about a Republican candidate advantages the Democratic opponent. This would not be so in all cases (such as in IEs aired during primary contests). Overall, however, this approach may provide a more complete picture of super PAC activities than one that assumes advertising that supports or opposes one candidate has no effect on another.

This report does not attempt to assess the practical effect of these expenditures on individual candidates or to fully document their implications in individual races. As such, the spending discussed here should be regarded as one measure of super PAC activity, but not a comprehensive accounting of super PACs' electoral influence.

Notes

1. For a discussion of current campaign finance issues generally, see CRS Report R41542, *The State of Campaign Finance Policy: Recent Developments and Issues for Congress,* by R. Sam Garrett.

2. On the definition of IEs, see 2 U.S.C. § 431(17).

3. 130 S. Ct. 876 [558 U.S. 310] (2010); and 599 F.3d 686 (D.C. Cir. 2010), respectively.

4. The information here is not intended to be exhaustive. For additional information, see, for example, 11 C.F.R. § 109.20 and 11 C.F.R. § 109.21.

5. As the term is commonly used, 527 refers to groups registered with the Internal Revenue

Service (IRS) as Section 527 political organizations that seemingly intend to influence federal elections in ways that may place them outside the FECA definition of a political committee. By contrast, political committees (which include candidate committees, party committees, and political action committees) are regulated by the FEC and federal election law. There is a debate regarding which 527s are required to register with the FEC as political committees. For additional discussion, see CRS Report RS22895, *527 Groups and Campaign Activity: Analysis Under Campaign Finance and Tax Laws,* by L. Paige Whitaker and Erika K. Lunder. All political committees, including super PACs, are Section 527 political organizations for tax purposes.

6. 130 S. Ct. 876 [558 U.S. 310] (2010). For additional discussion, see CRS Report R41045, *The Constitutionality of Regulating Corporate Expenditures: A Brief Analysis of the Supreme Court Ruling in Citizens United v. FEC,* by L. Paige Whitaker.

7. 599 F.3d 686 (D.C. Cir. 2010).

8. Federal election law and FEC regulations have not been amended to clarify the role of super PACs. *SpeechNow* and related FEC advisory opinions have held that super PACs cannot make contributions to candidates or parties.

9. This is particularly true, some argue, for super PACs that are believed to be organized primarily for supporting or opposing particular campaigns rather than several campaigns. See, for example, Fred Wertheimer, "Democracy Loses With Super PACs," *Politico,* September 28, 2011, p. 27.

10. See, for example, Federal Election Commission, "FEC Statement on the Supreme Court's Decision in Citizens United v. FEC," press release, February 5, 2010, http://www.fec .gov/press/press2010/20100205CitizensUnited.shtml.

11. The commission deadlocked in two 3–3 votes on draft NPRM documents 11-02, draft A, and 11-02-A, at the January 20, 2011, meeting. See Federal Election Commission, January 20, 2011, meeting minutes, pp. 4–5, http://www.fec.gov/agenda/2011/approved 2011_06.pdf. A vote to approve draft NPRM document 11-33 failed on a 2–4 vote at the June 15, 2011, commission meeting. At the same meeting, alternative draft NPRM document 11-33-A resulted in a deadlocked 3–3 vote. See Federal Election Commission, June 15, 2011, meeting minutes, pp. 3–4, http://www.fec.gov/agenda/2011/approved 2011_39.pdf. FECA requires that at least four commissioners vote affirmatively to approve NPRMs and final rules. For additional discussion, see CRS Report RS22780, *The Federal Election Commission (FEC) With Fewer than Four Members: Overview of Policy Implications,* by R. Sam Garrett.

12. Federal Election Commission, "Independent Expenditures and Electioneering Communications by Corporations and Labor Organizations," 248 *Federal Register* 80803, December 27, 2011.

13. AOs provide an opportunity to pose questions about how the commission interprets the applicability of FECA or FEC regulations to a specific situation (e.g., a planned campaign expenditure). AOs apply only to the requester and within specific circumstances, but can provide general guidance for those in similar situations. See 2 U.S.C. § 437f.

14. The AOs are available from the FEC website, at https://www.fec.gov/data/legal/advisory -opinions/.

15. For sample letters, see appendix A in AOs 2010-09 and 2010-11.

16. AOs do not have the force of regulation or law. Although AOs can provide guidance on similar circumstances in other settings, some may argue that AOs cannot, in and of themselves, create broad guidance about super PACs or other topics.

17. Majority PAC was formerly known as Commonsense Ten, the super PAC discussed earlier.

18. On limitations on contributions to PACs, see table 3.1 in CRS Report R41542, *The State of Campaign Finance Policy: Recent Developments and Issues for Congress,* by R. Sam Garrett. This section assumes a super PAC would achieve *multicandidate committee* status. Multicandidate committees are those that have been registered with the FEC (or, for Senate committees, the secretary of the Senate) for at least six months; have received federal contributions from more than fifty people; and (except for state parties) have made contributions to at least five federal candidates. See 11 C.F.R. § 100.5(e)(3). In practice, most PACs attain multicandidate status automatically over time.

19. Colbert's super PAC is popularly known as the Colbert Super PAC. It is registered with the FEC as Americans for a Better Tomorrow, Tomorrow. For a scholarly discussion, see R. Sam Garrett, "Seriously Funny: Understanding Campaign Finance Policy Through the Colbert Super PAC," *Saint Louis University Law Journal* 56, no. 3 (Spring 2012): 711–23.

20. On the press exemption, see 2 U.S.C. § 431(9)(B)(i); 11 C.F.R. § 100.73; 11 C.F.R. § 100.132; and discussion in AO 2011-11, pp. 6–8.

21. See AO 2011-11, pp. 7–9. AOs are available from the FEC website at https://www.fec .gov/data/legal/advisory-opinions/.

22. Ibid., p. 9.

23. See AO request (AOR) 2011-23, p. 5. The AOR was filed, as is typical, in a letter from the requester's counsel to the FEC General Counsel. See Letter from Thomas Josefiak and Michael Bayes to Anthony Herman, General Counsel, FEC, October 28, 2011, in the AO 2011-23 documents at https://www.fec.gov/data/legal/advisory-opinions/.

24. Coordination is discussed later in this report. On coordination and the three-part regulatory test for coordination, see, respectively, 2 U.S.C. § 441a(a)(7)(B) and 11 C.F.R. § 109.21.

25. Commissioners Bauerly and Weintraub issued a "statement of reasons" document explaining their rationale, as did Commissioner Walther and the three Republican commissioners. See Cynthia L. Bauerly and Ellen L. Weintraub, *Statement on Advisory Opinion Request 2011-23 (American Crossroads),* Washington, DC: Federal Election Commission, December 1, 2011; Steven T. Walther, *Advisory Opinion Request 2011-23 (American Crossroads): Statement of Commissioner Steven T. Walther,* Washington, DC: Federal Election Commission, December 1, 2011; and Caroline C. Hunter, Donald T. McGahn, and Matthew S. Petersen, *Advisory Opinion Request 2011-23 (American Crossroads): Statement*

of Vice Chair Caroline C. Hunter and Commissioners Donald T. McGahn and Mat-
thew S. Petersen, Washington, DC: Federal Election Commission, December 1, 2011.

26. Leadership PACs are PACs affiliated with members of Congress that provide an additional funding mechanism to support colleagues' campaigns. Although historically the
purview of members of the House and Senate leadership, many members of Congress
now have leadership PACs. Leadership PACs are separate from the candidate's principal
campaign committee.

27. This is FEC form 1. Essentially, it provides the FEC with information about how to contact the campaign and identifies the treasurer.

28. Political committees devoted solely to Senate activities file reports with the secretary of
the Senate, who transmits them to the FEC for public positing. In theory, if a super PAC
were devoted solely to affecting Senate campaigns, it is possible the super PAC would
file with the secretary rather than with the FEC. Nonetheless, the information would be
transmitted to the FEC.

29. Reporting typically occurs quarterly. Pre- and postelection reports must also be filed. Non-
candidate committees may also file monthly reports. See, for example, 2 U.S.C. § 434 and
the FEC's *Campaign Guide* series for additional discussion of reporting requirements.

30. As noted previously, unlike other political committees, Senate political committees (e.g.,
a senator's principal campaign committee) file reports with the secretary of the Senate,
who transmits them to the FEC. See 2 U.S.C. § 432(g).

31. The occupation and employer requirements apply to contributions from individuals.

32. The FECA contains some exceptions. For example, all disbursements used to make contributions to another political committee must be itemized, regardless of amount. See 2
U.S.C. § 434(b)(4).

33. FEC policy guidance has stated that "when considered along with the identity of the
disbursement recipient, [the purpose of the disbursement] must be sufficiently specific to
make the purpose of the disbursement clear." In general, however, political committees
have broad leeway in describing the purpose of disbursements. For example, the commission has noted that generic terms such as "administrative expenses" are inadequate,
but "salary" is sufficient. The quoted material and additional discussion appears in Federal Election Commission, "Statement of Policy: Purpose of Disbursement," 72 *Federal
Register* 887–89, January 9, 2007.

34. Quarterly reports are due to the FEC on April 15, July 15, and October 15. The final
quarterly report is due January 31 of the next year. Monthly reports are due to the commission twenty days after the end of the previous month. The year-end report is due by
January 31 of the year after the election. Preelection reports summarizing activity for the
final weeks of an election period must be filed with the FEC twelve days before the election. Monthly or quarterly reports are not required if their due dates fall near an otherwise
required preelection report. Post-general-election reports must be filed thirty days after
the election; postprimary reports are not required. Additional requirements apply to special elections. See 11 C.F.R. § 104.5(c)(1).

35. The reports are due to the FEC by July 31 and January 31, respectively. See 11 C.F.R. § 104.5(c)(2).
36. Separate reporting obligations apply to electioneering communications.
37. See, for example, 2 U.S.C. § 434(g).
38. 2 U.S.C. § 434(g)(3)(B).
39. Remaining amounts were apparently spent on items such as administrative expenses and nonfederal races. IE totals range from approximately $61 million to approximately $65 million, depending on whether one analyzes summary data provided by the FEC or sums individual IE filings. As discussed elsewhere in this report, various data sources and different filing schedules often yield slightly different numbers.
40. The FEC provided CRS with data on spending by individual committees. The text in this section is based on CRS analysis of those data, including aggregating the totals and calculating percentages listed in the text.
41. The FEC subsequently terminated administratively some super PACs that had no financial activity.
42. The 2012 findings are based on CRS analysis of total receipts and disbursements by super PACs as reported in the FEC committee summary file.
43. The FEC provided CRS with data on spending by individual committees. CRS aggregated the totals listed in the text. In the absence of additional regulations concerning registration for super PACs, it is not clear that all organizations are reflected in the figures in the text.
44. This information is based on CRS analysis of super PAC data in the FEC committee summary file.
45. Ibid.
46. Ibid.
47. Ibid. This figure excludes IEs supporting or opposing third-party and independent candidates.
48. Table 3.3 excludes 2010 data to conserve space, but the data are available from the author and in previous versions of this report.
49. The data represent total spending. Although not reflected in FEC reports, alternative measures might include, for example, the number of unique advertisements, gross rating points (in brief, a measure of advertising impressions) purchased, etc.
50. This section only shows data in the figures and table for spending in the twenty-five contests in which super PACs spent the most on IEs. The underlying CRS analysis is based on all super PAC IE spending.
51. These are the "CO Senate" through "AK Senate" entries on the top of the left side of the figure.
52. For example, traditional PACs, known as "separate segregated funds," originally arose from advisory opinions in the 1970s. Congress later incorporated the PAC concept into FECA amendments. For a historical overview, see, for example, Robert E. Mutch, *Campaigns, Congress, and Courts: The Making of Federal Campaign Finance Law* (New

York: Praeger, 1988), 152–85; and Anthony Corrado, "Money and Politics: A History of Federal Campaign Finance Law," in *The New Campaign Finance Sourcebook,* by Anthony Corrado, Thomas E. Mann, Daniel R. Ortiz, and Trevor Potter (Washington, DC: Brookings Institution Press, 2005), 7–47.

53. As noted previously, this report reflects common understanding of regulation and law as applied to super PACs. Subsequent changes in law or regulation that explicitly address super PACs could yield alternative findings.

54. See, for example, Nicholas Confessore, "Lines Blur Between Candidates and PACs with Unlimited Cash," *New York Times,* August 27, 2011, A1; Steven Greenhouse, "A Campaign Finance Ruling Turned to Labor's Advantage," *New York Times,* September 26, 2011, A1; and Kenneth P. Vogel, "Super PACs' New Playground: 2012," *Politico,* August 10, 2011, online ed. retrieved via LexisNexis.

55. For example, American Crossroads is a registered super PAC; Crossroads Grassroots Policy Strategies (GPS) is a (c)(4) tax-exempt organization. The same is reportedly true for perceived Democratic counterparts Priorities USA Action and Priorities USA, respectively. See, for example, the sources noted in the previous note; and Eliza Newlin Carney, "The Deregulated Campaign," *CQ Weekly Report,* September 19, 2011, 1922.

56. See, for example, Josh Boak, "Enter the Era of the Super PAC," *Campaigns & Elections,* September 2011, online ed., http://www.campaignsandelections.com/magazine/us-edition /257312/enter-the-era-of-super-pacs.thtml. On campaign concerns about outside messages generally, see, for example, Michael John Burton and Daniel M. Shea, *Campaign Mode: Strategic Vision in Congressional Elections* (Lanham, MD: Rowman & Littlefield, 2003); R. Sam Garrett, *Campaign Crises: Detours on the Road to Congress* (Boulder, CO: Lynne Rienner Publishers, 2010); and David B. Magleby, J. Quin Monson, and Kelly D. Patterson, eds., *Dancing Without Partners: How Candidates, Parties, and Interest Groups Interact in the Presidential Campaign* (Lanham, MD: Rowman & Littlefield, 2007).

57. The coordinated communication regulations are at 11 C.F.R. 109.21.

58. See, for example, Eliza Newlin Carney, "Republican Super PAC War Splits the Party," *Roll Call,* March 20, 2013, 1.

59. Civ. No. 11-259-RMC (D.D.C. 2011).

60. Federal Election Commission, "FEC Statement on *Carey v. FEC* Reporting Guidance for Political Committees that Maintain a Non-contribution Account," press release, October 5, 2011.

61. For additional discussion of disclosure matters generally, see CRS Report R41542, *The State of Campaign Finance Policy: Recent Developments and Issues for Congress,* by R. Sam Garrett.

62. See, for example, 11 CFR § 109.20-11 and CFR § 109.23.

63. See, for example, CRS Report R41542, *The State of Campaign Finance Policy: Recent Developments and Issues for Congress,* by R. Sam Garrett; Eliza Newlin Carney, "The Deregulated Campaign," *CQ Weekly Report,* September 19, 2011, 1922; and Diane Freda,

"Section 501(c)(4) Spending Expected to Hit New Records in 2012 Election," *Daily Report for Executives,* vol. 180 (September 16, 2011): J-1.

64. Members of Congress have taken a variety of positions over the appropriate level of disclosure for political committees and other organizations in recent years. This is particularly true for what level of disclosure should be required for contributions to organizations making IEs or electioneering communications—perhaps most notably in recent years through the 111th Congress debate over the DISCLOSE Act (2009–2010). See CRS Report R41264, *The DISCLOSE Act: Overview and Analysis,* by R. Sam Garrett, L. Paige Whitaker, and Erika K. Lunder. In the 112th Congress, Rep. Van Hollen filed a rulemaking petition with the FEC stating that the agency had improperly interpreted statute when writing regulations (11 C.F.R. § 109.10(e)) that required disclosure of contributions supporting independent expenditures only if the contributions were made "for the purpose of furthering" the IEs. See Federal Election Commission, "Rulemaking Petition: Independent Expenditure Reporting," 76 *Federal Register* 36000, June 21, 2011.

65. In particular, this included consultation with FEC disclosure database analyst Paul Clark.

66. Form 3X reports receipts and disbursements for entities other than authorized committees (e.g., PACs). Schedule E of form 3X reports itemized independent expenditures, including indications of support for or opposition to specific candidates. Electronic versions of schedule E are known as form 24.

67. The remaining IEs were reported by entities such as traditional PACs, parties, or individuals.

Discussion Questions

1. What are super PACs, and what Supreme Court decisions led to their emergence?
2. How do super PACs differ from traditional PACs?
3. What are some of the positive and negative consequences of super PACs for the American political process?

4

Reforming the Modern Congress

Donald R. Wolfensberger

ON SEPTEMBER 28, 2016, TWO ILLINOIS congressmen introduced a resolution to establish a Joint Committee on the Organization of Congress. Representative Darin LaHood (R-IL) and Representative Dan Lipinski (D-IL), were joined by thirty-seven cosponsors (ten Democrats and twenty-seven Republicans) in calling for "a full and complete study of the organization, operations, [and] functions" of Congress, "and relevant interactions of the Members." The joint committee would be charged with reporting its findings (and presumably any recommendations) to the House and Senate not later than the end of each session of its existence.[1]

The proposed joint committee is clearly patterned after three precursor committees of the same name in 1945, 1965, and 1993. The first two efforts were enacted into law in 1946 and 1970. The last joint committee's work, however, died aborning in the House Rules Committee in September 1994 when House Speaker Tom Foley (D-WA) pulled the plug on it in the middle of markup (the committee amendment process).[2]

If there is a common refrain running through the history of the republic, it is that Congress is not measuring up to what the founders intended of it: it is incapable of doing its job in an effective and accountable manner; it has been subordinated to the president and executive branch; and it is losing the faith and trust of the American people. Consequently, there has always been a chorus for reforming the institution, though the chorus emanates more often from the choir loft than on the floor of the two chambers.

Nevertheless, the chorus periodically builds to a crescendo that Congress can no longer ignore, and it is forced to act. Since World War II, Congress has undergone many changes. Some are a result of major reform efforts, such as the Legislative Reorganization Acts of 1946 and 1970. Other significant changes in the institution have occurred through more targeted efforts aimed at particular problems. Most notable are the War Powers Resolution of 1973, in response to the Vietnam War experience; the Congressional Budget and Impoundment Control Act of 1974, in response to President Nixon's impoundment policy of refusing to spend funds appropriated by Congress; and the Ethics Reform Act of 1989 (originally passed in 1978 as the Ethics in Government Act) in response to a spate of scandals on Capitol Hill. Still other changes have been accomplished through amendments to the standing rules of the House and Senate or through alterations in party-caucus rules.

In each case the changes made were in response to national crises, institutional failings, or scandals. The reforms are usually designed to make Congress better equipped to handle its responsibilities, or to improve public opinions about the legislative branch. While not all changes produce the desired results, and some even have unintended consequences and negative backlashes, taken together they evidence a willingness, albeit, often a reluctant inclination, to adapt to new developments and keep the institution relevant, dynamic, and worthy of public support.

The purpose of this chapter is to briefly trace the history of these reform efforts over the last seven decades—what precipitated them, what they aimed to accomplish, and how well they succeeded (or failed). Finally, the chapter will discuss some of the current problems Congress is having and how various reform efforts have contributed to them.[3]

The Legislative Reorganization Act of 1946

Coming out of World War II, Congress suffered the brunt of criticism in the media and elsewhere over the extent to which its powers and capabilities had not kept pace with the mounting complexities of the mid-twentieth century. The social welfare state and national security state rising out of the Great Depression and World War II, respectively, greatly enhanced the powers of the presidency and left Congress with relatively diminished strength and capabilities.

Demands arose both inside and outside the Congress to restore the institution as a coequal branch of government with respect to the presidency.

Responding to these demands, Congress established a Joint Committee on the Organization of Congress in 1945 to conduct a comprehensive study of the organization and operation of Congress "with a view toward strengthening the Congress, simplifying its operations, improving its relationships with other branches . . . and enabling it better to meet its responsibilities under the Constitution."

The bipartisan and bicameral committee of twelve members, cochaired by Senator Robert M. La Follette Jr. (Progressive-WI) and Representative A. S. "Mike" Monroney (D-OK) produced a set of recommendations to overhaul the basic structures of Congress. The most dramatic change in what was to become the Legislative Reorganization Act of 1946 was the reduction in the number of committees in the House from forty-eight to nineteen, and in the Senate from thirty-three to fifteen. Committee jurisdictions were codified and, for the first time, committees were provided with professional and clerical staff. Staffing at the legislative drafting office (now Office of the Legislative Counsel) and Legislative Reference Service (now the Congressional Research Service) was also increased.

Congress was encouraged to exercise better oversight of the executive branch, and a joint budget committee was established to produce an annual concurrent resolution on the budget by April 15. The act also bestowed on members a 25 percent pay increase. Finally, lobbyists were required to register with both the House and the Senate.

The 1946 act was not without unintended consequences. While the number of committees was substantially reduced, the law did not limit the number of subcommittees, and they proliferated like rabbits. The codification of committee jurisdictions did not necessarily untangle overlaps (ten of the nineteen House committees' jurisdictions were left untouched). Moreover, the stabilization and consolidation of committees, along with staff increases, both strengthened committees, as intended, but also heightened the importance of committee and subcommittee chairmanships based on seniority—the elevation to the top of members with the longest committee service. Seniority favored those members with the safest seats and lowest turnover rate, predominantly, Democrats from the one-party South.

Finally, the act's attempt to reclaim Congress's powers over the purse strings, by creating an annual budget resolution with enforceable spending caps, was abandoned after three years before being fully implemented, mainly due to resistance from appropriators. (A consolidated-appropriations-bill approach was tried in 1950 but soon abandoned as being too unwieldy.)

While the intent of the 1945–1946 reform effort was to increase Congress's esteem in the eyes of the public, majority Democrats were turned out of power in both houses in the 1946 elections—before the changes even took effect.[4]

The Legislative Reorganization Act of 1970

Notwithstanding the mixed results of the 1946 joint committee reforms, Congress established a nearly identical committee in 1965 with a similar mandate to study the institution and recommend changes to simplify its operations and improve its relations with the other branches. The twelve-member committee was headed this time by Senator Mike Monroney and Representative Ray Madden (D-IN).

The reasons for creating another congressional reform committee were similar to those behind the 1945 effort. Congress was again seen as falling behind the executive branch in its powers and performance and was again held in low public esteem.

Liberal reformers supported creating the joint committee for another reason, more sub-rosa in nature, and that was to use it as a vehicle for undermining the seniority system. However, they failed, both in committee and on the floor, to take down the seniority system directly. The closest they came was offering a House floor amendment to permit consideration of factors other than seniority in selecting committee chairs, and it was defeated.

Reformers were more successful in including changes that indirectly loosened the grip of committee chairs whom they considered out of touch with the majority caucus's more liberal policy preferences. At the heart of these was a "committee bill of rights" that enshrined in the rules a more democratic process that strengthened the hand of committee members.

The committee bill of rights required committees to adopt rules setting regular meeting days, allowing a majority of committee members to add items to the agenda, authorizing the broadcasting of House committee hearings, making publicly available a record of committee votes and meeting transcripts, permitting the filing of minority and additional views to committee reports, and enhancing minority party members' powers on committees, including the right to call witnesses and appoint minority staff.

Perhaps the most significant change made by the act was House adoption of a floor amendment offered by Representative Thomas P. "Tip" O'Neill Jr. of Massachusetts, who would become Democratic whip in 1971. The amendment authorized recorded votes in the committee of the whole, where most floor amending activity takes place. Previously such votes were taken by nonrecorded, teller votes in which members were head-counted for or against an amendment as they filed down the chamber's aisle.

Despite some defeats, the reformers were successful in the Legislative Reorganization Act of 1970 in establishing a more open and accountable committee and floor system. The act set the tone and laid the predicate for what was to become a very fertile decade for congressional reform, with both intended and unintended consequences.[5]

Committee and Subcommittee Reforms of the 1970s

The attack on the seniority system continued the year after the enactment of the Legislative Reorganization Act of 1970, when both party caucuses in the House adopted resolutions stating that seniority need not be the only criterion in appointing committee chairs and ranking minority members. By 1973, both House party caucuses had adopted rules permitting separate, secret ballot votes on the top committee slots. And by 1975, the new class of "Watergate Babies" (so named because President Nixon's Watergate scandal swept a horde of freshman Democrats into office) put the rule to good use by ousting three sitting chairs. The rest of the chairs were on notice that they would be held accountable to caucus wishes.

Moreover, in 1973 the House Democratic Caucus adopted a set of rules known as the "subcommittee bill of rights" that took away the authority of committee chairs to create subcommittees, appoint their chairs and members, and determine their jurisdictions. The rules also required all legislation referred to a committee to be referred to a subcommittee within two weeks unless the full committee voted otherwise. Taken together, these changes diminished considerably the authority of committee chairs and in its place erected a system of semiautonomous subcommittees that could set their own agendas, appoint staff, set their own budgets, and meet and act when they wanted.

One of the areas left relatively untouched by the 1970 reorganization act was the tangled and overlapping sets of committee jurisdictions. To address this, the House created a bipartisan, ten-member Select Committee on Committees in 1973 chaired by Representative Richard Bolling (D-MO). However, when the select committee reported a substantial jurisdictional reorganization proposal in March 1974, it was referred to the Democratic Caucus's Committee on Organization, Study, and Review for further study. When it finally emerged late in the session, a caucus substitute was made that eliminated most of the proposed changes. Some of the consolidations retained related to transportation, science, and foreign affairs. However, energy jurisdiction remained scattered among multiple committees.

One procedural item that survived allowed the Speaker for the first time to refer legislation to more than one committee. However, without a more rational jurisdictional structure, the new multiple-referral system only guaranteed a greater duplication of effort and more committee infighting over legislation.[6]

Another attempt at overhauling House operations occurred in 1976 with the creation of the Commission on Administrative Review chaired by Representative David R. Obey (D-WI). It came up with forty-two recommendations, many relating to the administrative services of the House, while others dealt with committee staff and operations. The House did adopt the commission's recommended ethics reforms but refused to take up its other bill making administrative changes in how the House is run. Republicans fought it because they feared coronation of a House administrative "czar." Ironically, nineteen years later, when Republicans took control of the House in 1995, they created their own version—a chief administrative officer. The intervening House bank and post office scandals convinced them a more professional and less patronage-driven internal operation was needed.

One final swipe at committee jurisdictional reform was made in 1979 with the establishment of a second Select Committee on Committees, this time headed up by Representative Jerry Patterson (D-CA). Rather than attempt a comprehensive realignment of committees, the select committee focused on energy alone and proposed a new House energy committee with exclusive authority over energy-related legislation. However, the modest proposal was again trumped by a substitute that simply clarified existing energy jurisdictions and renamed the Interstate and Foreign Commerce Committee the House Committee on Energy and Commerce.

Senate Reform Efforts

Meanwhile, the Senate was not moribund when it came to reforming itself. By 1975, both party caucuses had adopted rules providing that committee chairs and ranking members would be chosen without regard to seniority (though the Senate still tends to follow seniority more than the House in choosing chairs).

Beginning in the mid-1970s, the Senate undertook a series of special reform efforts to examine various aspects of its internal operations. The Commission on the Operation of the Senate in 1975–1976 was the brainchild of Senator John Culver (D-IA), but was composed entirely of non-senators, including its chairman, former senator Harold Hughes (D-IA) and vice-chair Archie Dykes, chancellor of the University of Kansas. The commission was concerned primarily with the administrative and support mechanisms for senators and did not address committee jurisdictions.

While the commission made a number of recommendations, most were not acted on. The exception was a strengthened code of ethics for the body. Additionally, the Senate amended its filibuster rule in 1975 to reduce the votes needed to invoke cloture (shut off debate), from two-thirds of those present and voting to three-fifths of those sworn (sixty senators).

In 1976–1977, the Senate created a twelve-member, bipartisan Temporary Select Committee to Study the Senate Committee System under the chairmanship of Senator Adlai E. Stevenson III (D-IL). After eight months of hearings and deliberations, the select committee issued a report recommending a major overhaul of the Senate committee system. Its recommendations were introduced in the first session of the following Congress, reported by the Committee on Rules and Administration, and adopted by an 89–1 vote in February 1977.

The revamp succeeded where the House's Bolling committee failed, by realigning committee jurisdictions along more rational lines. Additionally, three Senate standing committees, one select committee, and three joint committees were abolished. The committee's proposals also reduced the number of committee and subcommittee assignments per senator, reduced committee scheduling conflicts, and provided the minority party one-third of a committee's budget for staffing purposes.[7]

A two-member Senate Study Group on Senate Practices and Procedures in 1982–1983 attempted to address ongoing inefficiencies in Senate operations. However, its recommendations died in the Senate Rules Committee after a single hearing. In 1984 a new twelve-member bipartisan Temporary Select Committee to Study the Senate Committee System, under the chairmanship of Senator Dan Quayle (R-IN), was formed to reexamine the structure, size, jurisdictions, staffing, and rules and procedures of Senate committees. The committee was also charged with looking at the allocation of senators' time and oversight of the executive branch.

The broad set of recommendations by the Quayle committee got a hearing before the Senate Committee on Rules and Administration in January 1985 but was never reported. Further temporary changes were made in 2005 when a bipartisan "gang of fourteen" forged an agreement on allowing certain judicial nominations to be taken up after Senate Majority Leader Bill Frist (R-TN) threatened to use the so-called "nuclear option" to change the rules using a procedural gimmick to permit majority cloture on such nominations.[8]

In 2011 and 2013, bipartisan leadership agreements were again struck for the 112th and 113th Congresses to reduce the number of possible filibusters in exchange for greater fairness in allowing minority party amendments. This was in response to the growing practice by leaders of both party majorities of "filling the amendment tree" to block other senators from offering amendments. The reforms were never utilized.

The Senate took a turn away from bipartisanship in late in 2013 when Senate Majority Leader Harry Reid (D-NV) carried out Frist's earlier threat by pulling the trigger on the "nuclear option." He did this by appealing the chair's ruling that sixty votes were needed to invoke cloture on a pending judicial nomination. Reid prevailed in reversing the chair's ruling and imposing a new precedent that only fifty-one votes are needed to invoke cloture on any nomination (other than for the Supreme Court).[9]

Had Reid attempted to accomplish that end by amending Senate rules, it would have required a two-thirds vote to end debate on such a rule change instead of the simple majority needed to overturn a ruling of the chair.

Battling the Imperial Presidency in the 1970s

As previously indicated, the decade of the seventies was a time of great reform ferment in Congress, even if some of those efforts were for naught. Those reforms that didn't get adopted were simply recycled at the next iteration of a reform effort. Three major changes in Congress that were adopted can all be attributed at least in part to a reaction against the Vietnam War, the Watergate scandal, and other manifestations of what came to be known as the "imperial presidency." Those changes were the War Powers Resolution of 1973, the 1974 Budget Act, and the broadcasting of House floor proceedings beginning in 1979.

As far back as the Joint Committee on the Organization of Congress in 1945–1946, proposals were put forward to allow for televising committee hearings and House and Senate floor proceedings. The Senate had long allowed for committee television coverage, but Speaker Sam Rayburn stood athwart the practice in the House as a result of some of the dramatic circuslike hearings of the House Committee on Un-American Activities (HUAC) in the 1950s. As has already been pointed out, the House finally allowed broadcasting committee hearings as part of the Legislative Reorganization Act of 1970 (LRO).

One of the offshoots of the 1970 LRO Act was the creation of an ongoing Joint Committee on Congressional Operations in 1971 to conduct a continuing study of the operation of the legislative branch with a view to keeping it modern and adaptable to changing situations. In 1972 the chairman of the joint committee commissioned a study by the Congressional Research Service on how Congress might better communicate with the American people. The study was contracted out to John G. Stewart, a former aide to Vice President Hubert Humphrey, and then communications director for the Democratic National Committee. Stewart's 1974 report, *Congress and Mass Communications: An Institutional Perspective,* emphasized the extent to which the president had captured the airwaves in modern times, while Congress was virtually ignored.

The report also highlighted waning public trust in Congress, citing Harris Polls showing assessments of Congress dipping from 64 percent positive in 1965 to just 26 percent positive and 63 percent negative in 1971. Especially troubling to Democrats in Congress was the ability of President Richard Nixon to commandeer the networks for talks to the nation on Vietnam, while Congress had no right of response. In addition to recommending finding ways to assure Congress equal time to respond to presidential addresses, the report discussed the pros and cons of broadcasting House and Senate floor proceedings.

The temporary boost in Congress's approval ratings with the televised broadcasting of the Senate Watergate hearings in 1973 and House Nixon impeachment proceedings in 1974 lent further impetus to giving Congress greater exposure through the broadcast media. By 1975, the joint committee was urging a carefully conceived test of broadcasting House and Senate floor proceedings.

The House Rules Committee created an Ad Hoc Subcommittee on Broadcasting to explore the possibility, and numerous resolutions were introduced to implement broadcast coverage. Despite initial resistance from House Majority Leader Tip O'Neill (D-MA) to broadcasting floor debates, the House Rules subcommittee reported a resolution calling for a network pool to cover the floor. A competing panel (the House members of the joint committee) called for a House-owned and -operated broadcast system. The Rules Committee resolution was recommitted to subcommittee for further work.

In 1977, a different subcommittee of the Rules Committee was appointed to ensure the majority leadership's wishes were more carefully followed. That coincided with the election of O'Neill as Speaker and a change in course. Bowing to pressures from his young, more media-savvy Democratic Caucus colleagues, O'Neill agreed to move forward with a ninety-day test of a House broadcast system. Two years later, after more debate and votes on broadcast resolutions, the House-owned and -operated broadcast system went public in March 1979. O'Neill's major condition was guaranteed in the new rules: the Speaker would control the cameras, which could only focus on the person speaking and not show reaction shots of other members.

The Senate would not follow suit until seven years later, in 1986, when the one-man resistance squad, Senator Russell Long (D-LA), finally relented, on the eve of his retirement, to allow Senate-operated cameras to cover floor proceedings.

There is no hard evidence that opening Congress to broadcast coverage either enhanced or detracted from Congress's image. Some members worried that such coverage would only hurt Congress in the people's eyes because networks would tend to use only sensational clips on the nightly news showing members engaged in angry exchanges. The simultaneous emergence of the public-affairs cable network C-SPAN in 1979 made it possible for the viewing public to watch House proceedings (and later Senate debates) all day, from the opening gavel to adjournment.[10]

Just as President Nixon's successful use of the airwaves in defending his war policies prodded Congress into demanding more airtime and eventually televising its own proceedings, Nixon's criticisms of Congress's spending habits and his subsequent impoundment of appropriated funds spurred the Congress into establishing its own budget process. The $3.4 billion surplus in fiscal year 1969 had turned into a $2.8 billion deficit the following year and soared to $23 billion by mid-1972.

President Nixon responded by vetoing spending bills, and, if his vetoes were overridden, by impounding (withholding) the funds anyway. He used the device as a bargaining lever to get Congress to agree to a spending ceiling that he could enforce by impoundments if Congress exceeded the caps. The House originally went along with Nixon's request (over objections of the Democratic leadership), but the Senate balked at even a modified version.

As a compromise, a Joint Study Committee on Budget Control was created to recommend ways in which Congress could get a better handle on spending. Meantime, late in 1972, Nixon impounded funds for a water pollution control bill after Congress overrode his veto on it. Both houses struck back by passing differing bills to curb the president's impoundment authority.

The House Rules Committee tried to intervene by making an amendment to attach to the impoundment control bill the Joint Study Committee's recommendations for House and Senate budget committees and annual congressional budget resolutions. The amendment was rejected, but the idea lived on through further hearings.

When the House- and Senate-passed impoundment control bills became snagged in a conference committee over how best to deal with presidential impoundments (two-house approval versus single-house disapproval), the House Rules Committee again proceeded to explore the Joint Study Committee's proposal for a congressional budget process. This time the two ideas were joined into what became the Congressional Budget and Impoundment Control Act of 1974—ushering in the birth of the modern budget process.

Nixon signed the measure on his way out the door as president (to escape imminent impeachment over the Watergate scandal). He indicated in his signing statement accompanying the 1974 Budget Act that it not only would give Congress greater discipline over its own spending decisions, but would also provide presidents a centralized system through which to impose their spending caps and budget priorities.[11]

The other legislative legacy of the imperial presidency was the War Powers Resolution of 1973. Congress had come to regret its adoption of the Gulf of Tonkin Resolution of 1964, which authorized the president to respond to North Vietnamese attacks on U.S. gunboats. After the 1964 presidential election, President Johnson used the authority to implement a massive escalation of American ground troops in Vietnam.

It wasn't until after President Richard Nixon took office in 1969 that the United States began to draw down its troop levels in Vietnam. However, Nixon's subsequent military incursions into Laos and Cambodia in 1971 to clean out suspected North Vietnamese sanctuaries infuriated Congress further and prompted a new assessment of the balance of war powers between the president and Congress. The resulting War Powers Resolution, enacted over Nixon's veto, attempted to put time limits on any unilateral presidential commitment of troops into hostilities or imminent hostilities, and require congressional approval for any extended presence.

Although every president since Nixon has supported his argument that the act constituted a violation of the commander in chief's prerogatives, all presidents have usually supported the law's reporting requirements to Congress when troops are sent to new combat areas. Congress has been less than forceful in enforcing the act's requirements, and the courts have generally steered clear of attempting to arbitrate disputes between the branches—treating them as "political questions."

Related institutional legacies of the era of conflict over foreign policy differences included the creation of Senate and House intelligence committees in 1976 and 1977, respectively, and enactment of the National Emergencies Act in 1976 abolishing scores of presidential emergency powers.

Despite all of the congressional muscle flexing in the 1970s in response to the imperial presidency, close observers argue that Congress is just as deferential and acquiescent to the president today on national security and foreign policy matters as it was pre-Nixon.[12]

Ethics Reforms

There's nothing like a good scandal to get Congress's reform juices flowing. Just as generals tend to plan for the last war, Congress tends to react to the latest scandal by plugging whatever loopholes or personal foibles are exposed. The latter half of the twentieth century was an especially fruitful period for scandals and reforms to address them.

The bribery scandal surrounding the Senate Democratic Caucus secretary, Bobby Baker, in 1964 led to the creation of the first standing committee on ethics. In 1967 the House followed suit with its own Committee on Standards of Official Conduct in response to alleged misconduct of Representative Adam Clayton Powell Jr. (D-NY). Both houses adopted their own codes holding members to higher standards than mere compliance with the law. The House code charged members with conducting themselves "at all times in a manner that shall reflect creditably on the House."[13]

The creation of ethics committees and codes of conduct did not stop the parade of scandals that would follow: Koreagate, ABSCAM (in which FBI agents were disguised as Arab sheikhs bearing bribes to members), the House bank and post office scandals, the page scandals, the Keating Five, the Abramoff lobbying scandal, and on and on.

Each time a new scandal erupted, a new rule or law would be concocted to prevent repeats and restore public confidence in Congress. While there is little evidence that the remedial rule or legislation had the effect of boosting public respect for Congress, the disruptions emanating from these institutional embarrassments probably served as useful reminders to members to behave or risk the opprobrium of their colleagues and constituents, not to mention possible jail sentences and electoral defeat. Moreover, the reward for adopting tough new ethics rules (or other reforms like the Legislative Reorganization Acts) has often been a pay raise for members.

That was especially true for the Ethics in Government Act of 1989, which provided government-wide pay raises for high-ranking officials in return for abolishing honoraria.

In 2008, the House created an Office of Congressional Ethics to screen ethics complaints and refer to the House Ethics Committee those having merit. The ethics office, comprising eight nonmembers, was specifically designed to address long-standing criticism that members are too complacent and protective in policing their own. While some tension initially existed between the office and the ethics committee, in the last few years the two entities learned to accommodate each other.

Another Joint Committee on Organization

It seems that every twenty years or so Congress makes a sincere effort to reorganize, if not reinvent, itself, regardless of the perils and pitfalls of attempting to do so. Such was the case in July 1992 when both houses voted to create another Joint Committee on the Organization of Congress, patterned after the 1945 and 1965 committees. Although House Speaker Tom Foley had long resisted the creation of a reform committee as an antidote to the House post office and bank scandals, he finally relented with the understanding that it would not begin its work until after the 1992 elections.

While the House had adopted a provision permitting the House members of the joint committee to make reform recommendations to their respective caucuses by November 6 (in time for the early organizational meeting for the next Congress), the Senate dropped the provision and substituted one prohibiting the joint committee from beginning any work until November 15.

Minority House Republicans rolled out a major set of House reforms on the opening day of the 103rd Congress in January 1993—a preview of what would become the reform plank of the "Contract with America" in 1994. But majority Democrats prevailed with a modest set of House rules changes instead.

The twenty-eight-member joint committee, equally divided between the parties and chambers, began its work shortly thereafter in January 1993. Cochaired by Senator David Boren (D-OK) and Representative Lee Hamilton (D-IN), the panel followed the examples of its predecessor joint committees by conducting extensive hearings over the next six months as well as conducting the first survey of members and staff ever undertaken by a joint entity of Congress.

However, when the time came to deliberate over proposed changes in Congress, the joint committee split between the two houses over House committee Democrats' demands that the Senate address filibuster reform and non-germane amendments in their recommendations as the price for cooperation from the House. Consequently, the two houses proceeded with their own markups and separate reports containing recommendations. They did issue a shared final background report containing historical materials as well as factual analyses of the contemporary Congress and its perceived problems.

The House half of the joint committee managed to report the bill in November 1993 despite defections by four Republicans who were disappointed the reform package did not go far enough. Even though the joint committee had looked at twelve possible options for reforming committee jurisdictions, none was included in the final report—a clear reflection of Speaker Tom Foley's admonitions: he repeatedly reminded members of both parties that "there are still blood stains on the Democratic cloakroom floor" from the 1973–1974 committee jurisdictional reform battles.

On February 3, 1994, joint committee cochair Lee Hamilton introduced the bare-bones bill reported by the House half of the joint committee. His was the only name on the measure.[14] The House Rules Committee held eight hearings on the legislation over the months of February through April, then allowed the bill to languish for the next three months.

The Rules Committee considered the bill for amendments for one day in August (before the summer recess); then resumed markup in late September. The Rules Committee chairman Joe Moakley (D-MA) abruptly recessed the committee to meet with the Speaker in the middle of debate on a Republican amendment to abolish proxy voting in committees. Because that amendment and another one dealing with committee jurisdictional changes had some support among Democrats, the Speaker directed Moakley to immediately adjourn the markup process for good, thereby killing the bill for that Congress. The Senate counterpart bill fared no better, and the 103rd Congress adjourned without so much as a thank-you note to the joint committee for its efforts.[15]

The Contract with America and Beyond

Most Congress watchers attribute the Democratic loss of both houses in the ensuing elections of 1994 to the failure of the Clinton health-care-reform effort, the economy, and residual public bitterness over the scandals that had rocked Congress just two years earlier. House Republicans played off all of those influences on the electorate by projecting a positive alternative to Democratic rule in their Contract with America—a ten-part legislative agenda plus a congressional reform plank, all rolled out at a signing ceremony on the Capitol steps in August 1994. The package was formally introduced on opening day of the 104th Congress, setting the clock ticking on the promised hundred-day deadline for completing action on every item—some two dozen bills in all.

The contract's House rules reforms, taken up on opening day, included banning proxy voting in committees, opening all committee meetings to broadcast coverage, cutting committee staff by one-third, imposing three-term limits on committee and subcommittee chairs and a four-term limit on the Speaker, and guaranteeing the minority party a final amendment to bills in the motion to recommit with instructions.

The rules resolution also abolished three House committees and made minor changes in the jurisdictions and names of the remaining panels. Republicans also brought to a vote on opening day a separate vote on the Congressional Accountability Act of 1995 to apply to Congress the same workplace laws and rules that apply to the private sector—something Foley had taken away from the joint committee the year before and passed separately as a House rule rather than a law.[16]

House Democrats followed the Republicans' 1994 model in 2006 by running against a corrupt majority and by putting forward their policy and rules proposals for changing Congress which they promised to complete action on within one hundred legislative hours. Their rules reform package was adopted on the opening day of the 110th Congress in 2007. Likewise, when House Republicans retook control in 2011, they put forward another reform package that they incorporated into the rule book at the beginning of the 112th Congress.

No longer was either party talking about the need for another bipartisan joint reform committee—at least not until the LaHood-Lipinski joint committee resolution was dropped in the hopper in October 2016. However, it is important to note that the LaHood-Lipinski initiative was not endorsed or cosponsored by any elected leader of either party; nor was a companion bill introduced in the Senate.

Two other things are worth noting about the joint committee proposal. First, the resolution attracted roughly two and a half times as many Republican backers (twenty-eight) as Democrats (eleven), dispelling the notion that discontent with the institution was confined primarily to disgruntled minority party members. Second, nearly 50 percent (nineteen) of the thirty-nine sponsors and cosponsors were in their first or second terms in the House, including freshman sponsor LaHood. Only eight had served five or more terms, including sponsor Lipinksi (then in his sixth term).

Could it be that disillusionment with the institution falls on newer members the hardest? Or is it that the newbies tend to be more idealistic and optimistic about prospects for change?

The failure of the 1993–1994 joint committee's effort was a clear sign of how far things had come since enactment of the Legislative Reorganization Act of 1970. The majority party currently takes full responsibility for shaping the rules and procedures of the House and running it. It sees itself as solely responsible and accountable for the institution's successes and failures.

Minority parties tend to be the most vocal about the majority's abuse of power and are most committed to overhauling Congress if they regain power. However, the history of Congress over the last forty years shows that when party control changes, the former minority party's zeal for reform quickly fades. Calls for a return to the "regular order" soon yield as the new majority reverts to the old majority's governing pragmatism—quickly jettisoning reforms that are obstacles to legislative success. This has been true regardless of which party makes the transition from minority to majority status. When faced with a choice between reform and results, the majority inevitably opts for results before the next election rolls around.

Conclusions

Congressional reform is difficult to define and even more difficult to successfully implement with any long-term, lasting effects. Presumably it is about improving the capabilities and operations of the institution of Congress in carrying out its basic lawmaking, budgeting, representational, and oversight functions. As this account shows, though, even the best of intentions can lead to unexpected consequences. The congressional reform revolution of the 1970s managed to overthrow committee government, briefly install in its place an unworkable and sprawling subcommittee government, and eventually settle on party governance with elected leaders calling most of the shots.

The confluence of reforms in the 1970s helped spur the hyper-partisanship prevalent today. Providing for roll-call votes in the committee of the whole led to a proliferation of floor amendments, many of which were used by the minority party to embarrass the majority and score political points. Such behavior prompted the majority leadership, through the use of special rules from the House Rules Committee, to increasingly limit (or prohibit) floor amendments. This perceived abuse of power by the majority invited minority party retaliation, with tit-for-tat reprisals escalating into a never-ending spiral of procedural warfare.

The televising of chamber debates provided an enhanced venue for members on both sides to present their political arguments to a broader public, quite often through highly partisan one-minute floor speeches at the beginning of each day, and one-sided "special order" debates at the end.

In summary, greater transparency and accountability eventually led to legislating behind closed doors by party and committee leaders instead of by rank-and-file members. Committee deliberations took on less importance, as leadership involvement in setting legislative priorities, details, and strategies increased. One example of this is the near-elimination of House-Senate conference committees to resolve legislative differences between the bodies. Conference committees have been replaced by amendment ping-pong between the houses, with party leaders wielding the paddles.

The underlying lessons that emerge from most congressional reform efforts is that members and their leaders will resist being led by procedural changes to places they don't want to go—namely into political and electoral cul-de-sacs. Many congressional reforms, though touted as being critical to renewing public confidence in Congress, do not produce those results. As former House member Donald Rumsfeld (R-IL) once put it, "Congressional reform has no constituency."

When reforms go unrecognized and unappreciated by the public, they tend to fall by the wayside—misused, abused, or waived. For every well-intentioned rule change, there is an exception, and those exceptions tend to build and become the new order. Only genuine public outrage, broadly and forcefully expressed, can prod Congress into action on meaningful internal improvements that will lead to developing real policy solutions. Absent that, any reforms in today's hyper-partisan environment will tend to be ephemeral and fleeting.

Notes

1. H. Cong. Res. 169, 114th Cong., 2d sess., September 28, 2016, referred to the House Committee on Rules.
2. For an excellent account of the latter ill-fated effort, see C. Lawrence Evans and Walter J. Oleszek, *Congress Under Fire: Reform Politics and the Republican Majority* (Boston: Houghton Mifflin, 1997). This author also recounts the trials and tribulations of the 1993 joint committee, in *Congress and the People: Deliberative Democracy on Trial* (Baltimore: Johns Hopkins University Press and Woodrow Wilson Center Press, 2000).
3. For a superb examination of congressional reform efforts in the latter half of the twentieth century, see Julian E. Zelizer, *On Capitol Hill: The Struggle to Reform Congress and Its Consequences, 1948–2000* (Cambridge and New York: Cambridge University Press, 2006).
4. See *Organization of the Congress, Final Report of the Joint Committee on the Organization of Congress,* "The Congressional Committee System, Historical Overview," for background on this and the following two sections. Also see Roger H. Davidson, "The Advent of the Modern Congress: The Legislative Reorganization Act of 1946," *Legislative Studies Quarterly* 15, no. 3 (August 1990), 357–73.

5. See Walter Kravitz, "The Advent of the Modern Congress: The Legislative Reorganization Act of 1970," *Legislative Studies Quarterly* 15, no. 3 (August 1990): 375–99.

6. For an insightful look at the work of the Bolling committee, see Roger H. Davidson and Walter J. Oleszek, *Congress Against Itself* (Bloomington: Indiana University Press, 1977).

7. The House's Bolling resolution in October 1974 was amended to include a one-third minority staffing provision and abolition of proxy voting, but both were repealed by majority Democrats at the outset of the next Congress in their opening-day rules package in January 1975.

8. The term "nuclear option" was reportedly coined by Frist's predecessor, Senate Majority Leader Trent Lott (R-MS) in describing the likely reaction of the minority if their filibuster rights were curtailed or eliminated: they would go nuclear and blow up the place.

9. *Congressional Record,* November 21, 2013, S8417.

10. For a fuller description of the fight to televise Congress, see this author's "A Window on the House: Televising Floor Debates," chap. 8 in Wolfensberger, *Congress and the People,* 103–28.

11. See Don Wolfensberger, "Congress and the Politics of Deficits," Congress Project seminar, Woodrow Wilson Center, September 22, 2003, available at http://www.wilsoncenter.org/event/congress-and-the-politics-deficits#field_files, accessed February 20, 2013.

12. See Donald R. Wolfensberger, "The Return of the Imperial Presidency?," *Wilson Quarterly* (Spring 2002), 36–41.

13. See Don Wolfensberger, "Punishing Disorderly Behavior in Congress," Congress Project essay, Woodrow Wilson Center, January 16, 2006, available at http://www.wilsoncenter.org/sites/default/files/ethics-essay-drw.pdf, accessed February 20, 2013.

14. The Legislative Reorganization Act of 1994, H.R. 3801, 103rd Cong., 2d sess., introduced by Rep. Lee Hamilton, February 3, 1994.

15. As previously mentioned, the best rendering of the joint committee's travails is Evans and Oleszek, *Congress Under Fire.* Both authors served on the staff of the joint committee, Oleszek as a consultant from the Congressional Research Service, and Evans on leave as a professor at William and Mary.

16. Evans and Oleszek, *Congress Under Fire* also tells the story of how the joint committee's work was incorporated into many of the proposals Republicans put forward as House rules on the opening day of the 104th Congress.

Discussion Questions

1. What factors seem to motivate Congress to reform itself?

2. Have the transparency reforms in Congress helped or hindered its deliberative function?

3. Can any institutional reforms help to restore Congress's loss of public confidence and approval? If so, what changes would be most helpful?

5

Congress and Earmarks, 2006–2018:
A Decade of Reform

Richard Doyle

The Spending Landscape and the Congressional Budget Process

Spending by the federal government is an important part of the U.S. economy. The gross domestic product (GDP), reflecting total economic activity, includes such spending, measured at 21 percent in 2018 (fig. 5.1, far right). Broadly considered, federal spending consists of three types: mandatory, discretionary, and net interest on the federal debt, shown in the Congressional Research Service (CRS) chart (fig. 5.1). Earmarks reside within discretionary spending.

Mandatory spending, dominated by such entitlement programs as Social Security, Medicare, and Medicaid, is usually untouched by Congress as it works its way through its annual budget process. Unless and until Congress changes the legislation that established entitlement to the benefit payments provided by these programs, spending to provide such benefits occurs automatically. Similarly, spending to service the debt (net interest) occurs without congressional action.

Discretionary spending, as the name implies, is much more amenable to decisions made within the congressional budget process each year. That is, it allows for the actions of individual members of Congress, subject to the politics of the budget process. The primary constraint upon these decisions is the total amount of discretionary spending allowed under the general budget plan Congress is supposed to implement each year in the form of a congressional budget resolution. The Congressional Budget and Impoundment Control Act of 1974 required Congress to enact a budget resolution each year, indicating, among

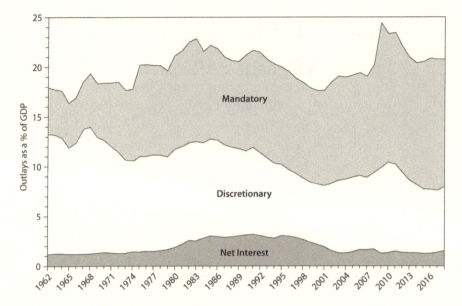

Fig. 5.1: Federal outlays by category since FY 1962.
Source: CRS, *Trends in Mandatory Spending: In Brief,* 2018.

other things, how much is to be spent on discretionary programs. The programs included within discretionary spending are displayed in the Peterson Foundation chart (fig. 5.2).

Appropriations bills begin at the subcommittee level within the Senate and House Appropriations Committees (the SAC and the HAC, respectively). Once the budget resolution is in place, the committees responsible for authorizing and then appropriating spending for discretionary programs are expected to develop and pass legislation distributing that spending. "Develop and pass" means that the subcommittees of the SAC and HAC will report out their bills to the full SAC and HAC and that those committees will in turn pass and forward them to the full Senate and House for approval. Within this decision-making regime, members of Congress have inserted earmarks, triggering controversy.

The Earmarking Problem

Earmarking, according to political scientist James Savage, "promotes ineffective government and bad public policy."[1] Earmarks are how legislators have designated either funds or resources for a particular purpose of interest to them.

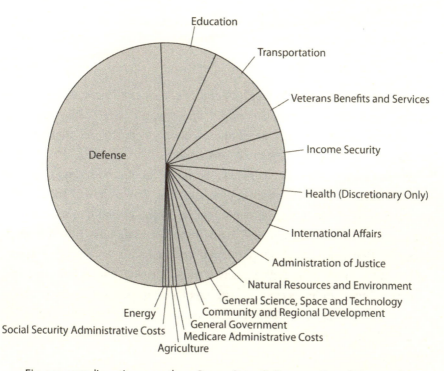

Education
Transportation
Veterans Benefits and Services
Income Security
Health (Discretionary Only)
International Affairs
Administration of Justice
Natural Resources and Environment
General Science, Space and Technology
Community and Regional Development
General Government
Medicare Administrative Costs
Agriculture
Energy
Social Security Administrative Costs
Defense

Fig. 5.2: 2017 discretionary outlays. *Source:* Peter G. Peterson Foundation, 2018.

They became more important in the first decade of the twenty-first century, for a variety of reasons. Irene Rubin noted that by 2007 earmarks had grown "beyond the ability of legislators to evaluate and prioritize," and that some of them "have been revealed as rewards for financial donors, contributing to the impression that government is corrupt." She also observed that the Bush administration "attacked congressional earmarks" as part of its "assault on congressional budgetary powers."[2] Brookings scholars saw the same problem in 2007, suggesting that earmarking got "out of hand and was used and abused in a fashion we have not seen before in recent years."[3] In 2010, the *Washington Post* noted that there were

a wave of investigations focusing on House appropriators' actions. The Justice Department has looked into the earmarking activities of several lawmakers, and, relying on public documents, the House ethics committee investigated five Democrats and two Republicans on the Appropriations defense subcommittee, finding that the lawmakers steered more than $245 million to clients of a lobbying firm under federal criminal investigation. The lawmakers collected more than $840,000 in political contributions from the firm's lobbyists and clients in a little more than two years.[4]

According to an editor at *CQ Weekly,* earmarks "have been cited as a symbol of everything that's wrong with Congress."[5] In a single week in 2008, three television network news broadcasts mentioned earmarks ninety-one times, nearly as often as they made reference to Afghanistan.[6]

Within Congress, key members have been critical of earmarking, including Senators Sam Nunn, William Proxmire, and John Danforth, and Representatives Bill Natcher and Edward Boland. More recently, a handful of senators and congressmen consistently attacked earmarks as spending bills moved through Congress. Congressman Jeff Flake referred to earmarks as "the currency of corruption in Congress,"[7] "no-bid contracts,"[8] and a "gateway drug to out-of-control spending."[9] Earmarking became something of a campaign issue in the congressional elections in 2006 and 2008, and Senator McCain employed his opposition to earmarks in 2009 "to rally conservatives reluctant to support his presidential campaign."[10]

Earmark reform began in 2006, impacting both the process to be followed by members of Congress seeking earmarks and the spending that results. Three sources of reform are examined here: House and Senate rules, the policies and procedures of the House and Senate Appropriations Committees, and the initiatives of congressional member organizations. The reforms are detailed and their impact on earmarks assessed.

Earmarks: A Means to What End, and for Whom?

Earmarking, a specific subset of "pork barrel politics," has been treated at length by students of Congress. Mayhew argued that members of Congress persistently engage in distributive policy-making, such as earmarking, in the belief that this will enhance their electoral fortunes.[11] This logic is stated explicitly by Law and Tonon: "A key element of every candidate's reelection strategy is to claim credit for services or programs that generate benefits for the voters in her district. Pork-barrel projects clearly serve this function."[12] There is the expectation, then, that earmarking will be used to advance the electoral fortunes of incumbents and that those best positioned to earmark (members of the majority party, the leadership, and the appropriations committees) will be disproportionately rewarded; for other, but related reasons, party leaders will reward vulnerable members with earmarks to retain control of those seats.

Engstrom and Vanberg looked at earmarks in the 110th Congress and found that the majority party received more earmarks than the minority, and that parties use earmarks to assist their most electorally vulnerable members and to reward members who hold "agenda-setting positions."[13] However, research on earmarks does not always or easily comport with these assumptions. Frisch, for example, notes that "empirical evidence connecting the provision of pork with improved electoral fortunes is hard to come by."[14] This is owed at least in part to the fact that voters are usually unaware of members' earmarking activities. Frisch found that in the 1994 congressional elections, "the amount of pork barrel spending during a Congress (in this case measured as the number of earmarks) is not positively related to the subsequent election margin."[15] Further, although seniority was positively associated with the number of earmarks, vulnerable members did not receive more earmarks than less vulnerable members. This conclusion regarding vulnerable members of Congress was supported by a study of earmarks in the 110th Congress conducted by Clemens and Finocchiaro, who found that members from competitive districts did not consistently receive more earmark funding than those from safe districts.[16]

Fisher and Rocca provide a potential solution to the problem posed by Frisch, that is, that voters are not aware of members' earmarking activities, hence will not reward them at the ballot box. They posit the possibility that earmarks provide a return to members of Congress by signaling potential campaign contributors "about the direction and intensity of their preferences."[17] Earmarks, they argue, are "another important form of non-roll call position-taking in Congress and, as such, are tools (1) for interest groups to acquire information about members' preference and (2) for legislators to advertise the direction and intensity of their positions to potential donors."[18] In this context, interest groups "provide the crucial link between distributive policy and electoral gain."[19] Reviewing the earmarks provided by the 110th Congress, the authors find "a strong relationship between earmarks and campaign contributions from defense groups."[20] Put otherwise, "members of Congress seem to be receiving a considerable wage for their earmarks and that wage provides ample incentive to engage in this sort of distributive and signaling behavior."[21]

Crespin and Finocchiaro examined earmarks in the Senate to test the general proposition regarding the distribution of earmarks. They found that by using "various procedural maneuvers," the majority party garnered a larger share of earmarks between 1995 and 2005.[22] Further, members of the appropriations committee did better than nonmembers, and committee chairs, ranking members, and party leaders all received more earmarked funding than others. This evidence regarding the role of the majority party is congruent, in part, with the findings of Balla and colleagues, who examined academic earmarks between 1993 and 2000. They concluded that by "giving the minority some pork, the majority party inoculates itself against charges of wasteful spending, but by granting the minority a smaller share of the federal pork pie, the majority party boosts the electoral fortunes of its own members and its collective reputation and prospects."[23]

Will earmark reform—changes affecting transparency and accountability—alter incentives, distribution, and more? Crespin and colleagues used appropriations data from Citizens Against Government Waste (CAGW) through fiscal year (FY) 2009 to argue that the earmark reforms initiated in 2006 have not been effective in preventing members from adding earmarks to the Joint Explanatory Statement of Managers, a document that accompanies conference agreements. That indictment leads them to conclude that the rules "are essentially meaningless."[24] "The only real outcome of the reforms," they note, "is a list of names attached to the appropriations bills designating who requested the earmarks."[25] They discount the effectiveness of this because it simply reinforces members' interest in publicizing their earmarks to voters at home.

Rebecca Kysar characterizes these earmark reforms as disclosure rules intended to provide transparency and accountability, or "self-referential rules."[26] They "aim to keep undesirable interest group influence at bay through the principled discussion of legislation and a heightened accountability of legislators" and to "surface previously hidden deals with interest groups." However, such rules are, in her view, "adopted by the foxes to govern administration of the henhouse."[27]They have only symbolic value, and "opportunities to defect from the regime are many."[28]

The Earmark Explosion

Before examining earmark reform, we must first note the expansion in spending within earmarks that has taken place over the past two decades. And before

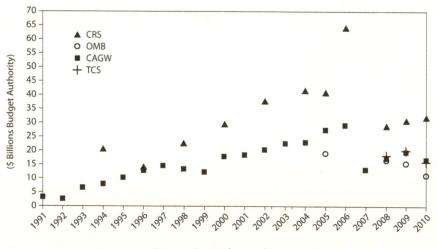

Fig. 5.3: Earmark spending.

we can measure the change in spending for earmarks and the impact of reform, we must wrestle a bit with the definition of an earmark. It also requires engaging multiple earmark databases, each offering a definition and a count. The definitional issue is minimized here, in favor of identifying major trends.[29]

In 2007 the Senate began referring to earmarks as "congressionally directed spending items," blurring the matter a bit further. That said, and allowing for such differences, a profile of earmark spending can be constructed, though with caution.

Spending for earmarks rose steadily and dramatically between the early 1990s, the first available data point, and FY 2006, after which it fell sharply. By FY 2010 it appears to have leveled off at FY 2002 levels. Data from two governmental offices (CRS and the Office of Management and Budget [OMB]) and two public interest organizations (CAGW and Taxpayers for Common Sense [TCS]) provide the best information on the nature and extent of earmark expansion and retreat. Trends in earmark spending are calculated by these four sources (fig. 5.3).

Because earmarks continue to be linked to the growth in federal spending (and thus deficits), this relationship should be made explicit. Frisch noted in 1998 that "there is virtual agreement in the more empirically based budgeting literature that congressional distributive spending is not the source of the growth of deficits."[30] But earmarks continue to be linked to spending growth and defi-

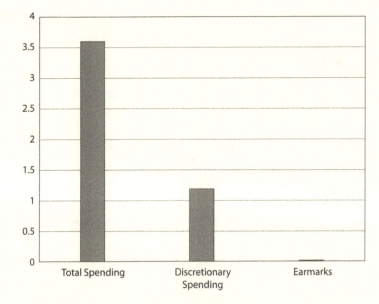

Fig. 5.4: Total, discretionary, and earmark spending, FY 2010 (budget authority in trillions). *Sources:* OMB Historical Tables, Taxpayers for Common Sense.

cits, frequently within a partisan context. According to the *Wall Street Journal,* "[n]othing highlighted Congress's spending problem in last year's [2006] election more than earmarks."[31] "It is no coincidence," Congressman Flake remarked, "that the growth of earmarks has paralleled the monstrous increase in overall federal spending."[32]

Earmarks were, indeed, at flood tide in 2006. However, their impact on total spending, never significant, diminished after 2006. If we compare earmarks in FY 2006, just before reforms were implemented, with their level in FY 2010, we discover that spending for earmarks fell 43.1 percent, while discretionary and total spending grew by 25.1 and 29.5 percent, respectively.[33] Total federal and discretionary spending is compared with spending for earmarks in FY 2010 (fig. 5.4).

CAGW

The earmark database available from CAGW is the most comprehensive, covering each of the twenty years between FY 1991 and FY 2010.[34] CAGW data indicate that spending for earmarks grew 432 percent over this period, while the number of earmarks grew even more rapidly, at 1,572 percent. By comparison, appropriated, or discretionary, spending (the category within which earmarks reside in the federal budget and the source used by CAGW) increased 128 percent during this period.[35] Thus earmarks not only expanded vertically, that is, in terms of numbers and cost, but also horizontally, consuming a larger share of each year's appropriated spending. As appropriated spending continued to grow through the end of this decade and earmark spending dropped and then leveled off, horizontal expansion ended.

CRS

The second-most comprehensive earmark database is provided by CRS. CRS does not compile earmark information on each year's spending bills, which explains the intermittent pattern shown in the trends (see fig. 5.3). The ten years of CRS data that include most of the same period covered by CAGW reveal much the same trajectory of earmark expansion through FY 2006, followed by a sharp drop and then a rough stabilization.[36] Because CRS and CAGW define (and therefore count) earmarks differently, and started counting at different points, they found different rates of growth. CRS data, which began at FY 1994, indicate that spending for earmarks grew by 57 percent by FY 2010, as compared with CAGW's 432 percent. Similarly, CRS data indicate that the number of earmarks grew by 174 percent by FY 2010, compared with growth of 1,572 percent in the CAGW database.

The CRS data show the same acceleration in earmark spending between the early 1990s and FY 2006 as revealed by the CAGW data, following which spending dropped dramatically. Between FY 2006 and FY 2010, the dollar value of earmarks dropped by 50 percent, while over this same period, discretionary spending went up by 25.1 percent.[37] That said, the CRS data also indicate three years of small but steady growth in earmark spending between FY 2008 and FY 2010.

OMB

The OMB earmark database was apparently intended to serve, at least for the executive branch, as an official government standard for tracking earmarks. OMB defined earmarks in 2007 in Executive Order 13457 (as will be addressed) and established a public, searchable online database on earmarks to "establish a clear benchmark for measuring progress" toward the Bush administration's goals of cutting their numbers significantly.[38] The database purports to provide "more information on earmarks in one place than has ever been available through the Federal Government."[39] However, complete OMB data on earmarks in appropriations bills are available for only four fiscal years—the FY 2005 baseline and FY 2008 through FY 2010. These data indicate a 41.3 percent reduction in earmark spending between FY 2005 and FY 2010, and a 31.9 percent drop in their number.

TCS

The newest contributor to earmark data was TCS, capturing information for FY 2008 through FY 2010. TCS numbers show the cost of earmarks dropping by 13 percent over this three-year period and their number falling by 26 percent.[40]

In sum, the data on earmarks spending indicate a significant expansion beginning in the early 1990s, which peaked around FY 2006, following which earmark spending dropped sharply and stabilized at about the FY 2002 level. This pattern is explained by an earmark moratorium on FY 2007 spending bills and subsequent earmark reforms (addressed in the next section). The conclusion of Crespin and colleagues that the new rules have had no meaningful impact is contradicted by this data.

Reform on Three Fronts

Earmark reform began in FY 2006 and had three sources. New House and Senate rules came first, followed by additional constraints put in place by the House and Senate Appropriations Committees. Congressional member organizations within Congress operated somewhere between these two fronts, primarily advocating earmark moratoria. These organizations were dominated by fiscally conservative House organizations.

It should be noted that individual senators and House members made many attempts to impact earmarks before and during the reform period. Among the most notable of these were Senators McCain, Coburn, DeMint, Feingold, and Inhofe, and Representatives Flake, Ryan, and Hensarling.[41] These efforts were less concerned with earmark reform than with earmark elimination. As such, they were met with limited, though ultimate, success. (In 2007, a motion in the House to eliminate all earmarks was defeated, 53 to 369, with majorities in both parties opposing it.)[42]

The role of presidents is minimized here, because presidents have very limited power to control earmarks. The exception occurred during the brief period when the line-item veto was available, which President Clinton used to veto, among other spending items, some congressional earmarks.[43] President Bush singled them out for criticism in his 2007 and 2008 State of the Union speeches, as did President Obama in 2010. President Bush issued Executive Order (EO) 13457, which applied to all bills passed after January 29, 2008, and remains in effect. This EO set out a series of detailed duties for agency heads in dealing with earmarks, encouraging agencies to implement only those included in appropriations bills rather than reports. There is little evidence that either administration used the authority provided by EO 13457 to impact earmark funding. In May 2010, President Obama proposed the Reduce Unnecessary Spending Act of 2010, a bill that would allow presidents to veto earmarks by incorporating them within legislation to be rescinded. Congress did not act upon this proposal.

Rule Reform

Following elections, each new Congress adopts rules to govern committee operations and the manner in which legislation is to be considered. Rules are enforced by parliamentary points of order. To address concerns about earmarks, the House changed its official rules late in 2006, at the end of a Congress rather than at the beginning. This was the least effective of four rule changes addressing earmarks adopted between 2006 and 2007.

As the majority party in the House and Senate in 2006, the GOP had promised "comprehensive earmark reform rules change."[44] House Resolution (H.R. Res.) 1000, adopted September 14 by a vote of 245 to 171, was the result. (Notably, of the twenty-four Republicans who voted against the rule change, twenty-two were members of the HAC.) According to this rule, earmarks inserted in appropriations bills in committee or in conference would have to be disclosed, along with the names of the members of Congress sponsoring them. Disclosure at this first step in the reform process meant inclusion within the reports that accompany appropriations bills.

But H.R. Res. 1000 was not retroactive, and the House had already passed all but one of its appropriations bills for the year when it took effect. Thus the rule would affect only this single bill and conference reports, and only in the House. No earmarks were disclosed as a consequence of the 2006 House rule change.[45]

The first earmark rule change to have an impact was implemented by the 110th Congress, January 5, 2007. Earmark reforms were incorporated in clause 9 of Rule XXI and clauses 16 and 17 of Rule XXIII of the House rules package (H.R. Res. 6). According to House Democrats, the new rules would help bring an end to a "'culture of corruption' that led to the GOP losing control of Congress after 12 years."[46]

The rule prohibited the House from considering bills unless a list of earmarks and their sponsors in such bills or the accompanying report was made available in specified public documents, that is, committee reports (for committee-reported bills) or the *Congressional Record* (for other legislation). Members requesting earmarks were required to provide to the chairman and ranking member of the HAC, in writing, the name and address of the earmark recipient, its purpose, and certification that neither the requesting member nor his or her spouse had a financial interest in the earmark.[47] House members were prohibited from considering special rules waiving the public-disclosure requirements.[48]

Implementing the new earmark rule became a severe problem, ultimately providing the incentive for the third rule change affecting earmarks. The conflict centered on the timely publication of earmark information on the House version of the Homeland Security appropriations bill for FY 2008 in June 2007. Chairman Obey said that the HAC staff had received in excess of thirty thousand earmark requests, as a result of which more time was needed to review them. Consequently, he indicated his intention to ignore the new House rule on the timing of the release of earmark information and "drop the earmarks into the bills when they move to the House-Senate conference committees before the August break."[49]

The resolution of this impasse produced H.R. Res. 491, the third congressional rule on earmarks. This rule addressed transparency issues affecting "air-drops," earmarks added to conference agreements that were not in either the House or Senate version of the appropriations bills at issue in the conference. The new House rule prohibited consideration of conference reports unless the joint explanatory statements accompanying them included a list of earmarks in the conference report or joint statement, and the names of the earmark sponsors.[50]

The final rule change impacting earmarks was the Senate version of the two rules changes that took effect in the House. The vehicle, an ethics reform bill that included a section on earmarks, became law September 14 as the Honest Leadership and Open Government Act of 2007 (P.L. 110-81). Section 521, Congressionally Directed Spending, incorporated the Senate earmark reforms, adding them to the standing rules of the Senate as Rule XLIV.

The Senate earmark rules were very similar to the House rules, but not identical. Rule XLIV made it out of order in the Senate to vote on appropriations bills containing earmarks until the chairman of the committee of jurisdiction or the majority leader provides a list of the names of senators sponsoring the earmarks. The information had to be "available on a publicly accessible congressional website in a searchable format at least 48 hours before such vote."[51] Senators requesting earmarks were required to provide to the committee of jurisdiction their names, the name and location of the intended recipient, the purpose of the earmark, and certification that neither they nor their immediate family had a financial interest in the earmark (Rule XLIV, 6(a)). As with the House rules, points of order were used to enforce the Senate rules.

Because the Senate rules did not take effect until late in the year, their applicability to FY 2008 spending bills could be questioned. Compliance issues aside, it should be noted that in April, before adoption of S.1, the SAC announced that it would adopt earmark reforms for the FY 2008 spending bills pending passage of the Honest Leadership and Open Government Act. The new policies called for clear identification of earmarks, their sponsor, amount, recipient, and purpose. Earmark information would be published on the website of the SAC and the Library of Congress. Senators would also have to certify that they had no financial interest in the earmark.[52]

The earmark rule changes put in place in 2007 were in effect for the 110th Congress (2007–2008) and were adopted again in 2009 by and for the 111th Congress (2009–2010).

Committee Reforms

The HAC and SAC initiated several earmark reforms, the most important of which have come from the HAC. These committee-initiated earmark reforms can be seen as operationalizing and sometimes complicating the reforms affected by House and Senate rules. Their objectives may be more stringent than those imposed by congressional rules, particularly as regards transparency, but committee-initiated reforms are also more problematic. These problems stem from the fact that the processes of promulgation and enforcement of committee-initiated rules are opaque, and because of the differences between reforms coming from the HAC and the relatively tepid steps taken by the SAC.

Committee-initiated reforms began in earnest as Representative Obey and the late senator Byrd prepared to assume their positions as chairs of the House and Senate Appropriations Committees, respectively, in the newly elected 110th Congress. In December 2006, the chairs announced an important committee decision affecting earmarks. That decision would affect the joint funding resolution (the final continuing resolution for most FY 2007 spending) left over from the 109th Congress, and ultimately the number of earmarks allowed. The decision stemmed in part from the campaign statements of the Democrats in Congress, including the incoming Speaker of the House, Nancy Pelosi, who, had "railed for months against wasteful 'special interest earmarks' inserted into bills 'in the dark of night.'"[53] This rhetoric, in conjunction with vocal opposition to passage of the FY 2007 omnibus appropriations bill from some congressional Republicans, led to the postelection statement on earmarks and the omnibus.

Senator Byrd and Congressman Obey indicated their decision "to dispose of the Republican budget leftovers by passing a year-long joint resolution," meaning there would be no new congressional earmarks in a bill providing $463.5 billion in new spending.[54] The measure would constitute "a moratorium on all earmarks until a reformed process is put in place."[55] When the joint funding resolution was filed in January 2007, Chairman Obey explained that most FY 2007 programs would be funded at the FY 2006 level, adjusted for increased pay costs, but the resolution "is free of earmarks."[56]

The measure became law February 15. Thus the only new earmarks in spending bills for FY 2007 were those in the two full-year appropriations bills approved in 2006 by the previous Congress. This is the primary explanation for the drop in earmarks and their cost between FY 2006 and FY 2007 (see fig. 5.3). This initiative, whatever its importance in constraining earmarks in FY 2007 appropriations bills, was a one-time event, hence of marginal policy consequence.[57] The data (see fig. 5.3) support this conclusion.

More meaningful committee-initiated reforms began in January 2009, when the HAC and SAC jointly announced additional transparency requirements. The key changes were to require posting of data about earmark requests, as opposed to earmarks that had been approved, and the requirement that members post this information on their own websites rather than committee websites. For FY 2010, members requesting earmarks in appropriations bills had to provide information on these items when the request was made, "explaining the purpose of the earmark and why it is a valuable use of taxpayer funds."[58] Further, the committees promised to make available earmark disclosure tables to the public the same day as the relevant appropriations subcommittees released their report, or twenty-four hours before full-committee consideration of bills that had not been marked up by a Senate subcommittee.

Some additional transparency resulted, though not without problems. Requiring members requesting earmarks to post their requests on their own congressional websites produced a variety of responses. In the House, compliance consisted of "a hodgepodge, with some members of each party proudly displaying their requests while many others apparently did their utmost to keep their requests out of public view."[59] Rarely did House member websites use the term "earmark" in providing the required information. Off the record, some member offices admitted relabeling, moving, or altering their initial online disclosures "after they were criticized or after their offices became concerned that they soon would come under scrutiny for how they first posted their spending requests."[60]

The SAC provided a link to the websites of individual senators, titled Congressionally Directed Spending Requests.[61] However, it was not always clear at those websites where to find senatorial earmark information, and some senators indicated the amount of their request while others did not.

The HAC also provided member earmark-request data by subcommittee bill. HAC subcommittees provided links for their bills, titled "Earmark Certification Letters," which provided access to a list of House members requesting earmarks within that bill. These letters reflected each member's interpretation of the need to rationalize earmark requests, including the need to indicate the amount requested.

Another constraint to House earmarks was adopted in March 2009.[62] House earmarks would now be reviewed by the executive branch, and those directed to for-profit entities would be subject to competition. The executive branch review, however, only required that agencies involved in executing earmarked funds were, within twenty days, "to check that the proposed earmark is eligi-

ble for funding and meets goals established in law."[63] The competition mandate was similarly vague, requiring that earmarks "directed to for-profit entities
will undergo a competitive bidding process."[64] This reform was not adopted by
the SAC.

OMB made no commitment to the twenty-day deadline imposed by the
HAC, which would have most likely been difficult to achieve. OMB agreed
only to provide "answers to factual questions articulated by chairs of relevant
House committees of jurisdiction in as timely a manner as possible," but these
responses "should not be construed as an evaluation or recommendation of
specific requests based on merit or value."[65]

Because the SAC had not agreed to submit for-profit earmarks to competitive
bidding, the issue had to be resolved when the Senate took up its FY 2010 appropriations bills. The resolution found in the defense appropriations bill indicates the problem agencies faced in implementing the requirement to submit
profit earmarks to competitive bidding. It also illustrates the fragmentation of
earmark-reform policy originating with committees. The HAC and SAC agreed
that earmarks to for-profit entities originating in Senate appropriations bills
would not be held to the HAC standard, but those originating in the House would.
Those (roughly 5 percent) with both House and Senate sponsors would be exempt from the House competition requirement the first year but would fall under
that requirement in subsequent years.[66]

As the FY 2011 appropriations season began, the chairman of the HAC set
the stage for the continuation of earmark reform. After reviewing the reforms
of 2007 and 2009, he informed his House colleagues that these rules would
be retained (and in one case, stiffened) for FY 2011 appropriations bills, and he
announced a goal of holding earmarks below 1 percent of discretionary spending. He then added two more conditions for FY 2011 appropriations: Rather
than mandating competition for earmarks to for-profit entities, such earmarks
were to be prohibited. Further, agency inspector generals would be tasked with
inspecting earmarks to nonprofit earmark recipients to ensure that for-profit entities would not receive earmark funding. The chairman also promised to provide additional transparency with the establishment by the HAC of an on-line
"one-stop" link to display all earmark requests from House members. This may
have made it more convenient to access earmark data, which had been previously provided by bill on the HAC subcommittee websites, though it was not
clear that any new information would result.[67]

The SAC did not consider these reforms necessary. The chairman of the SAC positioned the Senate above earmark problems, noting that he understood "the reasons why the House might feel it is necessary to adjust its practices in light of previous problems in that body."[68] Senator Inouye then indicated his satisfaction with Senate earmark policy: "The policies that the Appropriations Committee has adopted for the Senate safeguard the Senate's constitutional role in directing spending decisions while ensuring transparency and strict control on the practice of earmarking."[69]

The reforms of March 2010 capture nicely the problem with committee-initiated reforms. They materialized, as did many previous committee-initiated reforms, as announcements from a congressional committee. The *Wall Street Journal* reported this event as follows: "The ban was not voted on by the House, but was simply agreed to by Representative David Obey (D-WI) and Representative Norm Dicks (D-WA) who control the process for adopting House spending bills."[70] We can speculate regarding the motives for the change, but there is no public record. Similarly, the reform was unilateral, that is, the Senate did not follow, which means that the disposition of earmarks to for-profit entities would occur in the context of conference negotiations between the House and Senate on FY 2011 appropriations bills. It was also unilateral in that House Republicans had not been involved in the HAC decision. To compound the issue, House Republicans upped the ante the day after the HAC announcement, declaring their intention to ban all earmarks, not just those to for-profit entities.

Reform and Congressional Party Organizations

The decision by House Republicans just noted is an example of another front in the earmark reform conflict. The decision was taken by the House Republican Conference, in the form of a resolution. The House Republican Conference is the official representation of the Republican Party in the House. Other organizations within Congress also attempted to influence earmark reform. Most active in the House, these organizations included some ad hoc, informal, and temporary member groups and some congressional member organizations (for example, the Republican Study Committee [RSC]). Although these efforts have had minimal effect on earmark policy to date, they are worth noting as indicators of the political salience of this issue and perhaps of the direction for future reform.

The primary earmark-reform theme advanced by House Republican groups was a moratorium pending adoption of additional reforms to be developed by a bipartisan committee on earmarks. In November 2007, for example, Republican members of the HAC, supported by the RSC, proposed a moratorium on earmarks and the establishment of a bipartisan, bicameral select committee on earmark reform. This offer was renewed in January 2008, with the additional support of the Republican leader, whip and chief deputy whip, three members of the Republican Conference, and members from the National Republican Congressional Committee, the Republican Policy Committee, and the Rules Committee. These House Republicans notified the Speaker of their belief that "the earmark system should be brought to an immediate halt, and a bipartisan select committee should immediately be established for the purpose of identifying ways to bring fundamental change to the way in which Washington spends taxpayers' money." In the meantime, House Republicans indicated their intent to adopt "a series of earmark reform standards that we insist that all House Republican members honor."[71] These standards included the following:

1. No projects named for themselves
2. No airdrops
3. No "pass-through" earmarks (earmarks that disguise actual recipients)
4. More details provided with earmark requests
5. Earmark recipients must put up matching funds for projects.[72]

A Select Committee on Earmark Reform was eventually put in place in the House, but it was neither bipartisan nor bicameral. Its ten members were all Republicans. Its impact was primarily in the form of press releases and proposals, none of which were adopted by either Republicans or Democrats. It was charged with filing a report no later than February 16, 2009, with recommendations for reform, but no report was produced. Some of its activities were captured on a now-defunct website devoted to earmark reform launched by the House Republican leadership in February 2008 to support the committee.[73]

In March 2009, House GOP conference chairman Adam Putnam attempted (without success) to pressure his party leadership into denying committee leadership positions to House Republicans who did not adhere to the standards proposed by the House Republican leadership.[74] In May, the RSC circulated a letter asking House GOP leaders to adopt the RSC position on earmarks, that is, a one-year moratorium; the leadership, however, rejected a GOP-only moratorium, opting to propose a bipartisan moratorium instead. Speaker Pelosi declined this offer.

On the Senate side, a Fiscal Reform Working Group, chaired by Senator Lugar, was announced by the Republican leader in January 2008. The panel was "to review the earmark process for spending and revenue and recommend additional means for the Senate to bring greater transparency and fiscal responsibility to government spending."[75] The five senators issued their report March 11, recommending a set of principles for the Senate Republican Conference. After carefully acknowledging "the Constitutional responsibility of each Member of Congress to make decisions on the appropriation of federal taxpayer funds," the report recommended that

1. Senate rules should be modified to require that earmarks be put in bills rather than reports;
2. senators should provide detailed information about earmark requests on their individual websites as well as websites of relevant committees in searchable formats at least forty-eight hours before floor consideration; the disclosure data should include the name and address of the intended recipient, full justification (financial/budget plans, federal matching requirements, and reasons for a lack of nonfederal funding), evidence that the requesting member will not benefit financially, and whether or not the earmarked funds will be competed;
3. the administration should provide greater transparency for the earmarks it includes in the budget request to Congress;
4. savings from earmarks removed from legislation should be used to reduce the national debt.[76]

The Senate Republican leader hedged his bet regarding the prospect of proposing these reforms in the form of a rule and "would not say whether his conference would adopt the plan if Democrats do not want to go along."[77] Item two on this list is the only one that proved relevant, but it was, in part, moot. The rules adopted by the Senate for the 111th Congress before the report was issued addressed the primary earmark disclosure issue it raises. The Senate was not willing to adopt measures requiring the additional information recommended by the Fiscal Reform Working Group.

The possibility of a second moratorium on earmarks was raised by the approval of a unilateral ban on earmark requests for FY 2011 by the House GOP conference in March 2010.[78] The Republican leader threatened to use the power of the Republican Steering Committee over committee assignments to enforce the ban.[79] The fact that the endorsement came from the Republican Conference rather than a subordinate Republican-led group suggests a broader consensus among House Republicans on this issue (though some House Republicans went on record as disagreeing with the ban, indicating that they would request earmarks for FY 2011). A resolution inviting House Democrats to join the GOP moratorium, supported by 162 House Republicans, including their leadership, was introduced in the House but never came up for a vote. It included another call for a bipartisan, bicameral committee to study and then reform the earmark process.[80]

In March, the Senate defeated a proposal for a similar ban by a vote of 68 to 21, with fifteen Republicans voting against the ban.[81] The next month, a two-year prohibition on earmarks—to be achieved by requiring a two-thirds majority to approve bills containing earmarks—sponsored by a Senate Democrat was defeated by a 2-to-1 majority.[82]

Fiscal conservatives in the Senate (two Republicans and two Democrats) launched an oblique attempt at earmark reform by calling for "a new centralized earmark database."[83] The database would ostensibly provide better access to most of the same kind of data that had been mandated by congressional rules and committee reforms. It would address a need for consolidation and clarification of earmark information. Further, and as noted here, compliance with the existing disclosure rules remained a problem, though whether the proposed Earmark Transparency Act would solve those problems was uncertain. Key senators suggested that technical difficulties would prohibit passage of the bill, which died in committee.

As detailed here, Congress engaged in a multiyear struggle to reform earmarking, culminating in the March 2010 ban, which remained in place as of November 2016. Following two and a half decades of significant growth, spending for earmarks peaked in FY 2006, then dropped noticeably after the FY 2007 earmark moratorium. Subsequently, and most likely as a consequence of the reforms instituted for FY 2008 to FY 2010, earmark spending stabilized at

	Pre-reform (FY 1991–2006)	Post-reform (FY 2008–10)
Number of Earmarks	107.8%	-7.1%
$ Value of Earmarks	52.2%	-1.4%
Discretionary Spending	5.2%	1.9%

Fig. 5.5: Average annual rates of growth before and after earmark reform. FY 2007 is used as the dividing line between pre- and post-reform and is omitted because that was the year of the first and only earmark moratorium and because substantive reforms first became effective in FY 2008. *Sources:* CAGW data were used for the number and dollar value of earmarks, while discretionary spending data were taken from OMB's Historical Tables, 2010.

about $20 billion before the ban in 2010, approximately where it was in 2002. Discretionary spending continued to expand after 2007, minimizing the cramping effect of earmarks noted in the rise in earmarks before that year. Average annual rates of growth in the relevant variables are used to compare pre- and postreform periods (fig. 5.5).

The nonpartisan, nonprofit organization Citizens Against Government Waste reports that there are significant increases in the cost and number of earmarks since 2017. In FY 2019 the 282 earmarks represents a 21.6 percent increase over the number in FY 2018, and the cost of $15.3 billion is a 4.1 percent increase over the cost in FY 2018.[84]

The reforms implemented through congressional rules and committee policies during the 110th and 111th Congresses demonstrably increased transparency of and accountability for earmarks. It was possible to observe earmarks as they moved through the appropriations process, from request to approval, and, usually, to connect them to individual members of Congress. This visibility was almost certainly linked to the decline in spending for earmarks evident in the databases reviewed here.

Committee-initiated earmark reform was dominated by the HAC, with the SAC following, intermittently. Committee-initiated reforms expedited the availability of information on earmarks and bolstered the use of the Internet to provide transparency. It remains difficult to assess committee reforms because the committee reform process, including enforcement measures, is opaque. Where only one of the appropriations committees implements an earmark reform, the impact is diminished. Party-oriented congressional organizations had a minimal effect on earmark reform, notwithstanding their intentions and the publicity they have received.

A small subset within Congress continued to dominate earmark allocation before the ban. Among those key players are members of the HAC and the SAC, whose leadership is also critical to earmark reform.

The GOP earmark critique incorporated two potentially conflicting themes. Earmarks were (and still are, for some) considered inherently bad for the budget, either directly or indirectly, and as such, must be banned. The ban, however, is usually linked to the notion that reform, as yet imperfect, will somehow change the process and allow earmarks some redemption. For example, in announcing the 2010 earmark ban, the House Republican leader stated that it means the beginning of "a process for bringing more transparency and accountability to how we spend the American peoples' money . . . [;] what the American people want to see is a process that does have all the transparency and accountability it ought to have. But we're not going to get to a cleaned up process until we break with the past."[85]

Senator McCain made the same point as part of his endorsement of the Earmark Transparency Act of 2010, noting that "it is abundantly clear that the time has come for us to eliminate the corrupt, wasteful practice of earmarking. While we work toward that end, it is important that we give the American people the ability to see how their money is being spent."[86] By combining calls for earmark bans with calls for earmark reform, the distinction is blurred between a ban as a necessary prelude to reform and a ban as the reform itself.

The process once used to move earmarks through Congress can be compared with the one that provides for mandatory spending. Appropriations bills must be passed by committees, then the full House, Senate, and conference committees each year, and all of the information about earmarks had to be provided pursuant to the reforms of 2006–2010. Many votes and much information— who was asking for and receiving what—were involved in providing the 0.4 percent of total federal spending that earmarks represented in FY 2010, before the ban took effect. On the other hand, mandatory spending (mostly entitlements, dominated by Social Security, Medicare, and Medicaid), made up 65 percent of FY 2010 spending, and occurred without naming a name or taking a vote.[87]

After the Ban: Alternatives to Earmarks and Nostalgia for Their "Transactional" Benefit

Conventional earmarks were effectively reformed, following which they were banned, ostensibly the ultimate reform. Only a single organization (CAGW) now tracks them. The OMB earmarks database has no data after FY 2010, and the Department of Defense comptroller's earmarks data end at FY 2011. Congressional committee and member earmark data are no longer posted. The charts from CAGW (figs. 5.6 and 5.7) reflect the impact of reform and the ban, showing dramatic reductions in both spending for earmarks and number of earmarks themselves.

However, earmarks are not dead. As the CAGW charts reveal, some spending continues to occur that is likely included within one or more of the definitions of earmarks. This spending may be incorporated within some new means to the old ends of earmarking. For example, the *Washington Post* launched a project called Capitol Assets, which links financial disclosure reports by members of Congress to earmarks and other spending provisions.[88] The *Post* named fifty members of Congress who have been involved in directing millions of dollars in earmarks to "projects that either held the potential to enhance the

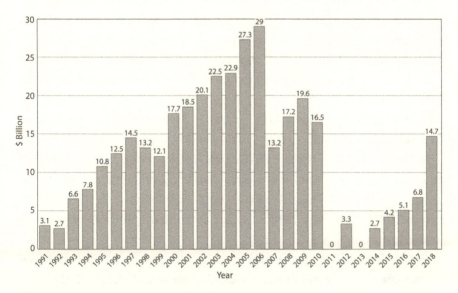

Fig. 5.6: Earmark spending, 1991 to 2018. *Source:* Citizens Against Government Waste.

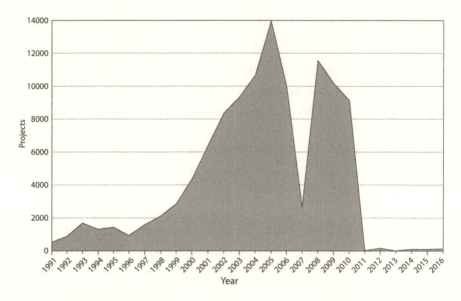

Fig. 5.7: Number of earmarks, 1991 to 2016. *Source:* Citizens Against Government Waste.

surrounding of a lawmaker's own property, or aided entities connected to their immediate family."[89]

Other sources point to efforts to manipulate the system to avoid the reforms by providing funding that will benefit individual members of Congress via "zombie" earmarks.[90] Funding is also being provided through "phone-marking,"[91] "letter-marking," "soft earmarks" and "undisclosed" earmarks."[92] Earmarklike expenditures no doubt, continue to occur, and the effort to identify and evaluate them is important.

More to the point, however, is the interest in ending the ban on conventional earmarks, and its motivations. Certain members of Congress, past and present, and students of Congress share this interest. In November 2016, members of the House Republican Conference were, apparently, prepared to vote to overturn the ban before Speaker Ryan convinced them to postpone the vote until early in 2017.[93] In January 2018, members of the House Rules Committee expressed interest in lifting the earmark ban. They were encouraged to consider this by President Trump, who noted that "there was great friendliness when you had earmarks."[94] The earmark ban remained in place as of October 2019.

Recall that it was House Republicans who transformed the earmark reforms of 2006–2008 into a ban. Evidence of a change of heart (not shared by all House

Republicans, of course) is in part driven by the notion that earmarks are essential to improving the way the budget process works. Transactional politics would trump fiscal policy here.

Arguments for reprising earmarks echo some of the themes just reviewed, for example, that earmarks are necessary for credit claiming and as such, essential to members' electoral fortunes. According to contemporary opponents of the earmark ban, "[e]armarks are the WD-40 that helped the gears of government grind forward."[95] Earmarks "provided a handy way for the leadership to buy votes and reward loyalists," Jonathan Rauch argues, hence "pork barreling, despite its much maligned status, gets things done."[96] Former congressman Jim Moran, a member of the House Appropriations Committee, stated that Congress "has not functioned since earmarks were prohibited."[97]

And getting things done in Congress, particularly with respect to budgeting, has become a very serious problem. Recall that earmarks are predominantly found within appropriations bills. Timely completion of these bills has become rare: all such bills have been passed before the start of the next fiscal year only four times in forty-six years since the Congressional Budget Act was put in place.[98] Absent these bills, programs are funded through continuing resolutions (CRs), punting decisions on programs and spending levels. Since FY 1997 (the most recent year that Congress completed all appropriations bills on time), CRs were enacted almost six times each year on average.[99] The result is increasingly "a mutation from the normal authorization and appropriation stand-alone bills to the mega constructs of omnibus appropriations bills . . . and its latest iteration, the cromnibus (a combination of a continuing resolution and an omnibus appropriation bill)."[100]

Similarly, Congress is finding it more difficult to agree on the overall level of annual spending, as reflected in failure to complete a budget resolution. After completing such resolutions each year from 1976 through 1998, only eleven were completed since, a stretch that includes five consecutive years without a congressional budget resolution (FY 2011–FY 2015).[101] It is perhaps notable that in 2016, the House Budget Committee refused to take testimony on the president's proposed budget for FY 2017, the first time that has occurred since 1975.

There are other, perhaps related, measures of congressional dysfunction. The number of bills each Congress passes has dropped significantly, from over eight hundred for the 95th Congress (1977–1978) to fewer than three hundred for the 115th (2017–2018).[102] On the flip side, the number of cloture votes has increased

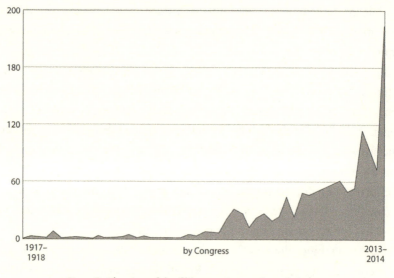

Fig. 5.8: The rise of the filibuster, in number of cloture
votes to end filibusters. *Sources: Vox,* U.S. Senate.

significantly, beginning, roughly, in the 1960s (fig. 5.8). Cloture votes are used
to end filibusters, the latter a legislative tactic used in the Senate to prevent
votes on legislation. The filibuster has now become common, "a tool that the
minority party used to routinely stymie the majority party."[103] There were a
record sixty-seven filibusters in 2009, twice the number that occurred in the two
decades between 1950 and 1969.[104]

It is argued that much of the congressional dysfunction apparent in the failure to legislate, especially evident within the congressional budget process, can
be attributed to the rise of party polarization. Data on the polarization of the
political parties in Congress suggest that as of 2018, Congress is more polarized
along ideological lines than it has ever been.[105] Ideological polarization in Congress is part of the problem of budget dysfunction, that is, it is likely contributing to the breakdown in the budget process outlined in the Congressional
Budget and Impoundment Control Act of 1974. But there is a dimension of this
polarization that is pertinent to the notion that bringing earmarks back might
help to break the stalemate between the parties in Congress and improve the
legislative process. The polarization in Congress is primarily the result of Republicans becoming more conservative, "a major partisan asymmetry in polarization."[106] This is particularly true in the House.

This matters insofar as earmarks are viewed as simply another example of government spending. As such, House Republicans, increasingly conservative, are not likely to favor the return of congressional earmarks, the November 2016 and January 2018 initiatives notwithstanding. (Should the ban be dropped by the House, the Senate may not agree, which would probably prolong the ban.) Given the size and nature of the gap between the parties in Congress and the impact it has had on the conduct of congressional budgeting as noted here, it seems highly unlikely that such small grease as earmarks might provide to that process would make a difference should a transparent earmark arrangement be resurrected.

Notes

1. Pamela Prah, "Emptying the Pork Barrel Would Hit Some States Especially Hard," *Stateline,* The Pew Charitable Trusts, December 10, 2010, https://www.pewtrusts.org/en/research-and-analysis/blogs/stateline/2010/12/10/emptying-the-pork-barrel-would-hit-some-states-especially-hard.
2. Irene Rubin, "The Great Unraveling: Federal Budgeting, 1998–2006," *Public Administrative Review* 67, no. 4 (July–August 2007): 608–17.
3. Thomas Mann, Sarah Binder, and Norman Ornstein, "Is the Broken Branch on the Mend?" Brookings Institution, September 4, 2007.
4. Paul Kane, "House Bans Earmarks to For-Profit Companies," *Washington Post,* March 11, 2010.
5. Susan Benkelman, "Money Chase," *CQ Weekly,* Oct 1, 2007.
6. Eric Alterman and George Zornick, "Think Again: Out, Out, Damned Earmark," Center for American Progress, September 18, 2008.
7. U.S. Rep. Jeff Flake, "Earmarked Men," *New York Times,* February 9, 2006.
8. U.S. Rep. Jeff Flake, "Of Pork and Payback," *New York Times,* February 24, 2009.
9. "Our View. Cuts In Military Pork Fall Short Of Rhetoric," *USA Today,* October 5, 2009.
10. Paul Kane, "Candidates' Earmarks Worth Millions," *Washington Post,* February 15, 2008.
11. David Mayhew, *Congress: The Electoral Connection* (New Haven, CT: Yale University Press, 1974).
12. Marc Law and Joseph Tonon, "The Strange Budgetary Politics of Agricultural Research Earmarks," *Public Budgeting and Finance* (2007), 6.
13. Erik Engstrom and Georg Vanberg, "The Politics of Congressional Earmarking," SSRN (2007), 2; available at http://ssrn.com/abstracts=1081654.
14. Scott Frisch, *The Politics of Pork: A Study of Congressional Appropriations Earmarks* (New York: Routledge, 1998), 143.
15. Ibid., 149.

16. Austin Clemens and Charles Finocchiaro, "Earmarks and Subcommittee Government in the U.S. Congress" (paper presented at the annual meeting of the Southern Political Science Association, January 7–9, 2010).

17. Stacy Fisher and Michael Rocca, "Earmarks and Campaign Contributions in the 110th Congress" (paper presented at the 2010 Western Political Science Association Meeting, San Francisco, CA), 2.

18. Ibid., 4.

19. Ibid., 7.

20. Ibid., 14.

21. Ibid., 17.

22. Michael Crespin and Charles Finocchiaro, "Distributive and Partisan Politics in the U.S. Senate: An Exploration of Earmarks," in *Why Not Parties? Party Effects in the United States Senate,* ed. Nathan Monroe, Jason Roberts, and David Rohde (Chicago: University of Illinois Press, 2008), 229–69.

23. Steven Balla et al. "Partisanship, Blame Avoidance, and the Distribution of Legislative Pork," *American Journal of Political Science* 46, no. 3 (2002): 515–25.

24. Michael Crespin, Charles Finocchiaro, and Emily Wanless, "Perception and Reality in Congressional Earmarks," *The Forum* 7, no. 2 (2009): 1–18.

25. Ibid., 25.

26. Rebecca Kysar, "Listening to Congress: Earmark Rules and Statutory Interpretation," *Cornell Law Review* 94 (2009): 520–86.

27. Ibid., 529, 522.

28. Ibid., 549.

29. According to the Congressional Research Service (CRS), "[t]here is not a single definition of the term earmark accepted by all practitioners and observers of the appropriations process, nor is there a standard earmark practice across all appropriation bills." Congressional Research Service, memorandum: "Earmarks in Appropriations Acts: FY 1994, FY 1996, FY 1998, FY 2000, FY 2002, FY 2004, FY 2005," January 26, 2006, p. 2.

30. Frisch, *The Politics of Pork,* 165.

31. "Earmark Cover-up," *Wall Street Journal,* March 26, 2007.

32. Flake, "Earmarked Men."

33. Earmark spending is calculated here using data from Citizens Against Government Waste. Discretionary and total spending data come from the OMB Historical Tables, https://www.whitehouse.gov/omb/historical-tables/.

34. Citizens Against Government Waste database, available at http://www.cagw.org.

35. OMB Historical Tables, https://www.whitehouse.gov/omb/historical-tables/.

36. Because of varying definitions and methodologies, CRS did not aggregate earmark data for all of the bills reviewed. Such differences are ignored here in the interest of providing a general sense of the evolution of earmarks. CRS memorandum: "Earmarks in Appropriations Acts," January 26, 2006; CRS memorandum: "Earmarks in FY 2006 Appropriations Acts," March 6, 2006; CRS report for Congress: *Bush Administration Policy Re-*

garding Congressionally Originated Earmarks: An Overview, November 17, 2008; CRS report: *Earmarks Disclosed by Congress: FY 2008–FY 2010, Regular Appropriations Bills,* April 16, 2010.

37. OMB Historical Tables, https://www.whitehouse.gov/omb/historical-tables/.

38. OMB, press release, "New Features Added to Earmarks Database," accessed July 10, 2007.

39. OMB database, Earmarks, accessed October 9, 2009.

40. Taxpayers for Common Sense, "Taxpayers for Common Sense Releases New Earmark Database," February 14, 2008, accessed February 18, 2010.

41. Earmark moratorium legislation was again introduced by Rep. Flake in the House (H.R. Res. 1101) and by Sen. DeMint (S. 2990) in the Senate in 2010.

42. Congress, House, Committee on Appropriations, press release: "Obey Statement on Earmarks," February 7, 2008.

43. Roy Meyers, "The Remarkable Case of the Disappearing (?) Earmarks" (paper prepared for the annual conference of the Association for Budgeting and Financial Management, October 25–27, 2007), 6.

44. Lirial Higa, "Earmark Rules to be Separate From Lobby Bill," *CQ Weekly,* September 11, 2006.

45. Steven Dennis, "House Changes Its Rules on Earmarks," *CQ Weekly,* September 18, 2006.

46. Steven Dennis, "House Adopts Budget, Earmark Rules," *CQ Weekly,* January 8, 2007.

47. House Rule XXIII, clause 17.

48. House Rule XXI, clause 9, section 4b.

49. Elizabeth Williamson, "Earmarks Dispute Bogs Down Homeland Security Bill," *Washington Post,* June 13, 2007.

50. H.R. Res. 491.

51. Rule XLIV, 1(a)(2).

52. Congress, Senate, Committee on Appropriations, press release: Senate Appropriations Committee Announces Earmark Reform Standards, April 17, 2007.

53. David Kirkpatrick, "As Power Shifts in New Congress, Pork May Linger," *New York Times,* November 26, 2006.

54. Congress, House, Committee on Appropriations, press release, "Byrd-Obey Announce FY 2007 Plan," December 11, 2006.

55. Ibid.

56. Congress, House, Committee on Appropriations, press release, "Democrats File Joint Funding Resolution for FY 2007," January 29, 2007.

57. House Democratic leaders discussed but did not agree to a party-wide moratorium affecting FY 2011 appropriations in March 2010. One factor contributing to this discussion may have been the concern that appropriations for FY 2011 might remain incomplete, as they were for FY 2007, the year of the earmark moratorium. If the earmarks would not take effect in the end, better perhaps to relinquish them publicly in advance. Tory New-

myer, "Majority Eyes Earmark Ban," *Roll Call,* March 8, 2010, http://www.rollcall.com, accessed March 8, 2010.

58. Congress, House, Committee on Appropriations, press release, "House and Senate Appropriations Committees Announce Additional Reforms in Committee Earmark Policy," January 6, 2009.

59. Jared Allen, "Earmarks: Online Hide and Go Seek," *The Hill,* April 7, 2009, http://thehill.com/, accessed October 10, 2009.

60. Jared Allen, "Earmark Scofflaws Get Pass," *The Hill,* April 22, 2009, http://thehill.com/, accessed October 10, 2009.

61. Congress, Senate, Committee on Appropriations, Congressionally Directed Spending Requests, http://appropriations.senate.gov/cdsr.cfm, accessed October 10, 2009.

62. Congress, House, Committee on Appropriations, press release, "Pelosi, Hoyer, and Obey Announce Further Earmark Reforms," March 11, 2009.

63. Ibid.

64. Ibid.

65. OMB, letter to the Honorable Nancy Pelosi, April 16, 2009.

66. David Clarke, "Democrats Are Ready to Move Appropriations Conference Agreements," *CQ Today,* September 25, 2009.

67. Congress, House, Committee on Appropriations, "Dear Colleague" letter, January 25, 2010; and press release, "Appropriations Committee Bans For-Profit Earmarks," March 10, 2010.

68. Congress, Senate, Committee on Appropriations, press release, "Senate Appropriations Committee Policy on Earmarks," March 11, 2010.

69. Ibid.

70. Corey Boles, "House Curbs Earmarks, Senate Balks," *Wall Street Journal,* March 11, 2010. It should be noted that Rep. Dicks replaced Rep. Murtha as chairman of the Defense Appropriations.

71. Ibid.

72. Ibid.

73. Congress, House, Select Committee on Earmark Reform, 110th Congress, 2nd sess., available at http://earmarkreform.house.gov/, accessed October 9, 2009.

74. Susan Crabtree, "Choose Reform or Panel Post, Putnam Warns," *The Hill,* March 5, 2009, available at http://thehill.com/, accessed October 9, 2009.

75. U.S. Sen. Richard Lugar, press release, "McConnell Announces Fiscal Reform Working Group," January 30, 2008.

76. Congress, Senate, Report of the Fiscal Reform Working Group, March 11, 2008, available at http://lugar.senate.gov/issues/indianaspending/pdf/Fiscal_Reform.pdf, accessed October 9, 2009.

77. Manu Raju, "Senate GOP Earmark Plan Hits Hurdles Quickly," *The Hill,* April 3, 2009, available at http://thehill.com, accessed October 9, 2009. One prominent earmark opponent in the Senate decided that "You don't save anything by cutting earmarks," and

"earmark-bashing misses the more important goal: reducing overall spending." Brian Friel, "Inhofe: Earmarks Are Good for Us," *National Journal,* March 6, 2010.

78. Edward Epstein and David Clarke, "House Republicans Embrace One-Year Moratorium on Earmarks," *CQ Today,* Online News, March 11, 2010. House Democrats also considered a party-wide ban on FY 2011 earmarks, calculated in part by the anticipation that earmarks would be scrapped for that year anyway because of the difficulties Congress would confront in completing appropriations bills using the regular process. No decision on this matter was taken by the Democratic leadership. Tory Newmyer, "Majority Eyes Earmark Ban," *Roll Call,* March 8, 2010.

79. Jackie Kucinich, "Boehner Warns of Consequences for GOP Members Seeking Earmarks," *Roll Call,* May 19, 2010.

80. Jackie Kucinich, "House GOP to Push Ban on All Earmarks This Year," *Roll Call,* April 21, 2010.

81. Emily Pierce, "GOP Splits as Senate Defeats Earmark Moratorium," *Roll Call,* March 16, 2010. Republican Sen. Bob Corker from Tennessee publicly withdrew his FY 2011 earmark requests, suggesting that the cost of those requests was less problematic than the process, "which is fundamentally flawed and lacks oversight." Dan Friedman and Humberto Sanchez, "Corker Becomes Latest Republican to Reject Earmarks," *CongressDaily/ AM,* April 15, 2010.

82. Bob Edgar and Bill Goodfellow, "The Real Problem with Earmarks," *The Hill,* April 19, 2010.

83. Paul Singer, "Coburn Bill Targets Earmarks," *Roll Call,* May 11, 2010.

84. Citizens Against Government Waste, "Introduction," *2019 Congressional Pig Book Summary,* https://www.cagw.org/reporting/pig-book.

85. House Republican Conference, press release, "Republican Leader Press Conference," March 11, 2010.

86. U.S. Sen. Russ Feingold, press release, "Senators Coburn, McCain, Feingold and Gillibrand Introduce Bill to Create Earmark Database Requested by President Obama," May 11, 2010.

87. This ignores votes on budget resolutions, which are not laws, but which can be seen as confirming the mandatory spending portions of the budget. Earmark spending for FY 2010 was taken from TCS; total and mandatory spending was taken from OMB's Historical Tables.

88. "Public Projects, Private Interests," Capitol Assets, *Washington Post,* http://www.washingtonpost.com/wp-srv/special/capitol-assets/public-projects-private-interests/.

89. Ibid.

90. Austin Wright and Jeremy Herb, "The Rise of the 'Zombie' Earmark," *Politico,* October 20, 2015.

91. Steve Ellis, "Earmarks Are Dead. Long Live Earmarks," *CNNMoney,* April 7, 2011.

92. Ron Nixon, "Lawmakers Finance Pet Projects Without Earmarks," *New York Times,* December 27, 2010.

93. Lindsey McPherson, "House GOP Postpones Decision on Whether to Restore Limited Earmarks," *RollCall,* November 17, 2016.

94. Sarah Ferris, "House GOP Mulls Lifting a Ban on Earmarks," *Politico,* Jan 9, 2018.

95. Chris Cillizza, "Let's Bring Back Earmarks, Please," *Washington Post,* Nov 20, 2016.

96. Jonathan Rauch, "How American Politics Went Insane," *The Atlantic,* July/August 2016.

97. Wright and Herb, "The Rise of the 'Zombie' Earmark."

98. Testimony of Philip Joyce before the House Budget Committee, May 25, 2016, p. 7.

99. Congressional Research Service, Continuing Resolutions: Overview of Components and Recent Practices, January 14, 2016.

100. Mark Strand, and Anca Butcaru, "The Case for Earmarks: Were They Really That Bad?," Congressional Institute, September 9, 2016.

101. Congressional Research Service, Congressional Budget Resolutions: Historical Information, November 16, 2015. Congress passed budget resolutions for FY 17 and FY 18 but failed to complete a budget resolution for FY 2019.

102. Govtrack, "Statistics and Historical Comparison," https://www.govtrack.us/congress/bills/statistics.

103. Ezra Klein, "Congressional Dysfunction," *Vox,* May 15, 2015.

104. Garrett Epps, "How the Senate Filibuster Went Out-of-Control—and Who Can Rein It In," *The Atlantic,* December 27, 2012.

105. Voteview Project, Jeffrey B. Lewis, project lead, "116th Congress (2019–2021): Representatives," University of California Los Angeles, available at https://voteview.com/congress/house.

106. Nolan McCarty, "What We Know and Don't Know about Our Polarized Politics," *Washington Post,* January 8, 2014.

Discussion Questions

1. Some who support earmarks argue for their restitution as part of a larger process of reclaiming for the legislative branch its appropriate spending role within the constitutional order. Speaker of the House Paul Ryan noted in late 2016 that the earmark reform debate "means stop giving all this power to unelected people to micromanage our society, our economy and our lives, and restore the Constitution. That's what this debate is about." What is the constitutional element here, and what are the stakes involved?

2. A common theme among earmark proponents is that members of Congress who propose earmarks know their states and districts better than the federal officials ("unelected bureaucrats") who otherwise allocate

discretionary spending. Assess this argument by comparing the decision-making processes used in both instances.

3. Consider the process by which earmarks became law, before the ban. Next figure out how the funding for Social Security is made available every year. What are the key differences between these two sets of processes and the types of public goods they provide?

6

The Business of America Is Lobbying

Lee Drutman

*It is grossly reckless to watch the long term business trajectory of the U.S.
to be at such risk. And we are part of the pathology that got us here.
We've all had our K Street lobbyists who are part of the problem.*
Paul Stebbens, CEO, World Fuel Services[1]

OVER THE PAST FOUR DECADES, large corporations have learned to play the Washington game. Companies now devote massive resources to politics, and their large-scale involvement increasingly redirects and constricts the capacities of the political system. The consequence is a democracy that is increasingly unable to tackle large-scale problems, and a political economy that too often rewards lobbying over innovation.

Prior to the 1970s, few corporations had their own lobbyists, and the trade associations that did represent business demonstrated nothing close to the scope and sophistication of modern lobbying. In the 1960s and the early 1970s, when Congress passed a series of new social regulations to address a range of environmental and consumer safety concerns, the business community lacked both the political will and the political capacity to stop it. These new regulations, combined with the declining economy, awoke the sleeping political giant of American business. Hundreds of companies hired lobbyists for the first time in the mid-1970s, and corporate managers began paying attention to politics much more than they ever did before.

When corporations first became politically engaged in the 1970s, their approach to lobbying was largely reactive. They were trying to stop the continued advancement of the regulatory state. They were fighting a proposed consumer protection agency, trying to stop labor-law reform, and responding to a general sense that the values of free enterprise had been forgotten and government regulation was going to destroy the economy. They also lobbied as a community. Facing a common enemy (government and labor), they hung together so they wouldn't hang separately. But as the labor movement weakened and government became much more pro-industry, companies continued to invest in politics, becoming more comfortable and more aggressive. Rather than seeing government as a threat, they started looking to government as a potential source of profits and assistance. As companies devoted more resources to their own lobbying efforts, they increasingly sought out their own narrow interests. As corporate lobbying investments have expanded, they have become more particularistic and more proactive. They have also become more pervasive, driven by the growing competitiveness of the process to become more aggressive.

External events may drive initial corporate investments in Washington. But once companies begin lobbying, that lobbying has its own internal momentum. Corporate managers begin to pay more attention to politics, and in so doing they see more reasons why they should be politically active. They develop a comfort and a confidence in being politically engaged. And once a company pays some fixed start-up costs, the marginal costs of additional political activity decline. Lobbyists find new issues, companies get drawn into new battles, and new coalitions and networks emerge. Managers see value in political engagement they did not see before. Lobbying is sticky.

Lobbyists drive this process. They teach companies to see the value in political activity. They also benefit from an information asymmetry that allows them to highlight information, issues, and advocacy strategies that can collectively make the strongest case for continued and expanded political engagement. Because corporate managers depend on lobbyists for both their political information and strategic advice, lobbyists are well positioned to push companies toward increased lobbying over time.

But what effect has it all had on public policy? Social science research on political influence has found no relationship between political resources and likelihood of success.[2] However, the lack of a direct, statistically significant correlation does not mean that there is no influence. It just means that the influence is unpredictable. The policy process is neither a vending machine nor an auction. Outcomes cannot be had for reliable prices. Policy does not go to the highest bidder. Politics is far messier and far more interesting than such simplistic models might suggest. And almost certainly, the increased competition for political outcomes has made it even more unpredictable.

Sometimes lobbying can be very influential, but its influence is contingent on so many confounding factors that it does not show up reliably in regression analysis. Yet the study of influence is a fundamental question of politics. Rather than looking for vote buying or expecting resources to correlate predictability with policy success, we must think bigger. We must understand the ways in which increases in lobbying activity shape the policy-making environment and how the changing environment may allow some types of interests to thrive more than others. The current political environment benefits large corporations for several reasons, which I will examine here.

The first reason is that the increasingly dense and competitive lobbying environment makes any major policy change very difficult. As more actors have more at stake, every attempt to change policy elicits more calls from more voices. In a political system whose many veto points already make change difficult, the proliferation of well-mobilized corporate lobbying interests, all with their own particular positions and asks, means that there are more actors with the capacity to throw more sand into the already creaky machinery of the multistage policy process. In order for any large-scale change to happen, lobbying generally must be one-sided.[3] To the extent that large corporations benefit from the status quo, a hard-to-change status quo benefits large corporations.[4]

But while the crowded political environment may make legislation harder to pass in general, it also makes the legislation that does pass more complicated (more side bargains). Large companies are more likely to have the resources and know-how to push for technocratic tweaks at the margins, usually out of public view. This contributes to what Steven Teles calls the "complexity and incoherence of our government." Teles notes that this complexity and incoherence has a tendency to "make it difficult for us to understand just what that government is doing, and among the practices it most frequently hides from view is the growing tendency of public policy to redistribute resources upward to the wealthy and the organized at the expense of the poorer and less organized."[5] The more complicated things become, the more of an advantage it is for corporate lobbyists looking to influence the out-of-sight, hard-to-understand, but sometimes highly consequential nooks and crannies of the U.S. code.

The increasing complexity of policy also makes it more difficult for generalist and largely inexperienced government staffers to maintain an informed understanding of the rules and regulations they are in charge of writing and overseeing. They typically have neither the time to specialize nor the experience to draw on. As a result, staffers must rely more and more on the lobbyists who specialize in particular policy areas. This puts those who can afford to hire the most experienced and policy-literate lobbyists—generally large companies— at the center of the policy-making process. Increasingly, corporations are not just investing in direct lobbying but also in think tanks and academic research and op-eds and panel discussions in order to shape the intellectual environment of Washington—to make sure that certain frames and assumptions come to mind immediately and easily when policy-makers consider legislation and rules. Lobbying efforts now tend to come buffeted by footnotes, white papers, and detailed estimates of how a particular member's constituents will be impacted. It is likely that most material winds up in the "circular file" (a round trash can), and most hosted policy discussions are sparsely attended.

But collectively, they take up time and attention and mindspace. Their ceaseless presence shapes the larger intellectual environment of Washington. They also often provide a necessary prerequisite for being taken seriously (however aggressive or dubious the number-crunching behind them). And they take time, effort, and—most importantly—money to produce.

A growing lobbying industry also siphons more and more talent from the public sector. The lobbying firms and corporate Washington offices that cluster around K Street generally provide better hours, better working conditions, and most of all better salaries than government, especially on Capitol Hill. Congressional staffers can usually at least double their salaries by "going downtown" (shorthand for becoming a lobbyist, since K Street is downtown). An increasing share of political and policy expertise increasingly resides in the law, lobbying, and strategic advice firms of Washington, DC, where a growing number of experienced political insiders and experts are available, for a fee, to the corporations (usually) who can afford to hire them (and by extension, their Rolodexes). Few diffuse interest groups, by contrast, can afford their fees.

Of course, nothing in the current Washington policy-making environment guarantees influence for any individual corporation. If anything, these changes probably reduce the expected return on investment to lobbying by raising the costs. On many issues, companies fight other companies to a standstill for years, with only the lobbyists on both sides benefiting. But this is not a sign that pluralism is alive and well. One also needs to ask, What issues are being left off the agenda? What groups and interests can't get into the fight without attaching themselves to a cause that large corporations also care about? How much of the policy capacity of the federal government is being used up refereeing parochial industry disputes, as opposed to dealing with other issues?

Nor are these changes generally good for business as a whole. Certainly, individual market leaders may benefit from the current environment, with its strong status quo bias and its rent-seeking possibilities (at least for those who can afford the right—and right number of—lobbyists). But overall, the increasing difficulty of political change reduces the capacity of the federal government to challenge the existing status quo, even when it is anti-innovation and anti-market. The current U.S. tax code, as former representative Bill Frenzel puts it, "is a hopelessly complex mess, antithetical to growth, and is crammed with conflicting incentives."[6] Yet comprehensive tax reform has been a political impossibility for a long time. The tax code may be the most compelling example of how the increased particularism of business lobbying undermines the interests of business as a community. Most everyone in the business community realizes that the U.S. tax code is, as a whole, bad for the economy. But while there is always talk of a "grand bargain" on taxes, nobody is willing to be the first to put their tax benefits on the table. Hence, the "grand bargain" remains largely talk.

"Individual American corporations have more political power in the early twenty-first century than at any time since the 1920s," writes Mark Mizruchi. But, "unlike their predecessors in earlier decades, they are either unwilling or unable to mount any systematic approach to addressing even the problems of their own community, let alone those of the larger society."[7] Consider what happened in 2013, when partisan warfare led to a sixteen-day government shutdown and threatened to let the United States default on its debt. In the run-up to the government shutdown, Paul Stebbens, the CEO of World Fuel Services who had been active in the "Fix the Debt" campaign, told the *Washington Post:*

> Let's start with the basic fact that business was part of the problem. In August of 2011, I was meeting with the Business Roundtable in D.C., and most business guys were running around the world being busy running their corporations and not

paying a lot of attention in a general way. . . . We have a higher duty of care to engage this issue. It is grossly reckless to watch the long term business trajectory of the U.S. to be at such risk. And we are part of the pathology that got us here. We've all had our K Street lobbyists who are part of the problem.[8]

While the business community was very unhappy about the budget brinksmanship in Washington, this was not the kind of issue that companies had experience lobbying. Instead, corporate lobbying has all gone to educate congressional offices about the particular concerns of specific industries and companies. As a result, members of Congress have done impressive work on behalf of particular companies and particular industries. However, they've been misled into thinking that the sum total of all their targeted support (essentially, picking winners through public policy) is somehow good for the economy, because each policy they support is promoted individually as good for the economy or good for business.

Even if fellow business leaders did agree with Stebbens that their K Street lobbyists were indeed "part of the problem," it seems unlikely that they would tell them all to go home. Large companies are unlikely to risk ceding any political advantages to competitors. After all, if they've invested significant resources in politics, they've surely been convinced that engagement is important. Why would they change their minds now? Especially when political engagement still remains cheap relative to what is at stake.

The Missing Reform Cycle?

While it is difficult to assess the power of business, a historical perspective does provide one possible lens: the concept of the political cycle. Arthur Schlesinger Jr. famously argued that political history tends to move in thirty-year cycles, with each period responding to the excesses of the previous period.[9] The laissez-faire Gilded Age led to the reformist Progressive Era, which led to the laissez-faire Roaring Twenties, which led to the reformist New Deal, which was followed by the relatively laissez-faire postwar period, which was followed by a reformist 1960s. The 1980s marked another era of laissez-faire politics. According to Schlesinger's theory, the next reform cycle should have come in the 1990s. It didn't. It still hasn't arrived. For all of the political Right's attempts to paint Barack Obama as a socialist, his landmark 2010 health-care reform bill (the Patient Protection and Affordable Care Act) was written and passed in close consultation with the pharmaceutical and health-insurance industries, and largely preserved both industries' market positions. It did not enact a "public option"—an entirely publicly funded health-care system that would have been a serious blow to the private health-care industry. Likewise, while the landmark 2010 Wall Street reform bill (Dodd-Frank) might have been billed as the most significant financial-sector reform since the series of bills that passed in the early 1930s, it did not challenge the fundamental structure of Wall Street (unlike the Glass-Steagall Act of 1933, which reshaped the organization of American finance in response to the financial collapse of 1929). Similarly, David Vogel argues that historically, reform tends to follow corporate profitability, because the public is most willing to support reforms when corporations appear to be doing well. But when American business is struggling financially, the public is more concerned with economic growth, and business does better politically as a result.[10] Certainly one of the most effective arguments of the business resurgence in the 1970s and the early 1980s was that government regulation was preventing an economic recovery. But then the economy recovered. The "Roaring Nineties,"[11] when business was booming in the 1990s, would have been a likely time for the forces of reform to reassert themselves.

But they did not, and they have not since the 1960s.

Both frameworks predict a reform era that never happened. Perhaps this missing reform cycle is the consequence of the density of the business lobbying presence in Washington. Perhaps the kind of large-scale turn toward government regulation that marked previous reform cycles is no longer politically feasible given the ubiquity of corporate lobbying. Perhaps corporations simply have too many lobbyists, and too many resources devoted to influencing political outcomes, to ever allow anything like the earlier reform eras to take place.

Is the Era of Lobbying Growth Over?

In 2011, reported lobbying expenditures experienced their first year-to-year decline since electronic disclosures began in 1998, falling from $3.55 billion in 2010 to $3.33 billion in 2011. The slide has continued into 2013, when reported lobbying expenditures fell to $3.21 billion. This decline has led to much speculation in Washington that lobbying hasn't really declined. Rather, there is more "shadow lobbying"—that is, there is more influence activity that doesn't meet strict Lobbying Disclosure Act definitions of lobbying, and more people who for various reasons prefer not to register as lobbyists and so structure their time and activity to avoid having to legally disclose.[12] For obvious reasons (the lack of disclosure), it is impossible to know for sure.

Still, there are good reasons why lobbying expenditures might actually have dropped 10 percent between 2010 and 2013. After all, congressional productivity has declined to record lows. The end of congressional earmarks put a damper on appropriations lobbying, and the end of two wars has made lobbying for defense procurement less lucrative. Given these factors, we might reasonably have expected even more than a 10 percent decline from 2010 to 2013. Perhaps the right question is, Why didn't lobbying decline even more?

One possibility is that while congressional activity declined, administrative rulemaking continued apace, even increasing in the wake of Dodd-Frank and the Affordable Care Act. A more plausible theory, based on the research presented in this book, is that large companies (which, as we have seen, account for a sizable share of the total lobbying expenditures) have become fully convinced of the importance of political engagement, and corporate managers now view lobbying as a long-term proposition. Gridlock may have overwhelmed Washington for the moment. But that just means that now is the time to do the spadework of further issue development and relationship-building on both sides of the aisle. That way, when the gridlock breaks, the companies that put in the hard work of building widespread support for their issues will be ready to move. Moreover, in a Congress that doesn't pass much, getting your issue onto the agenda requires even more work. Finally, the continued chatter of tax reform, budget cuts, and other austerity measures may have launched enough vague threats that corporations see the value in making sure that if there is going to be a chopping block, somebody else will be on it.

Additionally, in thinking about the long-term trends, it is important to note that while most of the very biggest companies have by now established major lobbying operations in Washington, the majority (close to 90 percent) of publicly traded companies still do not have their own lobbyists (preferring instead to leave representation to the trade associations). One reason may be that many corporate executives are still reflexively anti-government and still don't think they should be participating in politics. Some quotes from lobbyists help to illustrate this point. The first two come from contract lobbyists; the third comes from an in-house lobbyist:

- "Some companies are skeptical; they think lobbyists are con artists."
- "A lot of these companies think the last thing that they would do is to get involved in DC."
- "My very first day at the company, I hopped on a plane with the CEO to take a series of meetings. He has a true disdain for government. He thinks we can do it ourselves, that market forces work better."

As we've discussed, this distrust of government runs deep in American business culture.[13] Even companies that have decided to invest in government affairs frequently need to be convinced of its value, as multiple lobbyists told me. Even within the last twenty years, statements like this could be found in a how-to book on business lobbying: "Many managers, especially in highly regulated industries, view government as the enemy. You not only have to dispel that notion; you have to encourage the view that government can be influenced in ways that can advance company strategy."[14]

There are plenty of companies that have not yet been drawn into a public policy battle, and there are managers who have not yet been convinced that they need their own lobbyists in Washington. But my theory suggests that once they get drawn in, they tend to keep their lobbyists on. If Washington acts like a magnet, more and more companies will be pulled in as new policy battles arise. Consider the tech sector: one by one, the new giants of the sector—Google, Facebook, Twitter—have discovered Washington and are deepening their involvement. Google is now consistently one of the top spenders on lobbying. As new companies emerge in the economy, they will sooner or later add themselves to the ranks of major lobbying companies.

In all likelihood, the current trends are merely a temporary plateau (or a slight decline, depending on how much the reported numbers are to be believed). When partisan gridlock breaks, more companies will rush to take advantage of and/or respond to others trying to take advantage. And the increased competition will only raise the costs. Of course, the system may at some point reach capacity. There may be a moment where the government becomes incapable of taking any meaningful action given the pressures it faces on all sides. Hopefully, however, the system will find a way to reform itself before that happens. And if the system needs some help in reforming itself, the following section provides a way to start that conversation.

What to Do about Lobbying

In 2006, as Democrats fought to take back the U.S. House, then minority leader Nancy Pelosi promised that she would "drain the swamp" and on her first day as majority leader put in place new rules to "break the link between lobbyists and legislation."[15] And so, when the Democrats did come back into power, they passed a bill known as the Honest Leadership and Open Government Act (HLOGA).

HLOGA did a number of things to change the way lobbying worked. It put an end to meals, travel, and other gifts from lobbyists and special interests (campaign contributions, however, did not count as "gifts"). It upped lobbying disclosure filings to quarterly instead of biannually, and upped disclosure requirements for lobbyists who "bundled" multiple campaign contributions. It also slowed the revolving door: senators would have to wait two years to lobby Congress upon retirement, instead of just one. It also prevented retiring top-level Senate staff (defined as those making 75 percent of a member's salary) from lobbying the entire Senate for a whole year, and prevented retiring top-level House staff from lobbying their former office or committee for an entire year.[16]

The villain in mind as the bill passed was lobbyist Jack Abramoff, who had, in January 2006, been sentenced to prison for mail fraud, conspiracy to bribe public officials, and tax evasion. Abramoff was famous for taking members of Congress on golf trips, giving them free tickets to sporting events, and letting them eat for free at his upscale Washington restaurant, Signatures.[17] Thus, the implicit theory behind the 2006 reform was that if lobbyists could no longer provide special favors to members of Congress and their staff in the form of meals, trips, and other gifts, their influence would be reduced. Government would become less corrupt.

President Obama, who had made the power of lobbyists and special interests an issue during this campaign, took another approach. On his first day in office in 2009, he signed an executive order prohibiting registered lobbyists from serving in his administration.[18] While it sent a powerful political signal, there were some practical problems. Many in the nonprofit advocacy world who had registered as lobbyists (including some who had done so just to be careful, even

though they probably didn't have to) were disqualified from administration positions that they had hoped to obtain. The Obama administration was also
forced into a position of hypocrisy when it granted a waiver to William Lynn,
the former lobbyist for defense contractor Raytheon, so that he could serve as
the deputy secretary of Defense.[19] Moreover, the consensus in Washington was
that many who might otherwise have registered as lobbyists decided not to (or
simply adjusted their activities to avoid the legal definition of lobbying) for fear
that such registration would prohibit them from future administration jobs.[20]
Proponents of this theory have noted that the number of registered lobbyists in
Washington has decreased every year between 2007 and 2012 (from 14,849 in
2007 to 11,702 in 2012) after steadily increasing every year (save one) between
1998 and 2007 (*growing* from 10,408 to 14,849). However, there is also evidence to suggest that this decline may have been in response to the passage of
HLOGA.[21] Other than the optics, there is little evidence that executive branch
lobbying changed in the Obama administration (as compared to previous administrations). As James Thurber concluded:

> [Obama] has limited those who can be appointed to executive positions, but it has
> had little impact on those who actually influence the decision-making process.
> Moreover, President Obama has worked closely, often in a nontransparent way,
> with networks of "special interests" (lobbyists/advocates) in crafting the eco-
> nomic stimulus funding, health care reform, financial regulatory reforms, the fed-
> eral budget deficit and debt, climate change legislation, education reform, im-
> migration policy, and a wide array of other issues on his public policy agenda in
> 2009–2010.[22]

In other words, recent reforms have done very little to change the ways that
lobbying actually works. That is largely because these reforms have played to
popular conceptions of corruption, and in so doing have addressed the wrong
problems. Much public opinion on the subject of political influence suffers from
a confusing and counterproductive mix of hopeless idealism and fatalistic cyn-
icism. On the one hand, many people think that if only we could get special
interests out of politics, then we would have a government run by perfectly
rational Solomonic lawmakers, capable of divining the true public interest and
making wise and uncorrupted judgments. On the other hand, they look at the
political system and think that most politicians are at once craven and venal,

ready to sell their votes for the promise of a hosted fundraiser, or even more cheaply, a few thousand dollars in PAC contributions.

The reality is, of course, more complicated, but also much more interesting. Like everyone else, politicians are motivated by a mix of both noble and not-so-noble desires. There are some good ones and some not-so-good ones, but any attempts to cut them off from the pressures of society is a betrayal of both the idea of representative democracy and the potential for collective intelligence that widespread participation on the political process allows for. The Washington lobbying community is full of many bright policy minds, and the expertise and knowledge that the business community can provide makes for a more informed policy-making process.

Any attempt to directly limit the participation of corporate lobbyists in the political process runs immediately into the practical problem that other attempts to limit political influence have always encountered. If corporations (or other actors) are determined to influence the political process, they will find a way. If the history of political influence regulation has taught us anything, it should be this: that those determined to participate in the political process will find ways to do so.[23]

There are, however, three genuine problems that do need fixing, and that can be fixed in ways that work with, not against, the realities of politics. The first problem is the balance of power. When corporate interests spend thirty-four dollars for every dollar diffuse interests and unions *combined* spend on lobbying, it is not a fair fight. If we want a political system that is capable of responding to the broad societal interests, we want a political system where a broad range of societal interests are capable of presenting their most effective case. When large corporations are the dominant actors in Washington, policy attention will almost certainly reflect their priorities.

The second problem is the asymmetry of information and the related complexity. When government actors are forced to rely on outside lobbyists for policy expertise, and when that expertise is provided largely on behalf of a narrow set of actors, this is likely to distort outcomes. Additionally, policy complexity makes it easier for corporate actors with the most resources to make quiet changes with little to no scrutiny.

The third problem is particularism. Companies are increasingly oriented toward narrow, rent-seeking outcomes. Parochial intra- and interindustry battles take up an increasing amount of Washington bandwidth, and the increasing investments in this particularism crowd out the capacity of the political system to address larger problems. What may be good for some powerful companies is almost certainly bad for the economy as a whole.

These problems are all related, and any attempt to deal with one without dealing with the others is likely to fail. Sticking with the rule of threes, I propose three types of solutions. As with the problems, the solutions are interrelated. They would be most effective as a coherent program. Piecemeal application would almost certainly be far less effective.

The treatment of these solutions is admittedly limited here. These are, at this point, roughly drawn proposals. There is still much to be worked out in their details and implementation, and certainly, they are not meant to be cure-alls. They are presented in the hopes of starting a conversation, of trying to sketch out a few ways forward based on both the lessons I've learned in researching and writing this chapter and the book from which it is drawn, as well as the lessons of other recent attempts at reform.

The Madisonian Solution

I take very seriously James Madison's argument in Federalist No. 10 that the problem of faction is inherent to all political systems, and that any attempt to limit the participation of factions is a cure worse than the disease. Therefore, I share Madison's faith that the best way to deal with the problem of faction is for faction to counteract faction and to "enlarge the sphere."[24] Let everyone have a say, and hope that something resembling the public interests can emerge from the dust.

Of course, this approach depends on a rough balance of power. If unions and diffuse interest groups had roughly the same resources as business interests, we might reasonably expect that the two forces would keep each other roughly in check. This, however, is not the case. As we've seen, corporate interests now spend thirty-four times what diffuse interest groups and unions combined spend on lobbying. Not a single corporate lobbyist I interviewed identified a diffuse interest group or a union as the primary opponent on an issue on which he or she was lobbying. Faction is not counteracting faction.

This is not likely to change on its own for two reasons. One is the simple fact that it is relatively easy for businesses to mobilize politically since they can, with just a few executive decisions, allocate some of their already-existing resources to political activity.[25] And now that a growing number of business leaders have become convinced that politics matters, there is very little to stop them from continuing to spend substantial sums. Interested citizens, by contrast, must find a way to overcome the collective action problem, pulling together resources and commitments, and then sustaining those resources and commitments over time. This is difficult to accomplish.[26] Two, the nature of much political conflict, in which a particular policy affects a handful of companies greatly while affecting most citizens only marginally, means that individual companies and industries have the most concentrated stakes, and therefore the biggest incentive to remain vigilant and active.[27] Businesses have both the means and the motive to spend heavily. Both their stake in political outcomes and their ability to mobilize resources are far greater than the average citizen's. This is unlikely to change on its own. Fixing the participatory imbalance will require government to make an active investment. There is clearly a market failure.

Is there a public interest in fixing this imbalance? One analogy is to our legal system. Indigent criminal defendants are given court-appointed lawyers because we have decided that everybody should have the right to a lawyer when interacting with the justice system. Why does the same principle not apply to politics? Does not everybody whose interests are materially affected by the political system deserve the right to a lobbyist?

Certainly, there are difficulties in determining who has a legitimate claim for lobbying representation and how much representation they deserve. But here's one way it could work: Groups advocating for a diffuse interest would have to demonstrate that their perspective was shared by a threshold percentage of citizens, and that the existing lobbying community was not adequately representing this viewpoint. Imagine a three-stage process. First, an underrepresented perspective would have to gain a threshold number of signatures (perhaps twenty-five thousand), and advocates of the perspective would need to demonstrate that they were being outspent by at least a threshold ratio (perhaps 4 to 1), and that a diffuse group of citizens were affected. Then, that perspective could be included in a regularly occurring poll that the government conducts to test for widespread support in the country. If a threshold percentage of citizens agreed with the perspective (perhaps 25 percent), a federal subsidy would be awarded so advocates of that position could hire a lobbyist. Subsidies could be awarded based on the level of support and on the ratio by which advocates for that position were being outspent by powerful interests. A more aggressive version of this proposal would require well-funded interests on the other side to fund their opposition, in order to guarantee a fair fight.

Alternatively, rather than award a direct subsidy to the underrepresented perspective, the federal government could create an "Office of Public Lobbying," maintaining a team of public lobbyists who would then represent different public interest clients before the government. Zephyr Teachout has made the case for such an institution, noting that "Congress could hire, at a fraction of the expense paid to lobbyists, advocates to represent a range of opinions on any proposed legislation, and stage trial-like debates between them."[28] Serving as a public lobbyist might be a very appealing job for a congressional staffer whose boss lost an election or retired, or a congressional staffer just looking to do something different for a few years. Many congressional staffers may not necessarily desire to represent corporate interests, but may wish to stay in Washington and remain active in public policy. Working as a public lobbyist could provide an appealing alternative to a K Street job, while giving a voice to a set of societal interests that currently lack a voice in Washington. It may also provide an alternative to working for a nonprofit, because it would provide more variety and job security. Additionally, an "Office of Public Lobbying" could actively work to identify underrepresented voices, utilizing social media and other low-cost methods to tap into diffuse public concerns and give them voice.

The Genuine Public-Conversation Approach

In 1946, Congress passed the Administrative Procedure Act, which created "uniform procedures for rulemaking, adjudication, and transparency on federal agencies." Now most executive branch agencies have a structured rulemaking process. Before a rule can be finalized, all interested parties have a chance to comment. Those comments are public, and agencies respond to those comments in a public way. While there is certainly additional lobbying that takes place beyond formal commenting, the comments provide a useful way to see who is participating and whose concerns are being heard. In the age of the Internet, all agencies now post the comments online.

Lobbying Congress, by contrast, remains as haphazard as it has ever been. While organizations do have to file quarterly lobbying disclosure reports, these reports are vague. They may list specific issues, or they may not. Organizations that are lobbying do not have to disclose which offices they visited, nor do they have to disclose the positions for which they advocated or the draft legislation they left behind.

What if Congress passed a "Congressional Lobbying Procedure Act" that created a set of uniform processes for congressional lobbying? Such a system could take advantage of modern technology and require that any advocacy be posted within forty-eight hours on a central website. Each report would contain a short summary of the meeting, who attended, and what was advocated for.

Any white papers, draft legislation, or other leave-behinds would need to be posted in electronic form as well. The website would also serve as a repository for all arguments and advocacy. A series of clicks would take any interested member of the public to a corpus of arguments for or against particular public policies, creating a central clearinghouse.

Such a website could also make it much easier for citizens to offer input and register their opinions in an organized and traceable way (as opposed to the current sporadic and haphazard barrage of e-mails and phone calls, which may or may not get a response). Organizations like the Madison Project[29] and Popvox[30] have done impressive work exploring how the Internet could provide a forum for wider citizen participation in the legislative process, and both offer valuable frameworks for going forward.

This hypothetical "Congressional Lobbying Procedure Act" would change lobbying in several ways. First, it would level the playing field between corporate interests and diffuse interests. It would make lobbying less about hiring armies of well-connected lobbyists who can spread out all over the Hill, and more about developing convincing arguments and summaries that would inform congressional offices.

It would also become easier for diffuse interests to know what corporate interests are actually arguing, which would allow them to respond to those arguments in a timely manner (and vice versa). Ultimately, this website could serve as a kind of policy-making marketplace of ideas, where different interests would have the opportunity to respond to each other in real time. It could harness the competitive nature of lobbying in service of accountability. It would provide an instant source for all arguments on all sides and help congressional staffers new to an issue to know where they can find more information.

Such a process could also potentially reduce particularistic lobbying efforts. By bringing real-time transparency to attempts to insert narrow provisions into legislation, this system could alert watchdogs as these attempts happen, allowing them to blow the whistle and bring public scrutiny to deals that largely depend on nobody else paying attention to them. This could make members of Congress more wary of working to advocate particularistic benefits. In turn, lobbyists would be able to anticipate the consequences of such narrow asks. They would know that the risks would be high and the likelihood of success would be low. This would make them much less likely to make such asks in the first place. This could also have the effect of reducing lobbying, especially particularistic lobbying. This is admittedly optimistic, but it at least points in the right direction.

If lobbyists are able to put fewer particularistic policies in place, this would make it harder for them to demonstrate the bottom-line benefits of lobbying to corporate bosses. It would reduce the number of purely selective benefits in corporate lobbying. As lobbying moves more toward collective benefits, companies might pay less and hope to free-ride more. An added benefit of lobbying becoming less particularistic is that legislation could become simpler. There would be less need to address the narrow concerns of every single company with a lobbyist. It would be easier to move toward more coherent policy-making.

Such a system could also alter the information asymmetry between lobbyists and corporate managers. I've argued that one of the key reasons why corporations spend more on lobbying is because managers do not get to observe what lobbyists do and how their actions do or do not move the policy needle. Lobbyists can claim that they had substantive meetings with members of Congress and overstate their influence. If corporate lobbyists had to document everything that they do to try to influence political outcomes, managers would be in a better position to evaluate their lobbyists' activities. Doing so might allow savvy corporate managers to conclude that most of what they spend on lobbying is, in fact, wasted. They might spend less on lobbying. In principal-agent literature in economics, transparency is commonly seen as a way for principals to overcome information asymmetries and thus reduce their costs.[31]

Increasing Government Policy Capacity

A third approach would give Congress more of its own policy capacity. As I have argued, one of the reasons why lobbyists have become increasingly central to the policy process is that the policy capacity of the government, and especially Congress, has declined over time, while policy complexity and specialization have increased. Congressional staffers are always scrambling to play intellectual catch-up. They have to turn to lobbyists to explain increasingly complex policy for them. This gives lobbyists a tremendous advantage.

There are a number of potential ways to reduce congressional dependence on lobbyists. One is simply to improve the working conditions and salaries of congressional staff, making it a more attractive job for senior-level people. Rather than toil in anonymity at relatively low pay with long, unpredictable hours, congressional staffers should be given more acknowledgment, better pay, and more favorable working conditions. If congressional offices paid staff better, they could afford to attract and retain more top policy talent and make it less likely that congressional staffers would use their time on the Hill to plot their exits, potentially cozying up to lobbyists who might someday make them rich.

In most congressional offices, working conditions could be improved dramatically. Hours could be better, and staffers could be allowed to take more credit and ownership for the work that they produce. Instead of maintaining the fiction that it is the member of Congress who does everything, members of Congress could acknowledge that while they set the general direction and priorities for the office, voters are now electing a team of people to represent them, and that the entire team deserves some public credit.

While the private sector is likely to continue to be able to pay people more, elected officials ought to acknowledge that whom they hire has an impact on how well they can serve their constituents—and be willing to invest in good people. Some of this may seem like Management 101, but Congress could use a dose of institutionalized Management 101.

Congress could also improve its independent policy capacity externally. Already, Congress has some institutions designed to help it. The Congressional Research Service (CRS) and the Government Accountability Office (GAO) are both valuable resources and play an important role in providing independent expert advice and research. But both are limited in their capacities.[32] Perhaps, then, the most straightforward approach to improving congressional capacity is simply to significantly expand the budget for both of these organizations—allowing them to hire more people and work with congressional offices to make them as useful as possible.

Another possibility here is tapping into the knowledge and expertise that resides in American universities. House and Senate offices could officially partner with local universities, particularly public policy schools and law schools. Professors could serve as expert advisers. Universities could incentivize participation by giving formal credit to faculty who lend their expertise and lead students to help make national policy. Students could get excellent training serving as policy researchers and legislation drafters for congressional offices.

Shouldn't helping to improve the quality of public policy for the country be at least on par with publishing academic articles in small-audience, peer-reviewed journals? One approach in this direction comes from the Congressional Clerkship Coalition. More than one hundred law school deans have urged Congress to create a "congressional clerkship" program that would be a legislative analogue to the judicial clerkship program, giving young lawyers more legislative experience and congressional offices more legal help. But while legislation to create the program has passed the House twice and enjoys widespread bipartisan support, it has not made it out of the Senate.[33]

Heather Gerken and Alex Tausanovitch have suggested funding "policy research consultants" that would be available to congressional offices:

> What we have in mind is the lobbyist equivalent of public-interest law firms. The aim would be to allow legislators to hire "research consultants" who can provide information during the major stages of decision-making as well as during the period in which the bill is amended. These independent consultants would have a semi-permanent status, and thus be able to offer the "long-term commitment" that bears fruit in the lobbying world. They would be able to assist members with thinking through issues before they even get on the agenda of a particular committee, and they would be able to put their time and effort into developing good policies over the long-term.[34]

Congressional offices would be able to choose whomever they want as their consultants. They could choose lobbyists from the oil industry, but as Gerken and Tausanovitch argue, they would have no reason to do so, since they already get plenty of policy support from the industry, which happily provides it for free. Rather, these research consultants would allow them to get the legislative subsidies that they can't get elsewhere.

Though executive branch agencies tend to have better salaries and working conditions, and to also attract more policy expertise, even they are increasingly having a hard time maintaining the levels of internal expertise necessary to make policy in complex environments. They also suffer similar pay gaps and could benefit from more policy resources.

The basic thread of all these capacity-building reforms, however, is the same. In order to make the best policy, government needs the best people, and many of them. If key policy-makers don't have the resources to adequately evaluate policy and have confidence in their observations, they will be forced to rely excessively on those interests who have the most at stake.

How These Reforms Would Work Together

Perhaps the best way to understand how these reforms might work together is to see how they solve the possible objections that could arise from applying the reforms piecemeal. The most obvious objection to the Madisonian approach of enlarging the sphere is that Washington lobbying is already exceedingly competitive, and this competition is a source of gridlock. Wouldn't more competitive lobbying mean even more gridlock? This is a legitimate concern, especially if it means that congressional offices become even more overwhelmed by an onslaught of lobbying. But both moving lobbying into an online public conversation and giving offices more of their own policy capacity would help to better channel all the lobbying activity. Rather than being overwhelmed by all the arguments and advocacy, congressional offices would have the expertise and knowledge to sort through the information and pressures more productively. Moreover, the capacity of an online platform to organize the information would help staffers who often lack the time to stay organized. It would remind them of the bigger picture, rather than being susceptible to whomever they met with last.

The limitation of real-time, online lobbying is that the corporate interests with the most resources can simply overwhelm this process, as they overwhelm every other process. They can invest more resources in shaping the intellectual environment and more resources in responding to the opposing concerns. While the platform has some leveling effects, they are not nearly enough. In the absence of other reforms, this will almost certainly be the case. But if the government can take active steps to level the playing field by subsidizing diffuse interests, this will be less of a problem. If lawmakers have more capacity to evaluate the information without the help of lobbyists, this will also be less of a problem.

Even with expanded government policy capacity, government actors will still need the help of outside interests. They may need less help, but they will still require some assistance to develop, vet, and especially build external support for policy initiatives. After all, the "legislative subsidy" that lobbyists provide isn't only about policy expertise. It also covers the entire policy process. Without making some attempts to level the imbalance of lobbying resources, it will still be difficult for congressional offices to advance causes that lack organized lobbying resources. Government intervention to balance the playing field can help. Moving lobbying online and creating a repository of policy arguments can also help, because it will give congressional offices more resources on which to draw.

Another critique of this build-more-capacity approach is that expertise is never neutral, and just because members of Congress have access to more policy capacity doesn't necessarily mean that they won't simply use it in service of whatever narrow ends they might already be working toward and pick and choose studies that support their existing beliefs.[35] This is certainly a fair critique. Dreams of a perfectly rational, scientifically minded technocracy never end well, but all else being equal, more expertise and more policy capacity are almost certainly better than less. Certainly, there will be members of Congress who will be unaffected, but ideally this approach would push policy-making in a smarter direction. It would provide policy-makers with the resources to stand up to industry "experts" whom they might have reason to doubt, but whom the policy-makers lack the topic knowledge to confront.

In short, this package of reform would work best as a coherent program. One strength of this program, as compared to many other reform programs, is that it would embrace politics, rather than attempting to sublimate it. It is built on the premise that more lobbying and more political engagement are better, and more money and more resources (rather than fewer) ought to go into shaping public policy, and argues that it is possible to channel political competition in a constructive way. It also would not treat members of Congress as venal, corrupt individuals who are incapable of standing up to moneyed interests. It would acknowledge that they would like to serve a broader public interest, and could do so more effectively if they had some additional help.

Campaign Finance

This chapter has not devoted much attention to campaign finance, other than to acknowledge that contributing to campaigns is one of many strategies companies use to try to influence public policy. Companies spend roughly thirteen times more on lobbying than they do on PAC contributions. This is not to say that money is not important. It undoubtedly improves access and plays an important gatekeeping role in who can run for office and puts limits on what policies they can publicly support.

Members of Congress spend far too much time fundraising. As the costs of campaigns continue to rise, members of Congress spend more and more hours a day in "call time."[36] Increasingly, the main qualification for the job is having a unique personality trait that allows one to withstand several hours a day of begging rich people for money. In 2012, 28 percent of the nearly $6 billion in contributions from identifiable sources in the last campaign cycle came from just 31,385 individuals, a number equal to 1 percent of 1 percent of the U.S. population.[37] Those who can appeal to these kinds of donors can run for office. Those who can't appeal to these donors usually can't.

Appealing to wealthy donors involves both taking on policy positions that are comfortable for these donors and not wasting time with issues that do not concern them. It also involves listening to the donors' concerns, and at least acknowledging their arguments. As Senator Chris Murphy (D-CT) once described his campaign donors: "They have fundamentally different problems than other people. And in Connecticut especially, you spend a lot of time on the phone with people who work in the financial markets. And so you're hearing a lot about problems that bankers have and not a lot of problems that people who work at the mill in Thomaston, Conn., have. You certainly have to stop and check yourself."[38] Over time, this can lead to a kind of self-interested worldview osmosis, where candidates take on donors' perspectives as part of a need to appeal to them. If you hear an argument enough times, and you repeat it enough times to raise money, eventually you may even start to believe it. Or at the very least, whatever zeal you may have had on the other side of the issue is gradually replaced by doubt.

Certainly, proposals to create a small-donor matching system or to establish fully publicly funded elections (as is the norm in almost all other industrialized democracies) would level an unequal playing field, and almost certainly change the types of people who run for Congress in the first place. Politicians would spend less time nodding to the concerns of wealthy donors. They would be able to worry less about how various policy stances would affect their future fundraising.

However, even if elections were partially or fully publicly funded, this would not solve the expertise and experience problems we've discussed. It would not solve the complexity problem we've discussed. It would not change the revolving door. Corporations would continue to overwhelm the intellectual environment of Washington. There would continue to be an imbalance in the intensity of preference and attention on a wide range of highly technical issues. Taking high-dollar contributions out of campaigns would almost certainly push corporations to redouble their efforts in other areas of influence. Some public funding of election mechanisms should be included in any larger reform package, but focusing only on the electoral aspects of influence is limited.

American Business and American Democracy

Scholars have long argued over whether or not corporate participation in politics distorts American democracy. To the extent that corporations have an operating principle, it is to maximize profits while minimizing and externalizing costs. To the extent that democracy has an operating principle, it is to allow people to rule themselves. These two principles run into potential conflict when the corporate goal of maximizing profits spills over into the mechanisms designed to allow the people to govern themselves, which was Charles Lindblom's fundamental concern in *Politics and Markets* when he concluded that "the large private corporation fits oddly into democratic theory and vision. Indeed, it does not fit."[39] If, instead of attending to the concerns of dispersed citizens, the mechanisms of democracy are primarily taken up with responding to the concerns and interests of the small number of citizens who either lead corporations or own significant amounts of their stock, this would appear to be a distortion of democracy.

Of course, business lobbyists will argue that they are advocating on behalf of policies that benefit the economy, and thus all citizens. In their advocacy, they tell a convincing story about the jobs they will create or save, the ways in which consumers will benefit from their products and services, and why what they advocate is good public policy. In a competitive lobbying environment, they have to.[40] Companies work hard to polish their image and to show why what they want is good for all of America. Corporate lobbyists will also argue that they are not as powerful as they are often made out to be, and quite often they don't get what they want.

Such an argument can go back and forth indefinitely. Arguably, it has already been raging for many years. But what such a back-and-forth misses is that the process of widespread business political mobilization has changed the contours of policy-making. Corporate lobbying has become more proactive, particular-istic, and pervasive. The size and scope of the modern corporate lobbying oper-ations are unprecedented in American history. And the environment it has pro-duced is one that is very hospitable to corporate lobbyists.

These changes, however, do not mean that corporations automatically get what they want if they spend large sums of money. There is no evidence to sup-port this. However, these changes do make it more likely that large corporations that can spend large sums of money on lobbying will be more successful than the diffuse interests or groups that don't have the same resources to get their issues on the agenda. While individual policy outcomes are unpredictable, in the aggregate, policy outcomes lean toward the preferences of corporate inter-ests and wealthy donors.[41]

Over the last four decades, American corporations have learned how to play politics, and more and more corporate executives have come to view political engagement as an important part of their business. They have hired lobbyists who have told them to see politics as important. The large-scale result has not only been distortion of democratic priorities. It is also increasingly an immobili-zation of democracy. If the trends I have described continue, American democ-racy will continue to decline. And it will not be because corporations necessarily get the policy outcomes they want. It will undermine the functioning of Amer-ican democracy because it will diminish the problem-solving capacity of gov-ernment, which will mean that hardly anybody will get anything that they want. To quote an old Kenyan proverb, "When the elephants fight, it is the grass that suffers." Increasingly, that grass is the functioning of the democratic process.

There may be those who argue it is too late to change things. They may look at the current corporate investments in Washington, and the ways in which these investments have come to overwhelm the key government decision-making processes, and see no hope. Certainly, the narrative arc of the story told in this study of lobbying does not point in an optimistic direction.

But it is important to understand that reform is in everybody's long-term interests. Business as a whole does not benefit from the current system, which is widely criticized as being market-distorting and anti-growth. Business leaders frequently express frustrations with the inability of Congress to do anything. The only winners in the current system seem to be the lobbyists—but even they should have a long-term incentive for change. If the political system becomes incapable of accomplishing anything, companies will begin to question why they are investing in Washington and lobbying revenue will dry up. Arguably, this drying up has already begun.

Despite the general pessimism, I wish to close on a note of optimism. It is my sincere hope that my work will contribute to our collective understanding of how lobbying works, what motivates corporations to spend large sums of money on politics, and how these increasing sums have changed the ways in which the policy process operates. It is also my sincere hope that this knowledge can help to inform political reforms that will continue to strengthen the quality of American democracy and move us just a little closer to that "more perfect union" that always lingers just over the horizon.

Notes

1. Remarks made during the 2013 government shutdown. Lydia DePillis, "'Shame on Us': How Businesses Brought the Debt Limit Mess onto Themselves," *Washington Post,* 2013, http://www.washingtonpost.com/blogs/wonkblog/wp/2013/09/29/shame-on-us-how-businesses-brought-the-debt-limit-mess-onto-themselves/.
2. Stephen Ansolabehere, John M. de Figueiredo, and James M. Snyder Jr., "Why Is There So Little Money in U.S. Politics?," *Journal of Economic Perspectives* 17, no. 1 (January 1, 2003): 105–30; Frank R. Baumgartner et al., *Lobbying and Policy Change: Who Wins, Who Loses, and Why* (Chicago: University of Chicago Press, 2009); Frank R. Baumgartner and Beth L. Leech, *Basic Interests: The Importance of Groups in Politics and in Political Science* (Princeton, NJ: Princeton University Press, 1998).
3. Baumgartner et al., *Lobbying and Policy Change.*
4. Ibid.; Jacob S. Hacker and Paul Pierson, "Winner-Take-All Politics: Public Policy, Political Organization, and the Precipitous Rise of Top Incomes in the United States," *Politics & Society* 38, no. 2 (June 1, 2010): 152–204, doi:10.1177/0032329210365042.
5. Steven M. Teles, "Kludgeocracy in America," *National Affairs,* Fall 2013, https://www.nationalaffairs.com/publications/detail/kludgeocracy-in-america.
6. Bill Frenzel, "The Tax Code Is a Hopeless, Complex, Economy-Suffocating Mess,"

Forbes, April 4, 2013, http://www.forbes.com/sites/billfrenzel/2013/04/04/the-tax-code -is-a-hopeless-complex-economy-suffocating-mess/.

7. Mark S. Mizruchi, *The Fracturing of the American Corporate Elite* (Cambridge, MA: Harvard University Press, 2013), 4.

8. DePillis, "'Shame on Us.'"

9. Arthur M. Schlesinger Jr., *The Cycles of American History* (Boston: Houghton Mifflin, 1986); Andrew S. McFarland, "Interest Groups and Political Time: Cycles in America," *British Journal of Political Science* 21, no. 3 (July 1, 1991): 257–84.

10. David Vogel, *Fluctuating Fortunes: The Political Power of Business in America* (New York: Basic Books, 1989).

11. Joseph E. Stiglitz, *The Roaring Nineties: A New History of the World's Most Prosperous Decade,* repr. ed. (New York: W. W. Norton, 2004).

12. Thomas Edsall, "The Shadow Lobbyist," *New York Times,* 2013, http://opinionator.blogs .nytimes.com/2013/04/25/the-shadow-lobbyist/; Thomas B. Edsall, "The Unlobbyists," *New York Times,* December 31, 2013, https://www.nytimes.com/2014/01/01/opinion /edsall-the-unlobbyists.html.

13. David Vogel, "Why Businessmen Distrust Their State: The Political Consciousness of American Corporate Executives," *British Journal of Political Science* 8, no. 1 (January 1, 1978): 45–78.

14. Michael Watkins, Mickey Edwards, and Usha Thakrar, *Winning the Influence Game: What Every Business Leader Should Know about Government* (New York: Wiley and Sons, 2001), p. 101. One lobbyist quoted in this book said that "CEOs . . . will talk about themselves as victims of government. They never think of themselves as partners."

15. David Espo, "Pelosi Says She Would Drain GOP 'Swamp.'" Associated Press, October 6, 2006.

16. Bruce E. Cain and Lee Drutman, "Congressional Staff and the Revolving Door: The Impact of Regulatory Change," *Election Law Journal: Rules, Politics, and Policy* 13, no. 1 (March 1, 2014): 27–44, doi:10.1089/elj.2013.0213.

17. Peter H. Stone, *Casino Jack and the United States of Money: Superlobbyist Jack Abramoff and the Buying of Washington* (New York: Melville House, 2010).

18. Sheryl Gay Stolberg, "On First Day, Obama Quickly Sets a New Tone," *New York Times,* January 21, 2009, U.S./Politics sec., http://www.nytimes.com/2009/01/22/us/politics/22 obama.html.

19. Julian E. Barnes, "Raytheon Lobbyist Picked for Deputy Defense Post," *Los Angeles Times,* January 23, 2009, http://articles.latimes.com/2009/jan/23/nation/na-deputy-defense -secretary23.

20. James A. Thurber, "The Contemporary Presidency: Changing the Way Washington Works? Assessing President Obama's Battle with Lobbyists," *Presidential Studies Quarterly* 41, no. 2 (2011): 358–74, doi:10.1111/j.1741–5705.2011.03858.x.

21. Timothy M. LaPira, "Erring on the Side of Shady: How Calling out 'Lobbyists' Drove

Them Underground," *Sunlight Foundation,* April 1, 2014, http://sunlightfoundation.com /blog/2014/04/01/erring-on-the-side-of-shady-how-calling-out-lobbyists-drove-them -underground/.

22. Thurber, "The Contemporary Presidency," 139.

23. Heather K. Gerken and Alex Tausanovitch, "A Public Finance Model for Lobbying: Lobbying, Campaign Finance, and the Privatization of Democracy," *Election Law Journal: Rules, Politics, and Policy* 13, no. 1 (March 1, 2014): 75–90, doi:10.1089/elj.2013.0212.

24. James Madison, Federalist No. 10.

25. Robert H. Salisbury, "Interest Representation: The Dominance of Institutions," *American Political Science Review* 78, no. 1 (March 1, 1984): 64–76, doi:10.2307/1961249; David M. Hart, "'Business' Is Not an Interest Group: On the Study of Companies in American National Politics," *Annual Review of Political Science* 7, no. 1 (2004): 47–69, doi:10.1146/annurev.polisci.7.090803.161829.

26. Mancur Olson, *The Logic of Collective Action; Public Goods and the Theory of Groups,* vol. 124 (Cambridge, MA: Harvard University Press, 1965).

27. James Q. Wilson, *The Politics of Regulation* (New York: Basic Books, 1980); R. Douglas Arnold, *The Logic of Congressional Action* (New Haven, CT: Yale University Press, 1990); Theodore J. Lowi, *The End of Liberalism: The Second Republic of the United States,* vol. 2 (New York: W. W. Norton, 1979).

28. Zephyr Teachout, "Original Intent," *Democracy Journal,* 2009, http://www.democracy journal.org/11/6666.php.

29. The home page of the Madison Project can be found at http://madisonproject.com.

30. The home page of Popvox can be found at http://www.popvox.com/.

31. Bengt Holmstrom, "Moral Hazard and Observability," *Bell Journal of Economics* 10, no. 1 (Spring 1979): 74–91.

32. Lorelei Kelly, *Congress' Wicked Problem: Seeking Knowledge Inside the Information Tsunami* (Washington, DC: New America Foundation, 2012).

33. Dakota S. Rudesill, "Closing the Legislative Experience Gap: How a Legislative Law Clerk Program Will Benefit the Legal Profession and Congress," *Washington University Law Review* 87 (2010): 699. Also see http://www.congressionalclerkship.com.

34. Gerken and Tausanovitch, "A Public Finance Model for Lobbying," 88–89.

35. Gary Mucciaroni and Paul J. Quirk, *Deliberative Choices: Debating Public Policy in Congress* (Chicago: University of Chicago Press, 2006).

36. Ryan Grim and Sabrina Siddiqui, "Call Time for Congress Shows How Fundraising Dominates Bleak Work Life," *Huffington Post,* January 8, 2013, http://www.huffingtonpost .com/2013/01/08/call-time-congressional-fundraising_n_2,427,291.html.

37. Lee Drutman, *The Political 1% of the 1% in 2012* (The Sunlight Foundation, June 24, 2013), http://sunlightfoundation.com/blog/2013/06/24/lpct_of_the_lpct/.

38. Paul Blumenthal, "Chris Murphy: 'Soul-Crushing' Fundraising Is Bad for Congress," *Huffington Post,* May 7, 2013, https://www.huffpost.com/entry/chris-murphy-fundraising _n_3232143?utm_hp_ref=politics&utm_source=reddit.com.

39. Charles Edward Lindblom, *Politics and Markets: The World's Political Economic Systems* (New York: Basic Books, 1977), 356.

40. Nicholas W. Allard, "Lobbying Is an Honorable Profession: The Right to Petition and the Competition to Be Right," *Stanford Law and Policy Review* 19, no. 1 (2008).

41. Martin Gilens and Benjamin I. Page, "Testing Theories of American Politics: Elites, Interest Groups, and Average Citizens," *Perspectives on Politics* 12, no. 3 (2014); Martin Gilens, *Affluence and Influence: Economic Inequality and Political Power in America* (Princeton, NJ: Princeton University Press, 2012).

Discussion Questions

1. How is business lobbying different today from the 1970s? Is businesses' influence or impact greater today, or is their presence in Washington larger and changed from before—or are both things happening? Explain.

2. How can the power of lobbyists and special interests be reduced by Congress? That is, how effective have reform efforts been, and can a Madisonian solution work?

3. What are the three problems that Drutman identifies as needing to be fixed to "work with, not against, the realities of politics" and the influence of lobbyists? What are the possible remedies he suggests?

PART THREE

CONGRESS AND THE SEPARATION OF POWERS

7

The Legislative Role of the President

Paul Weinstein Jr.

Introduction

Over time the relationship between the president and Congress has evolved considerably, as have the tools that the president utilizes in attempting to manage that relationship. While in the early stages of the Republic the president played second fiddle to Congress in terms of setting the policy and legislative agenda, the modern presidency far outweighs the power and influence of Congress when it comes to policy-making.

There are a number of reasons for this seismic shift in the balance of power between the president and Congress. First, the size and scope of the executive branch have grown to over two million full-time employees in recent years. These individuals (and the agencies for which they work) report to the president and offer a wealth of information and resources that far outweigh those available to members of Congress.

Second, Congress has chosen to place a number of highly influential agencies within the Executive Office of the President of the United States, including the Office of Management and Budget, which is responsible for producing the President's Budget and overseeing the management of the federal government. Third, as America's role in the world has risen, so too has the president's as commander in chief. Fourth, the president's executive authority has increased in proportion to the growth in the scope of government. As Congress has enacted legislation to cover more and more issues, a considerable amount of discretion has been granted to the president to "fill in the specifics." Finally, attempts by

Congress to rein in the president's growing power have tended to fail, or in some cases, such as with the War Powers Act of 1973 (formally known as the War Powers Resolution of 1973), actually backfired.

President's Legislative Responsibilities

Even though the president has become the de-facto "policy-maker in chief," the White House still needs to manage relations with Congress effectively and efficiently in order to attain its objectives. Which is why a set of formal systems and entities exist to assist the president in overseeing the legislative process with Congress. The Constitution is clear that when it comes to the legislative process, the Congress is supreme. As Article 1, Section 1, states:

All legislative Powers herein granted shall be vested in a Congress of the United States, which shall consist of a Senate and House of Representatives.[1]

Yet while the authority to make laws via the legislative process clearly resides with the Congress, the role and responsibilities of the president and executive branch have grown in relevance. In fact, although the president does not have a vote in Congress, one could argue his or her influence over the crafting and passage of legislation outweighs that of most members of the House or Senate.

The president has five primary legislative responsibilities. The first four of these are derived from the Constitution. The responsibility of submitting an annual budget was established by the Budget and Accounting Act of 1921. The responsibilities include:

1. Delivering the State of the Union (SOTU)
2. Recommending new laws or changes to existing ones
3. Signing or vetoing legislation
4. Calling for a special session of Congress and the power to adjourn the House and Senate in certain instances
5. Proposing a budget to Congress

In order to fulfill these duties, the president presides over a large policy-making and coordinating body known as the Executive Office of the President (EOP). The EOP consists of almost two thousand employees spread across the White

House Office, the Office of the Vice President, the National Security Council (NSC), the Office of Administration, and a number of agencies mandated by Congress, including the Office of Management and Budget (OMB) and the United States Trade Representative (USTR).

The White House office includes not only those people who maintain the White House residence but also the White House counsel, the chief of staff, the Office of Congressional Affairs, the press, the National Economic Council (NEC), and the Domestic Policy Council (DPC).

Given the large number of White House and EOP staff, the task of fulfilling the president's legislative responsibilities and coordinating policy between the president's staff and cabinet departments and smaller agencies is challenging and complicated. Since the 1990s, policy and legislative decisions within the EOP have taken place at two levels. At the highest level (those that may require the president's input), the White House policy councils (NEC, DPC, and NSC) develop and coordinate major policy decisions with input from the relevant agencies and departments. For other matters, the OMB coordinates. The resulting decisions are then run through a formal clearance practice conducted by the OMB, called the Legislative Referral Management (LRM) process.

Legislative Clearance

Any legislative proposal a federal agency wishes to put before Congress must run through OMB's Legislative Referral Memorandum (LRM) process. This process is set forth in OMB Circular A-19. The LRM clearance function not only covers legislation but is also used to coordinate agency review of testimony, enrolled bills, agency reports, and comments on pending legislation, which is usually delivered utilizing a Statement of Administration Policy (SAP).

This power is one that is closely guarded by the OMB and can sometimes be a point of contention between the OMB and the agencies of the executive branch. Some agencies believe the OMB focuses too much on budgetary matters and not on broader policy goals. The OMB would argue a discussion of the cost of proposals will lead to better and more precise policy.

The LRM process is designed to

1. provide Congress with a unified administration position;
2. identify presidential priorities;

3. ensure agency-developed proposals are consistent with existing law and administration policy;

4. create a process to resolve agency disputes; and

5. establish a process to carry out the president's agenda.

The clearance process requires the OMB to circulate bills and other items to those agencies they deem to be affected, along with the relevant White House staff. Agencies may agree or have no objection. They can also propose substantial or technical changes, and in some cases submit a radically different alternative.

Disputes between agencies are reconciled by the OMB through e-mail, telephone, or interagency meetings. If the issue is not resolved through this process, it can be bumped up to the White House policy councils.

Agency Testimony and Reports

Besides legislation it proposes, the administration regularly interacts with Congress. Because of its oversight responsibility, Congress will often ask agencies to testify before its various committees. Congress also requires the executive branch to produce reports and studies.

In these instances, the LRM process would be used to ensure agreement within the administration as well as to provide Congress with technical expertise it might need to ensure that a bill will actually be effectively implemented.

Statement of Administration Policy (SAP)

Because of the president's ability to veto legislation, Congress will often request the administration's views on legislation that is pending before the House or Senate. The OMB also prepares a Statement of Administration Policy (SAP) for major bills scheduled for House or Senate floor action as well as those to be considered by major congressional committees, such as the House Rules Committee. SAPs are also prepared for so-called non-controversial bills considered in the House under suspension of the rules—bills that are voted on without the opportunity for members to offer amendments.

The SAP process coordinates, systematizes, and rationalizes the administration and formulation of the president's policy. SAPs are important because they provide a direct and authoritative way for the administration to let the Congress and, via the press, the American people know the views of the president on a particular bill or legislative issue. The SAP may be used to indicate support for legislation by the administration and the president. It may also be used to clarify the president's position in support of the whole bill or specific components of the legislation. Alternatively, the SAP may be used to indicate the administration and the president's disapproval of all or part of a particular bill. When the disapproval is strong enough, the SAP may contain a veto threat from the president. There are three levels of veto threats used in SAPs. These are in order of strength: first, "The President will veto it"; second, "Senior Advisors will recommend to the President that he should veto this legislation"; third, "The Secretary of Treasury [or whichever is the relevant agency] will recommend to the President that he should veto this legislation."

The OMB prepares SAPs in coordination with the agency or agencies principally concerned and other relevant EOP units. Once the SAP has passed through the clearance process, it is sent to Congress by the OMB's Office of Legislative Affairs.

Enrolled Bills

Once Congress has voted on and passed a particular bill, it is enrolled, that is, sent to the president for his approval or disapproval. The Constitution provides that the president shall take action within ten days after receipt of the bill, not including Sundays.

To assist the president in deciding his course of action on a bill (whether to sign or veto a piece of legislation), a review process, which is similar to the LRM process for bills submitted to Congress by the president, is set into motion in which the OMB requests that each interested agency submit its analysis and recommendation to the OMB within forty-eight hours. These "views letters" are signed by the head of the agency or a presidential appointee. The OMB prepares a memorandum to the president on the enrolled bill that transmits these views letters and summarizes the bill, significant issues, and various agency and OMB recommendations. If an agency recommends disapproval or a signing statement, it is responsible for preparing a draft of an appropriate statement for the president's consideration.

State of the Union

Arguably one of the most important ways a president conveys his or her agenda to Congress is the SOTU. The SOTU is an annual address presented by the president of the United States to the United States Congress. The address not only reports on the condition of the nation but also allows the president to outline his legislative agenda and national priorities to Congress.

The SOTU is typically given before a joint session of the United States Congress and is held in the House of Representatives chamber at the United States Capitol. From Jefferson to Taft, the SOTU was delivered in writing and was a report on the general condition of government as well as the nation at large. During the modern era, the SOTU has transformed into a policy agenda for the president, with a list of recommendations that the chief executive requests Congress to act upon.

Work on the SOTU begins in earnest in mid to late summer, six months prior to the address, which usually occurs in late January. Typically, the EOP staff begins the process by organizing interagency working groups to develop recommendations for ideas to be included in the SOTU. Any ideas that are included are considered part of the president's agenda and are given priority by the White House for enactment, funding, and implementation.

The process of developing ideas for the SOTU lasts through the fall, in some cases into December. Initially a list of ideas from the agencies and EOP offices is compiled by the White House and analyzed and debated throughout the summer and early fall. If a consensus is not achieved, options are laid out in a decision memorandum to a principals meeting of top White House and cabinet heads. Their recommendations (and any disagreements), are then sent to the president for his decision. Once a policy agenda is complete, the ideas are included in a document accompanying the SOTU, which is sent to Congress, the press corps, and is published for the public at large. The president's top priorities are referenced in the SOTU itself.

For a policy idea from the outside to be seriously considered, it must actually be placed into the process at the beginning of the SOTU process, around July or August prior to the address's delivery. Policy ideas must go through many stages before they get to the president. This includes budget estimates, legal reviews, economic and policy impact assessments, political/legislative analyses, and sign-off from the appropriate agencies and EOP offices.

The President's Budget

Like the SOTU, the "Budget of the United States Government" (colloquially referred to as the "President's Budget") is also used as a tool for the administration to outline its policy and legislative agenda for the upcoming year. Because of the level of detail involved, the President's Budget is much broader and informative than the SOTU. It is important to note that the President's Budget is not a law, but rather a recommendation to the Congress.

In 1921, the Congress passed the Budget and Accounting Act. This law required the president to submit to Congress an annual budget for the entire federal government. The act also created the Bureau of the Budget, now called the Office of Management and Budget (OMB), to review funding requests from government departments and assist the president in formulating the budget. As a result of this law, the president gained a meaningful and statutory role in the legislative budget process, along with the resources that far outsized anything Congress had at its disposal. And despite the creation of the Congressional Budget Office (CBO) and the Joint Committee on Taxation (JCT), there remains a sizable resource gap between Congress and the executive branch on budgetary issues.

Current law requires the president to submit a budget no earlier than the first Monday in January, and no later than the first Monday in February. The President's Budget request constitutes an extensive proposal of the administration's intended spending and revenue plans for the following fiscal year. The budget proposal includes volumes of supporting information intended to persuade Congress of the necessity and value of the budget provisions. In addition, each federal executive department and independent agency provides further details and supporting documentation to Congress on its own funding requests.

While initially envisioned as a way to help rein in deficits and improve the coordination of budget policy-making, the President's Budget has become a tool of policy-making as well. As such, it is, along with the SOTU, the primary annual process through which new ideas are submitted for consideration by the executive branch. However, unlike the SOTU, the budget process is done on a much larger scale.

The budget process cycle can take almost two years. Roughly one year before publishing the President's Budget, the OMB issues its spring planning guidance to all executive branch agencies for the upcoming budget. For policy experts outside the government, this is the first window into the budget process for sharing new ideas, reforms, and so on. Often, during this time period, agencies will put together a memo on budget priorities that they will submit to the OMB.[2]

Conclusion

As the president's role in the legislative and policy-making process has grown, so too has the need for tools and systems to manage the executive branch's relationship with Congress. Understanding these tools and systems is vital if one is to gain insights into how laws are developed and managed through the legislative process.

Notes

1. The Constitution of the United States, Article I, Section 1.
2. Rick Mertens and Greg Henry, "Budget Process for Science and Technology," Office of Management and Budget, 2010.

Discussion Questions

1. The president is the chief executive but also exercises legislative responsibilities. What are the president's major legislative responsibilities?
2. What is "legislative clearance?" Why is it important?
3. What are the chief purposes of the State of the Union Address?

8

Letters of Pacificus and Helvidius

Pacificus [Alexander Hamilton] and
Helvidius [James Madison]

IN APRIL 1793, PRESIDENT GEORGE Washington issued a "Declaration of Impartiality," designed to keep the United States out of the war between Britain and France. Washington's Declaration touched off a debate pitting Alexander Hamilton and his supporters against Thomas Jefferson and his supporters, who included James Madison. The two sides differed on the direction of American foreign policy and on the question of which institution of government should control America's relations with other nations. In a famous series of essays, Hamilton, writing as Pacificus, made the case of presidential primacy in the realm of foreign policy. Madison, writing as Helvidius, argued that under the Constitution, Congress was to play the dominant role. While Washington's declaration is now ancient history, the issues raised by Hamilton and Madison seem very current.

Pacificus (Alexander Hamilton)

[Hamilton's argument appeared in the *Gazette of the United States,* published in Philadelphia on June 29, 1793. Excerpts are from the first letter.]

Number 1

. . .

It will not be disputed that the management of the affairs of this country with foreign nations is confided to the Government of the UStates.

It can as little be disputed, that a Proclamation of Neutrality, where a Nation is at liberty to keep out of a War in which other Nations are engaged and means so to do, is a *usual* and a *proper* measure. *Its main object and effect are to prevent the Nation being immediately responsible for acts done by its citizens, without the privity or connivance of the Government, in contravention of the principles of neutrality.*

An object this of the greatest importance to a Country whose true interest lies in the preservation of peace.

The inquiry then is—what department of the Government of the UStates is the prop[er] one to make a declaration of Neutrality in the cases in which the engagements [of] the Nation permit and its interests require such a declaration.

A correct and well informed mind will discern at once that it can belong neit[her] to the Legislature nor Judicial Department and of course must belong to the Executive.

The Legislative Department is not the organ of intercourse between the United States and foreign Nations. It is charged neither with making nor interpreting Treaties. It is therefore not naturally that Organ of the Government, which is to pronounce the existing condition of the Nation, with regard to foreign Powers, or to admonish the Citizens of their obligations and duties as founded upon that condition of things. Still less is it charged with execution and observance of those obligations and those duties.

It is equally obvious that the act in question is foreign to the Judiciary Department of Government. The province of that Department is to decide litigations in particular cases. It is indeed charged with the interpretation of treaties; but it exercises this function only in the litigated cases; that is where contending parties bring before it a specific controversy. It has no concern with pronouncing upon the external political relations of Treaties between Government and Government. This position is too plain to need being insisted upon.

It must then of necessity belong to the Executive Department to exercise the function in Question—when a proper case for the exercise of it occurs.

It appears to be connected with that department in various capacities, as the organ of intercourse between the Nation and foreign Nations—as the interpreter of the National Treaties, in those cases in which the Judiciary is not competent, that is in the cases between Government and Government—as the power, which is charged with the Execution of the Laws, of which Treaties form a part—as that Power which is charged with the command and application of the Public Force.

This view of the subject is so natural and obvious—so analogous to general theory and practice—that no doubt can be entertained of its justness, unless such doubt can be deduced from particular provisions of the Constitution of the UStates.

Let us see then if cause for such doubt is to be found in that constitution.

The second Article of the Constitution of the United States, section 1st, establishes this general Proposition, That "The EXECUTIVE POWER shall be vested in a President of the United States of America."

The same article in a succeeding Section proceeds to designate particular cases of Executive Power. It declares among other things that the President shall be Commander in Chief of the army and navy of the UStates and of the Militia of the several states when called into the actual service of the UStates, that he shall have power by and with the advice of the senate to make treaties; that it shall be his duty to receive ambassadors and other public Ministers and to take care that the laws be faithfully executed.

It would not consist with the rules of sound construction to consider this enumeration of particular authorities as derogating from the more comprehensive grant contained in the general clause, further than as it may be coupled with express restrictions or qualifications; as in regard to the cooperation of the Senate in the appointment of Officers and the making of treaties; which are qualifica[tions] of the general executive powers of appointing officers and making treaties: Because the difficulty of a complete and perfect specification of all the cases of Executive authority would naturally dictate the use of general terms—and would render it improbable that a specification of certain particulars was designed as a substitute for those terms, when antecedently used. The different mode of expression employed in the constitution in regard to the two powers the Legislative and the Executive serves to confirm this inference. In the article which grants the legislative powers of the Governt. the expressions are—"All Legislative powers herein granted shall be vested in a Congress of the UStates"; in that which grants the Executive Power the expressions are, as already quoted "The EXECUTIVE PO[WER] shall be vested in a President of the UStates of America."

The enumeration ought rather therefore to be considered as intended by way of greater caution, to specify and regulate the principal articles implied in the definition of Executive Power; leaving the rest to flow from the general grant of that power, interpreted in conformity to other parts [of] the constitution and to the principles of free government.

The general doctrine then of our Constitution is, that the EXECUTIVE POWER of the Nation is vested in the President; subject only to the exceptions and qu[a]lifications which are expressed in the instrument.

Two of these have been already noticed—the participation of the Senate in the appointment of Officers and in the making of Treaties. A third remains to be mentioned the right of the Legislature "to declare war and grant letters of marque and reprisal."

With these exceptions the EXECUTIVE POWER of the Union is completely lodged in the President. This mode of construing the Constitution has indeed been recognized by Congress in formal acts, upon full consideration and debate. The power of removal from office is an important instance.

And since upon general principles for reasons already given, the issuing of a proclamation of neutrality is merely an Executive Act; since also the general Executive Power of the Union is vested in the President, the conclusion is, that the step, which has been taken by him, is liable to no just exception on the score of authority.

It may be observed that this Inference w[ould] be just if the power of declaring war had [not] been vested in the Legislature, but that [this] power naturally includes the right of judg[ing] whether the Nation is under obligations to ma[ke] war or not.

The answer to this is, that however true it may be, that th[e] right of the Legislature to declare wa[r] includes the right of judging whether the N[ation] be under obligations to make War or not—it will not follow that the Executive is in any case excluded from a similar right of Judgment, in the execution of its own functions.

If the Legislature have a right to make war on the one hand—it is on the other the duty of the Executive to preserve Peace till war is declared; and in fulfilling that duty, it must necessarily possess a right of judging what is the nature of the obligations which the treaties of the Country impose on the Government; and when in pursuance of this right it has concluded that there is nothing in them inconsistent with a state of neutrality, it becomes both its province and its duty to enforce the laws incident to that state of the Nation. The Executive is charged with the execution of all laws, the law of Nations as well as the Municipal law, which recognises and adopts those laws. It is consequently bound, by faithfully executing the laws of neutrality, when that is the state of the Nation, to avoid giving a cause of war to foreign Powers.

This is the direct and proper end of the proclamation of neutrality. It declares to the UStates their situation with regard to the Powers at war and makes known to the Community that the laws incident to that situation will be enforced. In doing this, it conforms to an established usage of Nations, the operation of which as before remarked is to obviate a responsibility on the part of the whole Society, for secret and unknown violations of the rights of any of the warring parties by its citizens.

Those who object to the proclamation will readily admit that it is the right and duty of the Executive to judge of, or to interpret, those articles of our treaties which give to France particular privileges, in order to the enforcement of those priveleges: But the necessary consequence of this is, that the Executive must judge what are the proper bounds of those priveleges—what rights are given to other nations by our treaties with them—what rights the law of Nature and Nations gives and our treaties permit, in respect to those Nations with whom we have no treaties; in fine what are the reciprocal rights and obligations of the United States & of all & each of the powers at War.

The right of the Executive to receive ambassadors and other public Ministers may serve to illustrate the relative duties of the Executive and Legislative Departments. This right includes that of judging, in the case of a Revolution of Government in a foreign Country, whether the new rulers are competent organs of the National Will and ought to [be] recognised or not: And where a treaty antecedently exists between the UStates and such nation that right involves the power of giving operation or not to such treaty. For until the new Government is acknowledged, the treaties between the nations, as far at least as regards public rights, are of course suspended.

This power of determ[in]ing virtually in the case supposed upon the operation of national Treaties as a consequence, of the power to receive ambassadors and other public Ministers, is an important instance of the right of the Executive to decide the obligations of the Nation with regard to foreign Nations. To apply it to the case of France, if the[re] had been a Treaty of alliance offensive [and] defensive between the UStates and that Coun[try,] the unqualified acknowledgement of the new Government would have put the UStates in a condition to become an associate in the War in which France was engaged—and would have laid the Legislature under an obligation, if required, and there was otherwise no valid excuse, of exercising its power of declaring war.

This serves as an example of the right of the Executive, in certain cases, to determine the condition of the Nation, though it may consequentially affect the proper or improper exercise of the Power of the Legislature to declare war. The Executive indeed cannot control the exercise of that power—further than by the exer[c]ise of its general right of objecting to all acts of the Legislature; liable to being overruled by two thirds of both houses of Congress. The Legislature is free to perform its own duties according to its own sense of them—though the Executive in the exercise of its constitutional powers, may establish an antecedent state of things which ought to weigh in the legislative decisions. From the division of the Executive Power there results, in referrence to it, a concurrent authority, in the distributed cases.

Hence in the case stated, though treaties can only be made by the President and Senate, their activity may be continued or suspended by the President alone.

No objection has been made to the Presidents having acknowledged the Republic of France, by the Reception of its Minister, without having consulted the Senate; though that body is connected with him in the making of Treaties, and though the consequence of his act of reception is to give operation to the Treaties heretofore made with that Country: But he is censured for having declared the UStates to be in a state of peace & neutrality, with regard to the Powers at War; because the right of changing that state & declaring war belongs to the Legislature.

It deserves to be remarked, that as the participation of the senate in the making of Treaties and the power of the Legislature to declare war are exceptions out of the general "Executive Power" vested in the President, they are to be construed strictly—and ought to be extended no further than is essential to their execution.

While therefore the Legislature can alone declare war, can alone actually transfer the nation from a state of Peace to a state of War—it belongs to the "Executive Power," to do whatever else the law of Nations cooperating with the Treaties of the Country enjoin in the intercourse of the UStates with foreign Powers.

In this distribution of powers the wisdom of our constitution is manifested. It is the province and duty of the Executive to preserve to the Nation the blessings of peace. The Legislature alone can interrupt those blessings, by placing the Nation in a state of War.

But though it has been thought adviseable to vindicate the authority of the Executive on this broad and comprehensive ground—it was not absolutely necessary to do so. That clause of the constitution which makes it his duty to "take care that the laws be faithfully executed" might alone have been relied upon, and this simple process of argument pursued.

The President is the constitutional EXECUTOR of the laws. Our Treaties and the laws of Nations form a part of the law of the land. He who is to execute the laws must first judge for himself of their meaning. In order to the observance of that conduct, which the laws of nations combined with our treaties prescribed to this country, in reference to the present War in Europe, it was necessary for the President to judge for himself whether there was any thing in our treaties incompatible with an adherence to neutrality. Having judged that there was not, he had a right, and if in his opinion the interests of the Nation required it, it was his duty, as Executor of the laws, to proclaim the neutrality of the Nation, to exhort all persons to observe it, and to warn them of the penalties which would attend its non observance.

The Proclamation has been represented as enacting some new law. This is a view of it entirely erroneous. It only proclaims a fact with regard to the existing state of the Nation, informs the citizens of what the laws previously established require of them in that state, & warns them that these laws will be put in execution against the Infractors of them.

Helvidius (James Madison)

[Madison's rebuttal to Hamilton appeared in a series of articles that appeared in the *Gazette of the United States* between August 24 and September 18, 1793. Articles are excerpted.]

Number 1

. . .

Let us examine.

In the general distribution of powers, we find that of declaring war expressly vested in the Congress, where every other legislative power is declared to be vested, and without any other qualification than what is common to every other legislative act. The constitutional idea of this power would seem then clearly to be, that it is of a legislative and not an executive nature.

This conclusion becomes irresistible, when it is recollected, that the constitution cannot be supposed to have placed either any power legislative in its nature, entirely among executive powers, or any power executive in its nature, entirely among legislative powers, without charging the constitution, with that kind of intermixture and consolidation of different powers, which would violate a fundamental principle in the organization of free governments. If it were not unnecessary to enlarge on this topic here, it could be shewn, that the constitution was originally vindicated, and has been constantly expounded, with a disavowal of any such intermixture.

The power of treaties is vested jointly in the President and in the Senate, which is a branch of the legislature. From this arrangement merely, there can be no inference that would necessarily exclude the power from the executive class: since the senate is joined with the President in another power, that of appointing to offices, which as far as relate to executive offices at least, is considered as of an executive nature. Yet on the other hand, there are sufficient indications that the power of treaties is regarded by the constitution as materially different from mere executive power, and as having more affinity to the legislative than to the executive character.

. . .

[T]reaties when formed according to the constitutional mode, are confessedly to have the force and operation of laws, and are to be a rule for the courts in controversies between man and man, as much as any other laws. They are even emphatically declared by the constitution to be "the supreme law of the land."

So far the argument from the constitution is precisely in opposition to the doctrine. As little will be gained in its favour from a comparison of the two powers, with those particularly vested in the President alone.

As there are but few it will be most satisfactory to review them one by one.

"The President shall be commander in chief of the army and navy of the United States, and of the militia when called into the actual service of the United States."

There can be no relation worth examining between this power and the general power of making treaties. And instead of being analogous to the power of declaring war, it affords a striking illustration of the incompatibility of the two powers in the same hands. Those who are to conduct a war cannot in the nature of things, be proper or safe judges, whether a war ought to be commenced, continued, or concluded. They are barred from the latter functions by a great principle in free government, analogous to that which separates the sword from the purse, or the power of executing from the power of enacting laws.

. . .

Thus it appears that by whatever standard we try this doctrine, it must be condemned as no less vicious in theory than it would be dangerous in practice. It is countenanced neither by the writers on law; nor by the nature of the powers themselves; nor by any general arrangements or particular expressions, or plausible analogies, to be found in the constitution.

Whence then can the writer have borrowed it?

There is but one answer to this question.

The power of making treaties and the power of declaring war, are royal prerogatives in the British government, and are accordingly treated as Executive prerogatives by British commentators.

. . .

Number 2

. . .

Leaving however to the leisure of the reader deductions which the author, having omitted, might not choose to own, I proceed to the examination of one, with which that liberty cannot be taken.

"However true it may be, (says he) that the right of the legislature to declare war includes the right of judging, whether the legislature be under obligations to make war or not, it will follow that the executive is in any case excluded from a similar right of judging in the execution of its own functions."

. . .

A concurrent authority in two independent departments, to perform the same function with respect to the same thing, would be as awkward in practice, as it is unnatural in theory.

If the legislature and executive have both a right to judge of the obligations to make war or not, it must sometimes happen, though not at present, that they will judge differently. The executive may proceed to consider the question to-day; may determine that the United States are not bound to take part in a war, and, in the execution of its functions, proclaim that declaration to all the world. To-morrow the legislature may follow in the consideration of the same subject, may determine that the obligations impose war on the United States, and in the execution of its functions, enter into a constitutional declaration, expressly contradicting the constitutional proclamation.

In what light does this present the constitution to the people who established it? In what light would it present to the world a nation, thus speaking, thro' two different organs, equally constitutional and authentic, two opposite languages, on the same subject, and under the same existing circumstances?

But it is not with the legislative rights alone that this doctrine interferes. The rights of the judiciary may be equally invaded. For it is clear that if a right declared by the constitution to be legislative, leaves, notwithstanding, a similar right in the executive, whenever a case for exercising it occurs, in the course of its functions: a right declared to be judiciary and vested in that department may, on the same principle, be assumed and exercised by the executive in the course of its functions: and it is evident that occasions and pretexts for the latter interference may be as frequent as for the former. So again the judiciary department may find equal occasions in the execution of its functions, for usurping the authorities of the executive: and the legislature for stepping into the jurisdiction of both. And thus all the power of government, of which a partition is so carefully made among the several branches, would be thrown into absolute hotchpot, and exposed to a general scramble. . . .

Discussion Questions

1. What reasons does Hamilton give for believing that the executive should control America's foreign affairs?
2. What reasons does Madison give for thinking that the Congress should be the dominant force in America's foreign affairs?
3. Who makes the stronger argument? Why?

9

Bureaucrats and Their Constituents:
Congressional Monitoring in the Modern Era

John Ray

Introduction

In this paper I suggest that Congress in the modern era has developed an unorthodox and informal new set of tools to pursue its agenda in an era in which policy-making on the floor is difficult, and I describe one such set of tools: televised committee hearings, which allow individual legislators to interact with the bureaucracy in an era when individual legislators are relatively unable to generate new bills on their own. My work suggests that individual legislators are busier than they are often given credit for, and that in an era of polarization and gridlock, limiting congressional study to floor votes may miss a significant portion of legislative activity.

On September 15, 2016, at the culmination of a lengthy series of procedural maneuvers, the head of the House Judiciary Committee called off a vote to commence impeachment proceedings of Internal Revenue Service (IRS) commissioner John Koskinen.[1] A series of investigations conducted by the Government Accountability Office had found that the IRS not only may have improperly targeted certain political nonprofits for audits, but that it had been sluggish in changing its internal review process to prevent improper targeting of those nonprofits in the future.[2] The case against Koskinen was a "slam dunk," according to prominent conservative commentators, who lamented the seemingly inexplicable decision not to pursue impeachment.[3]

While Republican members of the Judiciary Committee may have been confident in the quality of their case, they never doubted that a successful impeachment vote was unrealistic. Enough Republicans in the House questioned the strategic value of the case to make a public vote an unwise choice for a party struggling to project unity in the immediate post-Boehner era. Long before the vote was officially called off, the Judiciary Committee leadership was planning another tactic: a series of lengthy hearings at which the IRS's malfeasance would be repeatedly laid bare on national television.

The "slam dunk" nature of the case resulted in a series of investigations conducted and reported on in Judiciary Committee hearings by one of Congress's investigative agencies, the Government Accountability Office. Ultimately, the committee decided it was better to rely on these reports so that a credible, nonpartisan source like the GAO would provide damaging information about the activities of the IRS. Rather than wage a lengthy conflict within the party to secure a floor vote, the committee's Republican leadership opted to go public with its concerns, and to let the GAO fact-finding missions do the talking on their behalf in the form of a series of investigations on which the committee would report.

In this paper, I argue that this strategy is increasingly important for individual legislators to pursue in an era of growing gridlock and decreasing congressional productivity. While by some measures Congress overall is less productive than it used to be, I demonstrate that legislators have compensated by shifting their individual time and effort to other activities. As the size and scope of the federal bureaucracy grow and the capacity of Congress to legislate on the floor shrinks, these alternative policy venues will grow in importance for governance studies.

In the next section, I review changes in the nature of congressional work that scholars have observed that differentiate the modern era from previous eras. I show that while Congress is less productive in the modern era than it has been in previous eras, individual legislators still campaign for, and win, their seats at similar rates to those of the past. I show that by some measures legislators are not outsourcing their productivity to private-sector lobbyists. I then show some evidence suggesting that Congress is increasingly invested in monitoring the behavior of the bureaucracy, which is growing as a share of overall federal activity. I conclude by suggesting that monitoring the bureaucracy allows individual legislators to circumvent the costly floor or legislating process while engaging in productive activities on which they can campaign.

Congress in the Modern Era

Congress produces less legislation in the modern era than it did in the past (Grant and Kelly 2008). Some attribute the decrease in new legislation to the rise of amendments fostered by the electronic voting system (Roberts and Smith 2003; Frantzich 1979), which made it easier to alter existing legislation rather than create new legislation. Generally, scholars of Congress view polarization as playing a fundamental role in the comparatively low volume of new legislation produced in the modern era (Howell et al. 2000). The Speaker of the House exerts stronger control over the agenda of the House now than in the past (Cox and McCubbins 2005, but see Lawrence, Maltzman, and Wahlbeck 2001) and over the committee system (Cox and McCubbins 1993). Individual legislators are less "important" as policy-makers than in the past.

I have plotted congressional productivity measured as the count of bills produced per Congress by congressional polarization, measured as the DW-NOMINATE distance between the medians of the two parties (fig. 9.1).[4] The relationship between productivity and polarization is negative ($\beta = -2.75$, $p < 0.001$).[5] A 0.1-unit shift in polarization between the median Democrat and the median Republican along the DW-NOMINATE scale, which ranges from -1 to

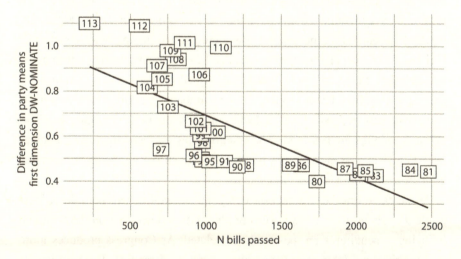

Fig. 9.1: Congressional productivity by polarization (1947–2013). *Notes:* Boxed labels represent the congressional session number corresponding to the productivity and polarization statistics. Numbers on the left are degrees of polarization.

1.0, is associated with Congress producing about 275 fewer pieces of new legislation per session.

As a consequence, individual legislators have relatively little control over the
daily activities of Congress. Some evidence shows that individual legislators
instead spend the vast majority their time fundraising for themselves and for
their party (Feigenbaum and Shelton 2013). Other work suggests that when
policy-making on the floor is not an option, some legislators will choose to out-
source policy-making to the private sector (Drutman 2015).

In that view, interest groups are relatively powerful actors because of the attention they pay to the rule-making process in the federal bureaucracy (Yackee
2011). Because the bureaucracy is growing as an overall share of federal activity, and because congressional activity is shrinking, lobbyists who are interested
in the details of policy implementation enjoy an advantage in the negotiation
phase of rulemaking (Yackee 2006). Absent new and specific language to con-
strain the activity of the bureaucracy, bureaucrats left to implement policy under
the aegis of concerned interest groups are thought to bear responsibility for
most new policy-making.

And yet legislators are as busy campaigning as they've ever been. Over the
past five years, the number of trips individual legislators have taken home has
been roughly constant (fig. 9.2). As most of those trips are for legislators to return home to campaign and maintain their name recognition (Leal 2002; Krehbiel and Wright 1983), the relative power reduction of nonparty leadership that
legislators have experienced has not reduced their personal need to return home
to campaign. Since the early 1980s, the typical House seat has gotten more
expensive (fig. 9.3). From 1983 to 2014, incumbent spending on reelection has
risen from just over $400,000 in 1980 dollars to about $1.4 million in 2014.
While legislators are passing less legislation, they are campaigning as much as
ever. Legislators, as measured by their floor productivity, are doing less and less
with more and more campaign resources.

At the same time, using data on lobbying expenditures at the federal level
(table 9.1) shows that congressional productivity as measured on the floor and
lobbying expenditures are positively correlated. As Congress produces more
(less) legislation, lobbying expenditures increase (decrease). The coefficients
(see table 9.1) indicate that the production of one additional piece of legislation
in the 1998–2012 period is associated with another $1.7 million in expenditures
by lobbying organizations on lobbying either legislators or the executive branch.

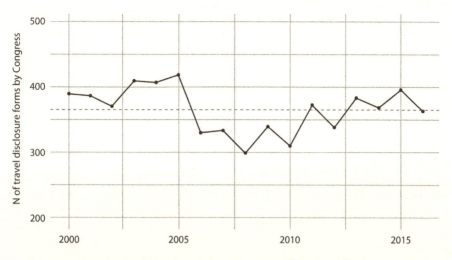

Fig. 9.2: Congressional travel statistics, 2000–2015. The dotted line represents the mean count of trips per year. *Source:* Data gathered from public financial disclosures available at "Congressional travel by approving members in the House," at https://www.legistorm.com/trip_browse_by_approver /index/office_type/HM/.html (accessed April 10, 2016).

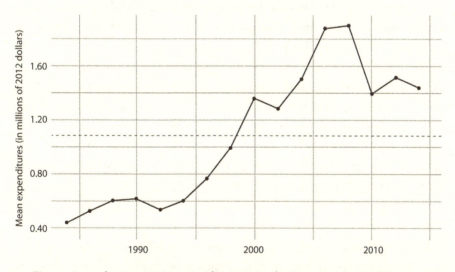

Fig. 9.3: Incumbent campaign expenditures on reelection campaigns, 1983–2014, measured in 2012 dollars. The dotted line represents mean expenditures over the 1983–2014 period. *Source:* Expenditures data from *Vital Statistics on Congress,* Washington, DC: Brookings Institution, 2016.

Table 9.1. Lobbying Expenditures and Congressional Productivity

	Dependent variable:		
	Lobbying Expenditures ($millions)		
	(1)	(2)	(3)
Bills	1.772**	1.746*	0.073
	(0.453)	(0.539)	(0.417)
Divided government		111.160	409.169
		(920.128)	(399.247)
Time trend			308.246***
			(63.982)
Observations	8	8	8
R^2	0.718	0.719	0.959

Notes: *p < 0.05; **p < 0.01; ***p < 0.001

The magnitude and precision of the estimate decrease slightly if we include a term for divided government, realized as a "1" in cycles in which the president and either chamber were held by different parties, and disappears if we include a linear term for time. If it were the case that lobbying activity and Congressional activity were *pure* substitutes—that is, if it were the case that for every new policy Congress failed to pursue, lobbyists pursued such a policy on their own—we would expect a negative correlation. While other theories model lobbying as a legislative subsidy (Deardorff and Hall 2006) rather than as a substitute, it remains to be fully explained how Congress has adapted to an era in which legislating on the floor is increasingly different. Congress is doing less, but it has not necessarily outsourced its role in the legislative process to the private sector.

The executive branch by contrast has grown steadily more productive over time, as measured by the volume of new rules promulgated by the cabinet-level agencies, such as the Departments of State, Health and Human Services, and Education. Federal agencies now promulgate more rules, and faster, than in the past (Webb Yackee and Webb Yackee 2009). The count of new "economically significant rules"[6] is plotted (fig. 9.4) and is defined as rules promulgated by any federal agency that the Office of Management and Budget (OMB) projects

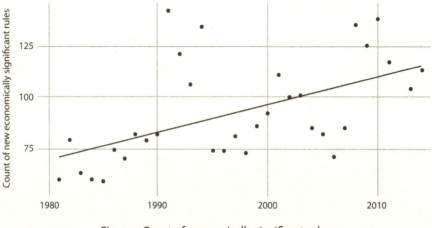

Fig. 9.4: Count of economically significant rules
promulgated by federal agencies, 1981–2014.

will cost at least $100 million in 1993 dollars over the ten years following their promulgation. Over time, the federal agencies have become more productive in promulgating rules, while Congress has become less productive as measured by the amount of new policies it passes.

A few innovations in congressional monitoring policy have attempted to correct for the growing imbalance between federal rulemaking and congressional lawmaking. The Congressional Review Act of 1996,[7] for example, was enacted along with the Gingrich-era "Contract with America" legislation and empowered Congress to "disapprove" new agency regulations and, absent a presidential veto, prevent new agency regulations from taking effect or passing into the federal registry. However, while prior work shows that legislators attempt to employ the Congressional Review Act to undo regulations of which individual legislators disapprove, they are rarely successful (Balla 2000). In practice, such resolutions are typically vetoed and the rules of which Congress disapproves promulgated.[8] While legislators exert some control over the bureaucracy in the design phase of new agencies (Huber 2007), presidential review of agency rulemaking is considered the most significant component of regulatory review in the modern era (Bruff 1988). The "presidential control model," as described in Schultz Bressman and Vandenbergh (2006), remains the prevailing model of bureaucratic governance in the modern era.

And yet while Congress is less productive in the modern era than it has been previously, its members are by some measures as busy working to raise funds

and interact with their constituents as in the past. Their reelection rates are un-
changed from previous eras, with roughly 90 percent of incumbent congresspeople winning reelection per cycle, and so incumbents campaign as effectively as they have in the past (Boatright et al. 2012; Boatright, 2013). Congress
has successfully adapted to a new equilibrium, in which individual legislators
raise money and campaign in their districts as in previous eras, but with fewer
legislative accomplishments for which they can claim credit or advertise (Mayhew 1974). By some measures, legislators have not outsourced lawmaking to
the private sector, and lobbying is not a pure substitute for legislating.

Some recent scholarship shows that individual legislators have grown more
creative in the nature of their credit-claiming activities, campaigning on relatively small accomplishments sometimes achieved years prior to when credit for
the accomplishment is claimed (Grimmer, Messing, and Westwood 2012). Legislators increasingly campaign on the promise of a broad agenda rather than on
specific accomplishments (Parmelee 2013). and in an era characterized by relatively strong parties, voters pay less attention to their individual legislators
and more to the "policy slates" they support (Lee, Moretti, and Butler 2014).
Legislators increasingly pursue low-cost activities about which they can claim
credit since they are largely prevented by either gridlock or their party leadership from passing new legislation, yet they still face fundraising pressure for
their personal reelection (Krasno and Seltz 2000).

Here, I describe one such form of low-cost but publicity-accruing activity
individual legislators may pursue at relatively low cost: televised congressional
hearings, specifically those hosted by House committees with some level of de
jure authority for oversight of the major executive agencies. A congressional
hearing is usually several hours long and involves legislators from a particular
committee asking prepared questions of particular guests of that committee,
who are often members of the federal agencies over which that committee holds
jurisdiction. While those hearings themselves are typically characterized by low
public attendance and by low viewership, legislators report that such hearings
are typically accompanied by some fanfare from its hosts, who will time their
hearings to coincide with campaign materials, press releases, and other television appearances legislators orchestrate to maximize the public impact of their
efforts.[9] While these hearings are of low salience by themselves, they allow
legislators to make their preferences known on a variety of issues over which

they have no practical policy power, and they provide free television footage to be used in advertisements (Docter, Dutton, and Elberse 1999).

Practically speaking, because congressional hearings are typically of low salience, the decision to host one is not predicted to be of great consequence to policy. Thus, while they are trivial in terms of generating public policy, they are attractive venues for committee ranking members and lower-level party members seeking to make their preferences known in a way that does not endanger their party's overall brand. Because gridlock in Congress is high, even these relatively inconsequential events serve as attractive alternatives to the costly and typically fruitless endeavor of authoring new legislation to pass on the floor.

Congressional hearings also allow individual legislators a chance to air their grievances about the federal agencies and federal policy implementation. Consider a recent example, the hearing held by the House Committee on Energy and Commerce on September 14, 2016, to discuss "the implementation and sustainability of the Patient Protection and Affordable Care Act (PPACA)."[10] There, several congressional Republicans and Democrats sitting on the Energy and Commerce Committee interviewed representatives of an executive agency, the Department of Health and Human Services (HHS). Consider an exchange that took place between Congressman John Shimkus (R-IL) and Andrew Slavitt, the acting administrator for the HHS subagency Centers for Medicare and Medicaid Services:[11]

JOHN SHIMKUS: . . . Mr. Slavitt, under the Affordable Care Act, if you like your health-care plan, will you be able to keep it? Yes or no?
SLAVITT: If it continues to be offered, yes, if not, then you'd switch to—
SHIMKUS: So the answer—so no. You can't. The plan that you had prior to the Affordable Care Act is no longer available to Americans.
SLAVITT: The plans available under the Affordable Care Act are—
SHIMKUS: Alright. Let me ask the second question. If you like your doctor, you'll be able to keep [him/her] with no changes, right? Prior to the Affordable Care Act, and now?
SLAVITT: I think it's always been true that physicians and health plans continually change their relationship—
SHIMKUS: There are limited provider networks who pay extra, so that's no longer true. Are premiums lowered by twenty-five hundred dollars for a family of four?
SLAVITT: I think if you're referring to the—
SHIMKUS: The promise by the president when he campaigned for this law.

SLAVITT: I believe this analysis is that it's lower than it would otherwise have been—

SHIMKUS: Then the answer is really no, the premiums haven't decreased. They've increased. The promise was premiums on average would decrease by twenty-five hundred dollars per family. Obviously, premiums have gone up. The other promise was, [for] 80 or 90 percent of all Americans, that their insurance would be stronger, better, and more secure. You think that's true?

SLAVITT: Yes.

SHIMKUS: Well let me read you two notes from constituents of mine who obviously are living it. . . .

A few features of this exchange are worth noting. One, Representative Shimkus is quoting the campaign promises of President Obama in his attempts to sell the Affordable Care Act to the public, which passed into law March 23, 2010, over six years prior to the hearing in question. Two, the hearing is being held not on new legislation to amend or repeal the Affordable Care Act, but on the implementation of new rules promulgated by HHS pursuant to the passage of the act. In other words, Representative Shimkus is fact-finding on his constituents' behalf due to his concern over bureaucratic policy, not over the contents of new law that might forcibly correct that policy.[12] Third, the hearing was prompted not by mandatory review of rules, but by an investigation by a congressional legislative agency, the Government Accountability Office, which found that it was possible to sign up for new health-care plans under assumed names.[13] By using a congressional agency's fact-finding mission and a subsequent hearing involving members of the executive agencies, legislators hoped to raise attention to concerns about the implementation of policy they were relatively powerless to reverse through the passage of new policy. Using the legislative agencies at their disposal, individual congresspeople investigated and found cause for a hearing at which to voice their concerns over executive policy implementation.

In the next section, I present more systematic data and models that show televised congressional hearings are growing as an overall share of congressional activity, and that House committees' deployment of televised hearings correlates with the promulgation of new economically significant rules. Focusing on the House of Representatives, I show that the rise of televised hearings is not attributable solely to overall changes in the amount of hearings held by Congress over time, which itself is decreasing. However, I also show that televised hearings are not more likely under divided government, suggesting that the purpose of televised hearings is not solely to antagonize the presidency.

Congressional Hearings: Data and Results

The Office of Information and Regulatory Affairs (OIRA) is responsible for gathering and reporting data on the passage of any new "economically significant" regulation, which is defined[14] as any new rule that the Office of Management and Budget projects will cost over $100 million in 1993 dollars over the course of ten years following the rule's promulgation into the Code of Federal Regulations. I start by scraping the OIRA repository of reports on new regulations to gather metadata on which agency is promulgating each rule, so that I may create a subset of only economically significant regulations.[15] In total, I find 3,166 economically significant rules proposed or promulgated from 1980 until 2015. I break down the share of new rules promulgated by the federal agencies through which they promulgate (fig. 9.5). Across the range shown, Health and Human Services (HHS) and the Environmental Protection Agency (EPA) were responsible for the most new major rules, totaling 43 percent of the new rules presented here. The top rule generators were HHS, with 678 of the total new rules in this period, EPA with 425, and the United States Department of Agriculture (USDA) at 360. The mean across all agencies promulgating economically significant new rules is 94.1 new rules in the 1980–2015 period, or about three per year.

Each major federal agency has a corresponding committee in the House of Representatives. That committee has either de facto or de jure jurisdiction over the agency in question and is tasked with monitoring and oversight of the implementation of rules and policy by that agency. A full list of agency-to-committee matches appears in the appendix. In total, I include data on twenty-seven federal agencies monitored by twelve different House committees, issuing major new regulations in the 1980–2015 period. Of the twenty-five agencies promulgating economically significant new rules in this period, the subset of six that I focus on—the Architectural and Transportation Barriers Compliance Board,[16] Department of Labor, Department of Transportation, Department of Housing and Urban Development, Office of Personnel Management, and the State Department—are under the monitoring jurisdiction of the Judiciary Committee. In a few cases committees share jurisdiction over an agency, but it is

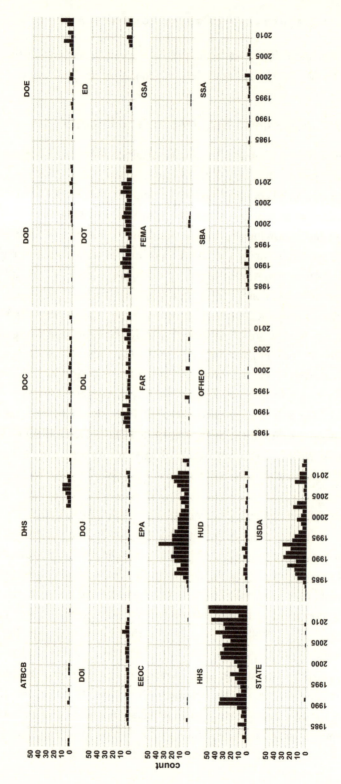

Fig. 9.5: Economically significant new rules promulgated in the 1980–2015 period, by agency and counts of televised committee hearings broadcast on C-SPAN, 1980–2015.

typically easy to assign an agency to a "primary committee." For example, the Homeland Security Committee oversees the implementation of all Federal Emergency Management Agency (FEMA) programs except for those pertaining to flood insurance, which are partially shared by the Oversight Committee. Because flood insurance is relatively small as a share of overall FEMA activity, I consider that agency as being overseen by the Homeland Security Committee. I attempt to match every rulemaking agency to a single overseeing committee.

Next, for data on televised hearings held in the House of Representatives, I turn to the C-SPAN archives, which record counts and metadata of all televised content produced by the federal government.[17] I gather counts of televised hearings held by each of the committees that hold jurisdiction over the federal agencies issuing rules in this period. Then I plot the count of televised committee hearings held by Congress over time, grouped by committee (table 9.2). The distribution of televised committee hearings is more even than the count of rules promulgated by agency, with the mean committee holding 26.4 meetings per year, the minimum zero, and the maximum 244, held by the Judiciary Committee in 2015. In total, the data set on which I run the models includes 376 observations.

After matching each federal agency promulgating major rules to the congressional committees that either nominally or formally oversee their rule implementation, I construct a measure realized as "1" when the agency-committee pair occurred in a year of divided government. and as "0" if not, and a measure to control for the size of committee, which is simply the count of sitting representatives on the committee. I include a time term, and a term to control for the overall rise of hearings in Congress, whether televised or not, which is simply the sum of committee hearings held by year as available in the Code of Federal Regulations. I use ordinary least squares (OLS) to measure the correlation between how many major rules an agency promulgates and how many televised hearings its jurisdictional committees hold.

I show the results of OLS specifications modeling the count of televised hearings by congressional committees across a variety of specifications (see table 9.2). One additional economically significant rule promulgated by a federal agency is associated with between 0.5 and 1 additional televised hearings. Every additional representative sitting on the committee is associated with about 0.6 more televised hearings. Surprisingly, there is no main effect of divided government on televised hearings. That is, Republicans do not hold more hearings

Table 9.2. Impact of Congressional Factors on the Count of Televised Hearings

	Dependent variable:		
	Count of Televised Hearings		
	(1)	(2)	(3)
Economically significant rules	0.743***	0.743***	0.501*
	(0.212)	(0.212)	(0.211)
Divided government		−0.102	5.783
		(3.478)	(3.523)
Committee size			0.646***
			(0.158)
Time	4.704***	4.707***	5.275***
	(0.408)	(0.417)	(0.416)
All-hearings count	−0.036***	−0.036***	−0.038***
	(0.005)	(0.005)	(0.005)
Observations	376	376	376
R^2	0.320	0.320	0.439

Notes: $*p < 0.05$; $**p < 0.01$; $***p < 0.001$

when Democrats control the executive, and vice versa. If we model the divided-government term as an interaction term with the count economically significant rules, we find no interaction effect between the two ($\beta = 0.113 + / - 0.423$, $p < 0.79$). In other words, the effect of divided government is not increasing in economically significant rules count, indicating that divided government does not become a more important component of congressional hearings as agencies promulgate more rules.

I recoded the data to consider whether televised hearings correlate with changes in the status of federal rules, which may be withdrawn, suspended, or reconsidered for review before being promulgated in the Code of Federal Regulations. I recoded the dependent variable as a count of the number of rules that each agency withdrew or suspended, and find that televised hearings have no statistically significant effect ($\beta = -0.001$, $p < 0.36$, using the full model specification) on whether or not rules are withdrawn or not. These hearings, while associated with federal rulemaking activity, do not correlate with substantive changes in the rulemaking process. While they generate television time for individual legislators, they do not substantively impact the daily operation of the federal government.

Discussion

In this paper, I have reviewed some evidence showing that Congress is less productive than it has been in the past. As gridlock in Congress has increased, it has become harder for legislators to pass legislation on the floor. At the same time, legislators continue to behave as they did in previous eras with respect to their reelection campaigns, traveling and raising money despite having less apparent importance to policy-making than in the past.

The strategies legislators use to accommodate the competing needs of their individual reelections and the demands of their party leadership continue to evolve. Here, I have suggested that actions legislators take to publicize the activities of the bureaucracy have some attractive features: they allow legislators some airtime upon which they can later campaign, but they are sufficiently minor to the overall process that they do not endanger the party's brand or the fundamental actions of government. I find that while Congress publicizes the activities it takes to monitor the federal agencies to a greater degree as those agencies become more important to the overall rulemaking process, the net effect of these hearings is not to stymie the rulemaking process.

This finding is consistent with the argument that legislators are single-minded seekers of reelection who must increasingly act as an organized group per the demands of their party leadership and of the preferences of the Speaker of the House. In response to this, legislators have begun developing technically minor procedural habits that raise their individual profiles without taking much responsibility for the nature of the party brand. Such activities, as televised hearings surely are, are likely to grow in importance as legislators seek to maneuver the conflicting demands of individual representation and collective action on the House floor.

The anecdotal contents of each of the hearings I discussed here concerned activity conducted on behalf of legislators and congressional committees by the Government Accountability Office (GAO), which experienced a significant staffing reduction under the Gingrich speakership but has recently begun expanding. The nature and content of those investigations will likely grow in prominence for congressional activity as individual legislators pursue new profit strategies on their own, for individual legislators can theoretically commission the GAO to investigate any policy implementation in the federal government on an ad hoc basis.

Some recent evidence suggests that legislators effectively lobby the bureaucracy to reverse certain policy outcomes on behalf of their constituents (Ritchie and You 2016). Further work will consider the temporal and polarization-related components of increasing effort by individual legislators on behalf of their constituents. As the bureaucracy continues to expand as a share of overall federal activity, and as individual legislators and the committee system decline, dyadic representation between legislators and constituents will increasingly be defined by how the bureaucracy represents the interests of individual legislators who are slowly adapting their tool kit to the modern era.

Appendix: Executive Agencies and Committees that Oversee Them

Table 9.3. Executive Agencies and Congressional Committees with Oversight of Them

Federal Agency	House Committee(s)
Architectural and Transportation Barriers Compliance Board	Transportation and HUD
Department of Homeland Security	Homeland Security
Department of Commerce	Commerce–Justice–Science
Department of Defense	Armed Services Committee
Department of Energy	Energy–Water
Department of the Interior	Interior–Environment
Department of Justice	Judiciary
Department of Labor	Labor
Department of Transportation	Transportation–HUD
Department of the Treasury	Financial Services
Department of Veterans Affairs	Veterans Affairs
Education Department	Labor–HHS–Education
Equal Employment Opportunity Coalition	Commerce–Justice–Science
Environmental Protection Agency	Interior–Environment

Federal Agency	House Committee(s)
Federal Emergency Management Agency	Homeland Security
General Services Administration	Financial Services–General Government
Health and Human Services Department (HHS)	Labor–HHS–Education
Housing and Urban Development Department (HUD)	Transportation–HUD
Office of Personnel Management (OPM)	Financial Services–General Government
Pension Benefit Guaranty Corporation	Labor–HHS–Education
Railroad Retirement Board	Labor–HHS–Education
Small Business Administration	Small Business
Social Security Administration	Ways and Means
State Department	State–Foreign Operations
United States Department of Agriculture (USDA)	Agriculture

Notes

1. Emmarie Huetteman, "House Calls Off Vote to Impeach I.R.S. Chief in Favor of Formal Hearing," *New York Times,* September 15, 2016, available at http://www.nytimes.com /2016/09/16/us/politics/house-impeach-irs-john-koskinen.html?_r=1.

2. See, e.g., Government Accountability Office, "IRS Return Selection: Wage and Investment Division Should Define Audit Objectives and Refine Other Internal Controls," December 17, 2015, available at http://www.gao.gov/assets/680/674313.pdf.

3. See, e.g., Brent Smith, "Republicans Cave on IRS Impeachment—Just as They Always Do," September 18, 2016, available at http://rightwingnews.com/column-2/republicans -cave-irs-impeachment-just-always/.

4. See Poole and Rosenthal 2001 on the subject of measuring congressional polarization.

5. DW-NOMINATE data gathered from Voteview (voteview.com). Congressional productivity statistics from *Vital Statistics on Congress;* see https://www. brookings.edu/wp -content/uploads/2016/07/Vital-Statistics-Full-Data-Set.pdf.

6. Data from "agency rule list" pages are available at https://www.reginfo.gov/public/do /eAgendaMain?.

7. 5 U.S.C., § 801–808, 1996.

8. See, e.g., Stuart Shapiro, "The Congressional Review Act, Rarely Used and (Almost Always) Unsuccessful," *The Hill,* April 17, 2015, available at http://thehill.com/blogs /pundits-blog/lawmaker-news/239189-the-congressional-review-act-rarely-used-and -almost-always.

9. For an example, see *Congressional Research Services* RL31835: "Reorganization of the House of Representatives: Modern Reform Efforts," October 20, 2003, available at https://archives-democrats-rules.house.gov/archives/RL31835.pdf.

10. Available at C-SPAN: "State-Based Health Care Exchanges," https://www.c-span.org/video/?415234-1/hearing-reviews-report-health-state-based-exchanges.

11. This exchange takes place from approximately 1:07:08 until approximately 1:10:00 of the hearing linked previously.

12. Most likely, the hearing in question refers specifically to the rules being passed collectively as the Nondiscrimination in Health Programs and Activities bundle, whose final language entered the Code of Federal Regulations on May 13, 2016. HHS Press Office, "For Immediate Release: HHS Finalizes Rule to Improve Health Equity under the Affordable Care Act," available at http://www.hhs.gov/about/news/2016/05/13/hhs-finalizes-rule-to-improve-health-equity-under-affordable-care-act.html.

13. See Government Accountability Office, February 23, 2016, "Patient Protection and Affordable Care Act: CMS Should Act to Strengthen Enrollment Controls and Manage Fraud Risk," available at https://www.gao. gov/assets/680/675340.pdf.

14. While this specific definition was made permanent in the Code of Federal Regulations in 1993 by Executive Order 12866, it had been standing practice since the Reagan administration (Croley 2003).

15. The data in question are available in raw format at http://www.reginfo.gov/public/do/eoPackageMain.

16. This organization is responsible for monitoring compliance with the Americans with Disabilities Act.

17. The archive I use is available at https://www.c-span.org/video/?420857-1/span-video-library.

References

Balla, S. J. 2000. "Legislative Organization and Congressional Review of Agency Regulations." *Journal of Law, Economics, & Organization* 16 (2): 424–48.

Boatright, Robert. 2013. *Getting Primaried: The Changing Politics of Congressional Primary Challenges.* Ann Arbor: University of Michigan Press.

Boatright, R., M. Malbin, M. Rozell, and C. Wilcox. 2012. Interest Groups and Advocacy Organizations after BCRA. In *The Election after Reform: Money, Politics, and the Bipartisan Campaign Reform Act,* edited by M. Malbin. Lanham, MD: Rowman & Littlefield, 112–38.

Bruff, Harold. 1988. "Presidential Management of Agency Rulemaking." *George Washington Law Review* 57 (3): 533–95.

Cox, G., and M. McCubbins. 1993. *Legislative Leviathan: Party Government in the House.* Cambridge: Cambridge University Press.

Cox, Gary, and Mathew McCubbins. 2005. *Setting the Agenda: Responsible Party Government in the U.S. House of Representatives.* Cambridge: Cambridge University Press.

Croley, Steven. 2003. "White House Review of Agency Rulemaking: An Empirical Investigation." *University of Chicago Law Review* 70 (3): 821–85.

Deardorff, Alan, and Richard Hall. 2006. "Lobbying as a Legislative Subsidy." *American Political Science Review* 1 (1): 69–84.

Docter, Sharon, William Dutton, and Anita Elberse. 1999. "An American Democracy Network: Factors Shaping the Future of On-Line Political Campaigns." *Parliamentary Affairs* 52 (3): 535–52.

Drutman, Lee. 2015. *The Business of America Is Lobbying: How Corporations Became Politicized and Politics Became More Corporate.* London: Oxford University Press.

Feigenbaum, James, and Cameron Shelton. 2013. "The Vicious Cycle: Fundraising and Perceived Viability in US Presidential Primaries." *Quarterly Journal of Political Science* 8: 1–40.

Frantzich, S. 1979. "Computerized Information Technology in the U. S. House of Representatives." *Legislative Studies Quarterly* 4 (2): 255–80.

Grant, J., and N. Kelly. 2008. "Legislative Productivity in the U.S. Congress, 1789–2004." *Political Analysis* 16 (3): 303–23.

Grimmer, Justin, Solomon Messing, and Sean Westwood. 2012. "How Words and Money Cultivate a Personal Vote: The Effect of Legislator Credit Claiming." *American Political Science Review* 106 (4): 703–19.

Howell, William, Scott Adler, Charles Cameron, and Charles Riemann. 2000. "Divided Government and the Legislative Productivity of Congress, 1945–94." *Legislative Studies Quarterly* 25 (2): 285–312.

Huber, Gregory. 2007. *The Craft of Bureaucratic Neutrality: Interests and Influence in Governmental Regulation of Occupational Safety.* Cambridge: Cambridge University Press.

Krasno, Jonathan, and Daniel Seltz. 2000. *Buying Time: Television Advertising in the 1998 Congressional Elections.* Washington, DC: Brennan Center for Justice.

Krehbiel, Keith, and John Wright. 1983. "The Incumbency Effect in Congressional Elections: A Test of Two Explanations." *American Journal of Political Science* 27 (1): 140–57.

Lawrence, Eric, Forrest Maltzman, and Paul Wahlbeck. 2001. "The Politics of Speaker Cannon's Committee Assignments." *American Journal of Political Science* 45 (3): 551–62.

Leal, David. 2002. "Home Is Where the Heart Is." *American Politics Research* 30 (3): 265–84.

Lee, Daniel, Enrico Moretti, and Matthew Butler. 2014. "Do Voters Affect or Elect Policies? Evidence from the U.S. House." *Quarterly Journal of Economics* 119 (3): 807–59.

Mayhew, David. 1974. *Congress: The Electoral Connection.* New Haven, CT: Yale University Press.

Parmelee, J. H. 2013. "The Agenda-Building Function of Political Tweets." *New Media & Society,* 1–17. http://nms.sagepub.com/cgi/doi/10.1177/1461444813487955.

Poole, Keith T., and Howard Rosenthal. 2001. "D-Nominate after 10 Years: A Comparative Update to Congress: A Political-Economic History of Roll-Call Voting." *Legislative Studies Quarterly* 26 (1): 5–29. http://www.jstor.org/stable/440401.

Ritchie, Melinda, and Hye Young You. 2016. "Legislators as Lobbyists." *Semantic Scholar.* https://www.semanticscholar.org/paper/Legislators-as-Lobbyists-Ritchie-You/6b1cb8c8d 338ee9439ebe2c44b62f01a6dca6b49.

Roberts, Jason, and Steven Smith. 2003. "Procedural Contexts, Party Strategy, and Conditional Party Voting in the U.S. House of Representatives, 1971–2000." *American Journal of Political Science* 47 (2): 305–17.

Schultz Bressman, Lisa, and Michael Vandenbergh. 2006. "Inside the Administrative State: A Critical Look at the Practice of Presidential Control." *Michigan Law Review* 105 (1): 47–99.

Webb Yackee, Jason, and Susan Webb Yackee. 2009. "Administrative Procedures and Bureaucratic Performance: Is Federal Rule-Making "Ossified?" *Journal of Public Administration Research and Theory* 20 (2): 1–22.

Yackee, Susan Webb. 2006. "Sweet-Talking the Fourth Branch: The Influence of Interest Group Comments on Federal Agency Rulemaking." *Journal of Public Administration Research and Theory* 16 (1): 103–24.

———. 2011. "The Politics of Ex Parte Lobbying: Preproposal Agenda Building and Blocking During Agency Rulemaking." *Journal of Public Administration Research and Theory* 22 (2): 1–21.

Discussion Questions

1. Why is Congress thought to be "less productive" in the modern era? Is an unproductive Congress good for congresspeople? Doesn't that mean they don't have to work as hard?

2. Why would we think of lobbyists as providing a "substitute" for legislative activity? What does a lobbyist do, anyway?

3. Is it good or bad for American democracy that legislators are spending their time on activities that are ultimately less "productive" than they were in the past?

Appointment Politics and the Ideological Composition of the Judiciary

Edward H. Stiglitz

SCHOLARS HAVE ADVANCED A WIDE range of theories regarding the role of Senate confirmation in judicial appointments. In this article, I directly test the predictions of these models using a novel measure of the ideology of judges on the U.S. Courts of Appeals. The main results indicate that the filibuster and majority party have predominated in appointment politics. Prompted by recent events, I also conduct a simulation-based exercise to examine the ideological composition of the judiciary under a confirmation regime in which the filibuster is not present. This exercise suggests that the Senate filibuster induces moderation in judicial appointments; the elimination of the filibuster is likely to result in a more contentious, if less dilatory, confirmation process and a more polarized judiciary.

Introduction

Then professor Elena Kagan may have been right when she noted that Senate confirmation hearings sometimes take on "an air of vacuity and farce" (1995). But the confirmation *process*—the constitutionally required advice-and-consent procedure, as distinguished from the hearing itself—importantly influences the composition of the judiciary. Or so senators appear to believe. This much is evident by the impassioned debate over whether to eliminate the filibuster with respect to judicial appointments in 2005, and in Senator Reid's decision to follow through with that threat for many judicial appointments.[1]

Over recent years, students of Congress and the judiciary have developed sophisticated theories of the advice-and-consent process (Epstein and Segal 2005). The pioneering theories posited that congressional preferences systematically influenced the nature of judicial appointees. In subsequent efforts, scholars developed refined theories of congressional influence, focusing variously on specific Senate institutions: for example, the "blue slip" practice in which senators from a nominee's state can submit a favorable or unfavorable opinion of the nominee (Jacobi 2005), the floor median (Moraski and Shipan 1999), the filibuster (Rohde and Shepsle 2007), and the majority party (Cox and McCubbins 2005; Primo, Binder, and Maltzman 2008).[2]

But which of these theories holds merit? It is possible to find support for the importance of each of these Senate institutions in the cases of specific appointments. A more systematic assessment, however, has been elusive. Consider, for instance, the role of the filibuster in judicial appointments, the most hotly contested institution in appointment politics, and a topic of pressing importance given the recent (partial) demise of the filibuster. Existing empirical studies of judicial appointments either (1) do not analyze the filibuster as a potential constraint on judicial appointments, (2) do not compare the predictions of a model with a filibuster to the predictions from a model without the filibuster, or (3) rely on indirect tests of the models' implications. In fact, among the many articles on judicial nominations, only Johnson and Roberts (2005) and Primo, Binder, and Maltzman (2008) examine the role of the filibuster empirically.[3] Much the same can be said for the other theories of judicial appointments.

This article provides a direct comparison of the predictions from various theories of judicial appointments. In particular, I ask, Which appointment model, or hybrid of models, best predicts the observed ideology of judges on the U.S. Courts of Appeals? In its comprehensive focus, the article thus follows Primo, Binder, and Maltzman's (2008) effort to empirically test a wide range of judicial selection models. The difference between the current effort and Primo, Binder, and Maltzman's is that I offer a direct comparison of the models' predictions. I project the models' predictions onto an ideological space and compare these predictions with the estimated ideology of judges. By contrast, Primo, Binder, and Maltzman provide an indirect test of the models that correlates variation in the size of the gridlock interval implied by a model with the failure rate of nominees.

The direct approach offered in this essay offers advantages—and also some disadvantages—relative to the indirect approach. Centrally, the direct approach provides a closer connection between the theoretical models and the data. A second important benefit of this direct approach is that it allows us to examine a conventional hypothesis about the influence of the confirmation process on the judiciary. Using the word "fair" instead of "moderate," for instance, Senator Leahy observed on the Senate floor that "[the filibuster] help[s] ensure that life-time appointees have wide, rather than narrow, support because consensus nominees are more likely to be fair than extremely divisive ones" (*Congressional Record* 2003). Using a direct approach, I inspect Senator Leahy's suggestion, a task that is infeasible through an indirect method. The primary disadvantage of this direct approach is that it requires developing a measure of judicial ideology for the courts of appeals. To do so, I must commit to several assumptions that do not burden the indirect approach. As I will discuss, both the indirect approach and the direct approach of this article rely on different contestable but plausible assumptions.

The main results from this empirical exercise indicate that over the period studied, the filibuster and majority party predominate in appointment politics. These results correspond to a striking degree with those from the earlier indirect effort to test theories of appointment politics—striking, that is, given that the approaches have different foundations and rely on different assumptions. I also examine a counterfactual confirmation regime in which the filibuster is not present. The results from this exercise suggest that consistent with Senator Leahy's statement, the filibuster appears to have promoted moderate judicial appointments.

This article proceeds as follows: First, I identify the predictions of the prevailing models of judicial appointments. Second, I describe the data and measurement approach of the article and validate the measure of judicial ideology. Third, I report results from tests of the models' predictions. Fourth, I conduct an extension involving a counterfactual exercise to examine the role of the filibuster in shaping the ideological composition of the judiciary. My discussion and conclusions follow.

Models of Appointment Politics

Scholars have developed at least four central models of the role of the confirmation process in judicial appointments: a model of "blue slips," a Senate median model, a filibuster model, and a majority-party model.[4] It is also possible to construct hybrids of these models: it may be, for example, that both blue slips and the filibuster matter. But at its core, each model identifies a key player or set of players in the Senate that the president must satisfy to win Senate confirmation. The structure of the interaction is similar across models, and I first briefly describe this general setting. I then apply this structure to each of the main theories.

Consider a legislature with N-odd members. I make the common simplifying assumption of a one-dimensional policy space, $X \subset R$. Let xi represent the ideal point of member i. Denote the ideal point of the median in the legislature as xm. Member i's preference over a judge with policy preference x is given by $f(x, xi)$, continuous, symmetric, and strictly decreasing in the distance between x and xi.[5] The general interaction in the appointments game is governed by the following sequence:

- Nature removes one member of the court, creating a vacancy, and establishes a status quo reversion policy, xq, implied by the vacation.
- The president proposes a judicial nominee, $xn \in X$.
- Each pivot decides whether to veto the nominee. If any pivot exercises the veto, no new member is appointed to the court, xq prevails as the policy outcome, and the game ends. Otherwise:
- Senators vote on the president's proposal and the game ends.

Beyond this general structure, the appointments models also tend to assume an environment of complete and perfect information, and researchers employ subgame perfection as the solution concept. Further, researchers generally assume that both the Senate and the president care about the policy preferences of the nominee, as such, rather than the downstream implications of confirming one or another nominee for the body median.[6] I follow this focus on the preferences of the nominee. The central differences among the models rest in the identities of the key pivot players.

The blue-slip model refers to an informal norm in the Senate Judiciary Committee that allows home-state senators to veto the appointments (Jacobi 2005). Thus, if an appointee hails from Virginia, the two Virginia senators have a say over whether the appointment goes through (Primo, Binder, and Maltzman 2008). This convention applies both to senators of the same party as the president and to senators of the opposing party.[7]

Scholars have also developed theories based on formal Senate rules. The foundational model is premised on the fact that a majority of senators must support a nominee for confirmation. Thus, the majoritarian model, or the median model, maintains that the median senator holds a veto over possible judicial appointments (Moraski and Shipan 1999). More recently, scholars have examined the roles of other Senate rules.

Most prominently, scholars have developed models in which the filibuster pivots—the fortieth and sixtieth senators—have a veto over possible appointments. The identity of these pivots is derived from the cloture rule, which requires a three-fifths majority to stop a filibuster (Rohde and Shepsle 2007). Notice that the recent filibuster reform removes these pivots in the context of lower-court nominations.

A fourth main perspective focuses on partisan politics. In particular, it is possible that the majority party holds a veto over appointments. This party influence is modeled by endowing the median of the majority party with pivotal status. This operationalization ensures that a "majority of the majority" approves of any appointment (Cox and McCubbins 2005). This partisan perspective on Senate decision-making has received considerable empirical support in the context of ordinary legislation (for example, Cox and McCubbins 2005; Stiglitz and Weingast 2010).[8]

It is also possible to formulate hybrids of these models. A hybrid model might, for instance, endow both the filibuster pivots *and* the home-state senators with vetoes over appointments. In the empirical tests below, I consider several salient hybrid models, following Primo, Binder, and Maltzman (2008).

The basic algorithm for solving these appointments games is straightforward. First, identify the most liberal and most conservative pivots. These pivots *bind* on a president's appointments. Second, if the status quo is located between the president and any binding pivot, the president must nominate someone with policy preferences equivalent to the status quo; any other appointment provokes a veto by a pivot. Third, if a non-status-quo appointment is possible, the president nominates the individual with policy preferences closest to the president's own views who also makes all of the binding pivots at least indifferent between the nominee and the status quo.

The results from this simple algorithm represent the models' equilibrium predictions regarding appointees' policy preferences.[9] A bit of algebra shows that these models partition the policy space (fig. 10.1).

$$x_n^*(x_q) = \begin{cases} x_q & \text{if} & x_L \leq x_q \leq x_R & \text{region} & 1 \\ 2x_L - x_q & \text{if} & (2x_L - x_p) < x_q < x_L & \text{region} & 2 \\ 2x_R - x_q & \text{if} & (2x_R - x_p) > x_q > x_R & \text{region} & 2 \\ x_p & \text{if} & (2x_L - x_p) \geq x_q & \text{region} & 3 \\ x_p & \text{if} & (2x_R - x_p) \leq x_q & \text{region} & 3 \end{cases}$$

Fig. 10.1: Equations for different equilibrium predictions.

Where x_q is the status quo, x_L is the ideal point of the binding left pivot and x_R is the ideal point of the binding right pivot, and x_p is the president's ideal point. The difference between the appointments models is in the identities of these left- and right-binding pivots. Thus, region 1 represents a "grid-lock interval": any appointment other than one equivalent to the status quo provokes a veto by at least one veto-wielding constitutional actor. Region 2 represents a "semiconstrained" region of the policy space, over which the president is able to move the appointment toward his ideal position but must moderate the appointment to satisfy a pivot. Finally, region 3 represents an "unconstrained" interval of the policy space, in which the president is able to appoint his most preferred nominee. As I will explain in detail, my objective is to examine the relationship between each theoretical model's predictions and observed appointee preferences.

Data and Measurement

My data derive from appointments to the U.S. Courts of Appeals (CoA). Nominations to the CoA represent an ideal testing ground for theories of judicial appointments. The CoA is sufficiently important that senators and interest groups take keen interest in an appointment. Priscilla Owen, a George W. Bush nominee to the Fifth Circuit, for example, was one of the central figures in the 2005 filibuster row, in part due to interest-group mobilization by pro-choice organizations (for example, Perine 2006). Likewise, three contested and delayed appointments to the D.C. Circuit provided the final impetus for the 2013 filibuster reform. Yet unlike the nominations to the Supreme Court, the CoA contains a sufficient number of appointees each term to facilitate empirical analysis. Whereas presidents, on average, appoint one or two Supreme Court justices per four-year term, recent presidents appoint about forty circuit judges per four-year term.

The central challenge to testing appointment theories on CoA appointments is that no appropriate ready-made measure of lower-court judges' policy preferences exists. My basic approach is a familiar one: separately develop a measure of lower-court-judge policy preferences and then estimate a mapping from this measure of judges' preferences to a preexisting measure of congressional policy preferences. This is the approach of the widely used Judicial Common Space (JCS) scores (Epstein et al. 2007); unfortunately, the JCS scores cannot be used in the current study because the JCS measure of CoA preferences is based on an assumed model of judicial appointments (Giles et al. 2001). I first detail my measurement approach; I then discuss several key assumptions; finally, I conduct a series of validation tests.

Consider first the approach to measuring lower-court judges' preferences. I follow Epstein and Segal (2005) and use the percent of liberal opinions on civil rights, First Amendment, and criminal cases to characterize the policy preferences of an appointee.[10] I focus on appointments initiated in 1976 or later to avoid complications raised by the 1975 modification of the Senate cloture threshold. The appointments analysis extends to 2001, the last year covered by the available data. All told, the data set contains 218 nominations, with the average judge's ideology determined by 51 relevant cases.[11]

After developing this measure of lower-court judges' preferences, I connect it with preexisting measures of congressional policy preferences. I use Bailey's (2012; see also 2007) data to characterize policy preferences of senators and the president. Of course, the CoA measure of ideology is not on the same scale as Bailey's common-space estimates. I use a bridging technique to project the CoA measure of ideology onto Bailey's common-space scale (see Poole and Rosenthal 1997; Shor, McCarty, and Berry 2008). A total of fourteen judges served on the CoA and also on the Supreme Court or in the House or Senate.[12] Ideally, a larger number of judges would satisfy the bridging condition; unfortunately, sparsity of data is endemic to this area of research. The bridge used for the JCS scores, for example, is based on fifteen observations; Johnson and Roberts's (2005) empirical application is based on twenty-eight observations. All the same, this sparsity increases the importance of validation. I estimate the bridging coefficients by regressing the judges' common-space policy pref-

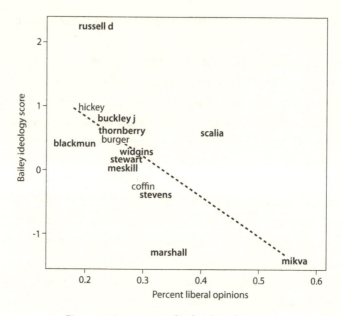

Fig. 10.2: A measure of judicial preferences.

erences against the measure of their preferences derived from behavior on the CoA.[13]

To visualize the construction of this measure, I plot the Bailey scores against the opinion behavior of the fourteen judges in the bridging set (fig. 10.2). I display each observation using the last name (and first initial if the last name is ambiguous) of the judge. The dashed line represents the fi (that is, the dummy variable) from the bridging regression. The first point to observe from this plot is that the model fi is reasonably linear, and the model appears to capture an underlying relationship between these two measures of ideology. By applied standards, the Bailey scores and the opinion behavior appear to represent a common latent attribute of the judges.

But this procedure invokes a number of assumptions, and it is important to validate the measure. First, the procedure assumes that a measure of percent liberal cases in one circuit is comparable to the percent liberal cases in another circuit; that is, *x* percent liberal represents the same policy preferences regardless of whether the judge sits on, for example, the Ninth Circuit or the Seventh Circuit. However, forum shopping, in which parties seek to have their cases heard in sympathetic forums, threatens this assumption.[14] Without knowing the prevalence of forum shopping, it is difficult to gauge the extent to which the activity influences the measure of CoA judge ideology. Second, we must trust the validity of the underlying Bailey scores themselves, as comprehensively detailed in Bailey's original article. Third, we must believe the transformation from percent liberal opinions to the Bailey common space. Each of these points is, to some extent, a genuine assumption—that is, a premise not possible to directly verify at present. However, I attempt to validate the measure in a variety of ways below. To the extent these points represent highly unrealistic assumptions, it will be difficult to validate the measures. It is also important to note that the purpose of developing this measure is to test a series of models. In this sense, the operative concern is not that the measure is imperfect. Instead, the relevant concern is that some form of bias in the measure unfairly privileges one or another theoretical model.

Now consider several approaches to validation. Focus first on individual judges. Does the transformed score correspond to legal observers' views of each judge's ideology? To examine this question, I mine the current *Almanac of the Federal Judiciary (AFJ)*.[15] This publication includes background information on each federal judge: education, dates of appointments, descriptions of key cases, and so on. It also includes a section in almost all entries that describes the "Lawyers' Evaluation" of the judge. In this section, the almanac summarizes interviews with lawyers who have argued before the judge. The interviews often focus on the judge's courtroom demeanor: for example, "She is a no-nonsense questioner." But most interviews also touch on the ideology of the judge. For example, one lawyer said of Judge Easterbrook, a highly regarded judge on the Seventh Circuit, "He is conservative." Based on these almanac entries, I develop a simple representation of lawyers' views of judges: the number of times the judge is referred to as "conservative" less the number of times he or she is referred to as "liberal." I then classify a judge as "conservative," if he is in the top third of this metric; "moderate" if in the middle third; and "liberal" if in the bottom third.

Transformed scores approximate lawyers' views of judges (fig. 10.3). There, I plot the mean score for judges whom lawyers classify as liberal, moderate, and conservative. The dot represents the mean score; the gray bar represents +/− one standard error. The mean score of a liberal judge is about −.5; the mean of a moderate is about 0; and the mean of a conservative is about .5. It is also the case that the mean score for each class of judge—liberal, moderate, conservative— is statistically distinguishable from the mean score for every other class of judge.

EDWARD H. STIGLITZ

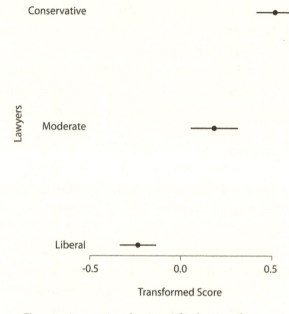

Fig. 10.3: Lawyers' evaluations of judges' preferences.

This pattern suggests that transformed scores bear a meaningful relationship with the evaluations of those who know judges best—the lawyers who argue before them.

Another question is whether the transformed judges' scores relate in a meaningful way to the scores of other institutional actors, such as senators. Using the novel measure of judicial ideology, I first calculate the median judicial ideology in each circuit. I then plot these medians alongside the median policy scores for Senate Democrats, Senate Republicans, and members of the Supreme Court (fig. 10.4), as estimated by Bailey (2012). I focus on the medians in the 106th Congress (1999–2001) to provide a relatable snapshot of preferences across institutions.[16] I denote circuit medians with black points and the institutional references with gray points.

The figure suggests that the circuit medians align with the institutional references in a sensible way. The Second, Third, and Ninth Circuits have the most liberal medians, around the location of the median Senate Democrat. The Fifth, Seventh, Eighth, and Eleventh Circuits have the most conservative medians, near the location of the median Senate Republican. The Supreme Court median is near the center of the distribution, or somewhat to the right, and close to the

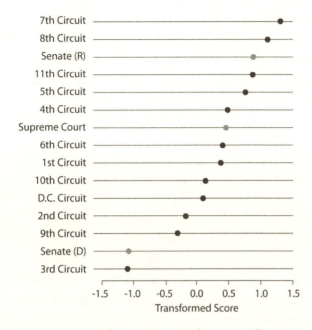

Fig. 10.4: Institutional comparison: medians in 106th Congress.

medians in the First, Fourth, and Sixth Circuits. These points correspond to the popular views of the preferences in the circuits and largely corroborate the results from previous efforts to generate common-space measures of lower-court judges' preferences (Epstein et al. 2007).

Together, these validation exercises indicate both that the judicial ideology scores bear a meaningful relationship to observers' assessments of judges' preferences—that is, to lawyers' evaluations—and that the scores sensibly relate to preexisting measures of ideology in other institutions. In the empirical applications below, I use this new measure of judicial ideology to directly test predictions of models of appointments.

Application: Comparing Models of Judicial Appointments

The empirical strategy is straightforward. I start with the most basic institutional model, with only a veto at the Senate median. I then consider adding, in sequence, various Senate institutions: the blue slip, the filibuster, and political parties. After evaluating the addition of each institution, I then consider multiple institutions: adding the blue slip to the filibuster, for example. The question at each stage is whether adding the institution in question improves the ability to predict observed appointee ideology.

I conduct these tests using decompositions. The appointee ideology predicted by theory i can be decomposed into the corresponding predicted appointee ideology of theory j plus the deviations between the predictions of theory i and theory j.[17] That is, $pi = pj + (pi - pj)$, where pi is the prediction for theory i and similarly for theory j. I then estimate,

$$xn = \alpha + \gamma pj + \beta(pi - pj) + \varepsilon.$$

Throughout, our focus is on the coefficient β, which will be positive and significant if the institution represented in theory i influences judicial appointments, beyond the influence of the institution represented in theory j. For instance, if theory j implicates the median and theory i implicates the filibuster, then β will be positive if the filibuster influences appointments—in this case, $pi - pj$ helps explain observed appointee ideology. By contrast, β will be 0 if the influence of the Senate median fully captures the data-generating process and the filibuster is irrelevant—in this case, $pi - pj$ does not help explain observed appointee ideology.[18]

In total, I consider eight theoretical appointment models: the median model (M), the filibuster model (F), the majority-party model (P), the blue-slip model (BS), the majority-party and filibuster hybrid model (PF), the blue-slip and filibuster hybrid model (BF), the blue-slip and party model (BP), and the filibuster and blue-slip and party hybrid model (BFP).

I follow the existing literature and adopt a circuit-based conception of the status quo policy (Krehbiel 2007; Moraski and Shipan 1999; Snyder and Weingast 2000).[19] In his study of the Supreme Court, Krehbiel, for example, argues that status quo is the median of the body before the vacation (2007). This conception of the status quo rests on the idea that whatever policy the court created before the vacancy remains in place. Another possibility, adopted by Snyder and Weingast (2000), is that the prevailing status quo policy is given by the median of the body after the vacancy is created. This conception of the status quo, therefore, involves the body actively revising policies after the vacancy is created. In general, it is not clear which of these two conceptions is correct. However, the practical difference between the two conceptions is trivial: the correlation between the previous median status quo and the current median approach is .98. Here, I report results based on the previous median approach, under the view that it typically takes years to adjust policy through litigation.[20]

Consider now the median model and possible institutional augmentations. The results indicate that the median model is easily improved upon (reported in the left panel of fig. 10.5). I plot the relevant β coefficient on the deviations implicated by each institution: the solid dot represents the point estimate, and the lines extending from the circle represent the 95 percent confidence interval. I array the coefficient relevant to each institution next to the abbreviation for the institution. Adding the filibuster, the figure demonstrates, produces significantly improved predictions. The coefficient on deviations predicted by the filibuster is positive and significant. Similarly, adding a majority-party veto to the median model produces a significant improvement over the simple median model. The blue-slip model, on the other hand, returns with an insignificant coefficient, suggesting that the blue slip does not influence appointments once we account for the floor median.

One interpretation of the blue-slip result, however, is that measurement error results in an attenuated coefficient. I address this possibility by instrumenting for the theories' predictions, a standard solution to the errors-in-variable problem. In particular, I instrument for the theories' predictions using the year of appointment and circuit of appointment, variables measured without error and hence suitable instruments in this context. The results from this exercise (reported in the right panel of fig. 10.5) suggest that even the institution of the blue slip helps predict appointee ideology. The coefficients relevant to the filibuster and majority party likewise shift away from zero, suggesting that these coefficients were likewise attenuated in the ordinary-least-squares (OLS) regressions.

The median thus appears insufficient to describe the appointments process. It remains unclear, however, which combination of institutions best describes the appointments process. To address this question, I now consider, in turn, the filibuster, party, and blue-slip models as base-lines. I then augment each of these institutions with each of the remaining institutions, thus examining the possible combinations of Senate institutions.

The results from this exercise (reported in fig. 10.6) suggest that once we account for the filibuster or majority party, little is added by considering other institutions. That is, using the filibuster predictions as a baseline, we cannot say

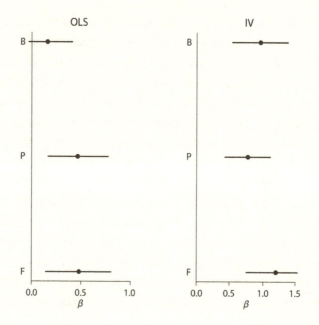

Fig. 10.5: Augmenting the median model. *Notes:* The figure represents the β coefficient associated with adding as possible constraints the filibuster (F), the majority-party median (P), and the blue slip (B) to the median model. A positive β coefficient indicates that adding a constraint generates improved predictions of observed appointee ideology.

that adding majority-party vetoes, or the blue slip, or the blue-slip and majority-party vetoes improves the ability to predict appointee ideology. However, the coefficient on the party-induced deviations is large, with a large standard error, reflecting the small number of deviations implied by party institutions in this context. Indeed, adding party institutions to the filibuster model changes only 15 of 218 observations. The same cannot be said when evaluating the blue-slip institution as the baseline. It is evident (see third panel of fig. 10.6) that adding *any* institution to the blue slip improves performance. These results therefore suggest that the blue slip, standing alone, inadequately describes the then-prevailing appointments process.[21]

Accounting for measurement error clarifies the picture further. Adding party or the blue slip to the filibuster appears unhelpful (fig. 10.7), as earlier, though again we cannot say much about adding parties to the filibuster. Here, though, adding the blue slip *and* the party pivot is now significant, if by a hair. On the other hand (see middle panel of fig. 10.7), this exercise reveals that the majority party standing alone does not appear to describe adequately the appointments

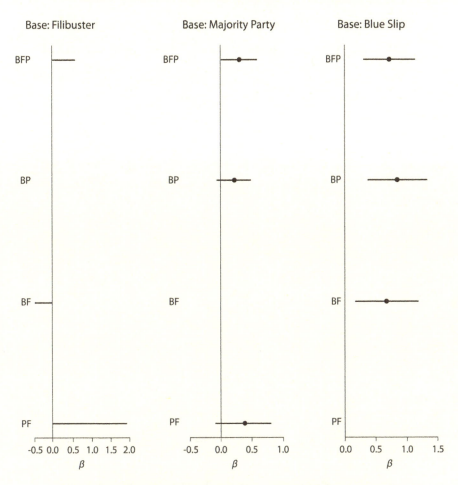

Fig. 10.6: Generating hybrid models (OLS). *Notes:* The β represents the
β coefficients associated with adding as possible constraints combinations
of the filibuster (F), the majority-party median (P), and the blue slip (B) to the β
model (left panel), the majority-party model (center panel), or the blue-slip model
(right panel). A positive β coefficient indicates that adding a constraint
generates improved predictions of observed appointee ideology.

process: adding the institutions of the filibuster or the blue slip (or both) improves model performance. The conclusions with respect to the blue slip do not
change as a result of correcting for measurement error.

The results so far indicate that the filibuster represents the strongest base
model. Including the institution of the blue slip adds little once we have accounted for the filibuster's influence on appointments. Adding a majority-party

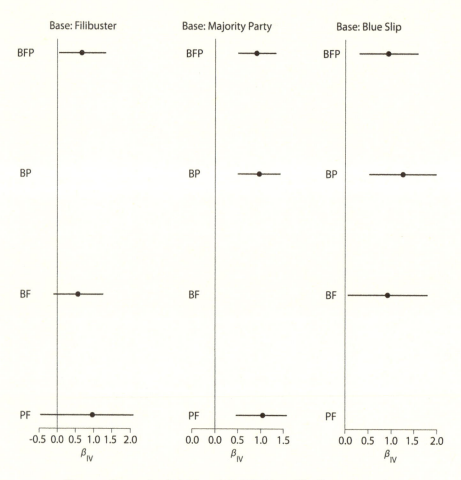

Fig. 10.7: Generating hybrid models (IV). *Notes:* The fi represents the
β coefficient associated with adding as possible constraints combinations
of the filibuster (F), the majority-party median (P), and the blue slip (B) to the fi
model (left panel), the majority party model (center panel), or the blue-slip model
(right panel). A positive β coefficient indicates that adding a constraint
generates improved predictions of observed appointee ideology.

veto, on the other hand, may or may not improve performance: we have only
a large yet imprecisely estimated coefficient to guide us. As a final iteration,
consider adding the blue slip to the model already representing the party *and*
filibuster. That is, once we have the filibuster and majority party, does adding
the blue slip improve model performance? It appears not. In this model, the
coefficient representing deviations implied by the blue slip is a mere .11 with a
standard error of .21

Several conclusions thus emerge from this exercise. First, the blue slip performs poorly. Regardless of baseline model, we cannot say that also including the institution of the blue slip improves model performance.[22] Second, the most apt model almost surely includes the filibuster. Regardless of the baseline model, including the filibuster improves performance. Third, adding partisan institutions to the filibuster produces unclear results. Doing so changes relatively few appointment predictions and results in a suggestively large yet imprecisely estimated coefficient.

The Bork "Break"

Congress observers often lament the contentious nature of confirmation battles. Early eras, it is supposed, operated in a more collegial environment. That is, earlier eras operated under a different appointments model. To examine this possibility, I generate a variable that takes 1 for appointments before 1989 and 0 otherwise. This point of partition follows Primo, Binder, and Maltzman (2008) and reflects observers' view that the failed Bork nomination produced a discontinuity in appointment politics.[23] I then rerun the regressions, this time interacting both pi and $[pj - pi]$ with the Bork period variable. Our central interest is in the coefficient on the interaction with $[pj - pi]$, which informs us whether the influence of deviations implied by pj depends on the Bork period.

The coefficients on these interaction terms suggest that little changed following the failed Bork nomination, results largely in line with previous research efforts (Primo, Binder, and Maltzman 2008). I report the results with respect to the median model and possible institutional augments (fig. 10.8).[24] As indicated by the nonsignificant coefficients (see left panel of fig. 10.8), adding the filibuster appears to have roughly the same influence before and after the Bork nomination. The same can be said for adding partisan institutions or the blue slip. Moreover, here, accounting for measurement error does not appear to matter much (suggested by the right panel in the figure).

Extension: Appointments without the Filibuster

A virtue of the direct approach in this article is that it allows us to question how the ideological composition of the judiciary would change in response to different institutional appointment regimes. The most relevant comparison in-

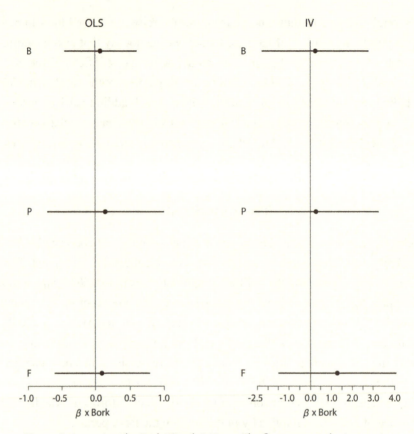

Fig. 10.8: Assessing the Bork "Break." *Notes:* The fi represents the interaction of a post-Bork indicator with the deviations in predicted appointee ideology implied by adding as possible constraints the filibuster (F), the majority-party median (P), and the blue slip (B) to the median model. A non-zero coefficient on the interaction term indicates that a candidate institutional constraint operated differently before or after the failed Bork nomination.

volves appointments with and without the filibuster. Following a long line of largely failed efforts to marginalize the role of the filibuster in Senate politics (see, for example, Gold and Gupta 2005), the Senate dramatically shed the filibuster for most judicial appointments in 2013, raising the natural question of how this reform is likely to influence appointment politics and the composition of the judiciary. With an eye on a filibuster-free future, therefore, we consider how the filibuster has shaped appointment politics in the past.

Many have the sense that the controversial institution of the filibuster, in fact, produces a moderate judiciary. Legal academics have followed this view, arguing that the Senate filibuster helps temper the preferences of extreme presidents (Maltese 2003; McGinnis and Rappaport 2005). Analytically, the intuition is simply that forcing the president to satisfy a more extreme Senate constraint induces him to appoint moderate judges. The appointment that renders the fortieth senator indifferent between the appointment and the status quo is more liberal than the appointment that renders the median senator indifferent. As such, the filibuster compels relatively conservative presidents to nominate more liberal judges than they would under a regime without the filibuster. And just the opposite goes for liberal presidents. This is the intuition.[25] However intuitively appealing, our ability to examine the magnitude of the filibuster's moderating influence has been limited by the absence of data connecting the status quos in the vacated circuits with the preferences of senators and presidents.

I examine Senator Leahy's intuition by using the observed status quo policies to predict the ideology of judicial appointments using models with and without the filibuster. In particular, I consider the predicted appointments from the model with the filibuster constraints as the baseline. I then compare these predictions to the predictions that result from the model with only the median constraint—the model, that is, produced by dropping the filibuster as a possible constraint. Thus, this exercise provides insight into the historically counterfactual of a world without a filibuster—a world that we now enter. Given the observed vacancies between 1976 and 2001, does the ideological profile of appointees depend on the existence of the filibuster?

By the lights of this exercise, the filibuster has had a striking influence on the composition of the judiciary (fig. 10.9). I plot the simulated distribution of 1976–2001 appointments with and without the filibuster. I also include the locations of notable reference points, such as President Clinton's policy preference. The distribution for the predictions of the model with the filibuster, which appears in the solid line, is basically unimodal centered upon a midpoint of zero. It is centered, that is, around the ideal policy of Senator Snowe. Now consider the model without the filibuster. The distribution of predictions for this model, which appears in a dashed line, is bimodal, with one mode just to the right of President Clinton's ideal policy and another just to the left of Senator Frist's ideal policy. This exercise indicates that, consistent with Senator Leahy's idea, the filibuster is a force of moderation in the context of judicial appointments.[26]

It is, in fact, likely that this exercise understates the degree to which the filibuster moderates judicial appointments. The predictions discussed earlier, of

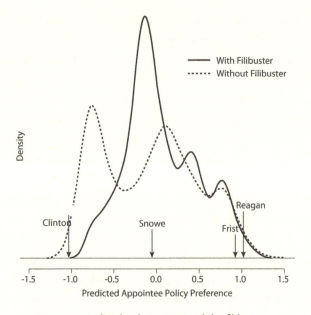

Fig. 10.9: Judicial polarization and the filibuster.

course, derive from observed status quo policies created by retirements under a confirmation regime with the filibuster. The filibuster dampens the incentives for strategic retirements by constraining presidents from appointing ideological judges. Absent the filibuster, judges will have a stronger incentive to retire only when the president is ideologically aligned. This incentive follows both from the stick of the ideological appointments of misaligned presidents and from the carrot of ideological appointments of aligned presidents. An increase in strategic retirements prompted by the elimination of the filibuster threatens to further exacerbate judicial polarization.

Discussion

This article adopts a direct approach to assessing the central models of appointment politics based on a new measure of ideology for judges on the courts of appeals. In particular, I develop a measure of judicial ideology for judges on the courts of appeals and use these measures to compare various appointment models' predictions against the observed appointee ideology. The results support the notion that the filibuster and, quite possibly, majority-party institutions predominate in appointment politics.

Compare these results with the results from Primo, Binder, and Maltzman, to date the most comprehensive effort to test models of judicial appointments. Their results derive from an indirect test of the appointment models' implications that turns on the observation that different models imply different gridlock intervals—intervals, that is, in which the status quo policy cannot be altered without provoking a veto from at least one veto player. Their central hypothesis is "that the larger the gridlock interval, the more likely is any given nomination to be contentious and to fail" (2008, 475). In this manner, their article examines both successful and failed nominations, whereas the present effort contends only with confirmed appointments. Yet, as with all studies, this design invokes a number of assumptions: centrally, that the distribution of status quos is uniform, that presidents have a harder time finding a nominee that satisfies the binding Senate constraints when the size of the gridlock region increases, and that the appropriate appointments model is static. None of these assumptions is self-evidently unproblematic. For example, if judges time their retirements to correspond with ideologically sympathetic presidential administrations, the distribution of status quos is unlikely to be uniform (see, for example, Spriggs and Wahlbeck 1995).

Yet it is striking that the results from the direct exercise in this article align to a considerable extent with those from the indirect exercise in Primo, Binder, and Maltzman. They conclude that "Senate decisions seem disproportionately affected by the preferences of the majority party and potential filibustering senators" (2008, 485). The direct tests of this article, likewise, support the view that the most relevant potential Senate constraints involve the filibuster and majority party. Moreover, as in this article, the constraints involving the filibuster and majority party predominate both before and after Bork's failed appointment. The fact that both articles reach similar conclusions despite using quite different approaches lends credibility to the basic conclusion that the filibuster and party pivots play the central role in appointment politics. Both sets of results also give low marks to the median and blue-slip models, at least in the context of appointments to the U.S. Courts of Appeals.

The ambition of this article was to assess the central theories in circulation. In closing, however, it is worth pausing to reconsider these theories. One important shortcoming of existing theories of judicial selection is that they posit one-period models, as recently emphasized and studied by Jo, Primo, and Sekiya (2013). A central implication of this modeling choice is that senators live with the status quo if they vote down a nominee, a fact that often compels veto players to compromise. However, appointment politics often involves more than one period: indeed, the next presidential election is always just around the corner. The fact that appointments take place in such a setting may influence senators' behavior and hence the president's choices over nominations.

Consider, for example, an unpopular Republican president nominating a judge to the liberal Third or Ninth Circuits. The status quo policies for these circuits may, indeed, be so liberal as to allow the president, in a one-period interaction, to appoint a conservative judge with preferences near the president's. However, in a dynamic setting, the relatively liberal Senate filibuster pivot, for example, may object to such an appointment. Such a liberal pivot may, instead, reason that a Democratic president has a strong chance of winning the next election given the unpopularity of the sitting president. Recognizing this, the unpopular Republican president may moderate his appointment to account for the liberal pivot's expectation of the liberal presidential candidate winning the next election.

It is possible that such dynamic considerations distort our perspective of the relevant pivots. For example, in the simple example mentioned, the appointee will have preferences closer to the status quo than would be predicted by a one-period model that features the true pivots. If we focus on one-period models, therefore, this status quo favoritism may lead us erroneously to infer the predominance of relatively extreme pivots; in reality, the binding pivots have more moderate preferences but operate in a dynamic setting. The manner in which such dynamic considerations influence the appointments process, and our inferences regarding binding pivots, depend on a variety of factors alien to most current models: the probability that the president wins the next election, the amount of time until the next election, the rate at which members discount time periods, and so on. These considerations hold relevance for future research (see, for example, Jo, Primo, and Sekiya 2013).

That said, we have at least one important indication suggesting the results reported in this article do not fall too far astray. The ragged debate over the filibuster with respect to judicial appointments suggests that senators, at least, view the institution as central to appointment politics. It is reasonable to suppose the nature of this debate reflects the fact that the filibuster has exerted a substantial influence over the nature of appointments, the central conclusion supported by the results reported earlier. It is also reasonable to suppose that whatever its faults, the filibuster promoted moderation in the ideological composition of the judiciary.

Appendix

Appointment Politics and the Ideological Composition of the Judiciary

The tables included in this appendix report the results displayed in figures 10.5–10.8 of this article.

Table 10.1. Augmenting the Median Model (fig. 10.5)

	M + F	M + P	M + B
Constant	0.19	0.23	0.22
	(0.05)	(0.05)	(0.05)
γ	0.78	0.65	0.66
	(0.11)	(0.09)	(0.1)
β	0.48	0.47	0.16
	(0.17)	(0.16)	(0.13)
N	218	218	218
R-squared	0.20	0.21	0.18

Notes: The dependent variable is observed judicial ideology. See the main text for interpretation of β (γ is also a coefficient). Estimated with OLS.

Table 10.2. Generating Hybrid Models (fig. 10.6)

	Left			Center			Right		
	F + P	F + B	F + BP	P + F	P + B	P + BP	B + F	B + P	B + FP
Constant	0.14	0.14	0.12	0.19	0.19	0.17	0.1	0.12	0.08
	(0.05)	(0.05)	(0.05)	(0.05)	(0.05)	(0.05)	(0.05)	(0.05)	(0.05)
γ	0.77	0.78	0.81	0.74	0.71	0.77	0.67	0.6	0.7
	(0.11)	(0.12)	(0.12)	(0.11)	(0.1)	(0.11)	(0.12)	(0.1)	(0.11)
β	0.95	0.04	0.21	0.36	0.22	0.3	0.69	0.85	0.73
	(0.52)	(0.21)	(0.2)	(0.23)	(0.14)	(0.14)	(0.26)	(0.24)	(0.21)
N	218	218	218	218	218	218	218	218	218
R-squared	0.2	0.18	0.19	0.21	0.21	0.22	0.13	0.15	0.15

Notes: The dependent variable is observed judicial ideology. See the main text for interpretation of β (γ is also a coefficient). Estimated with OLS.

Table 10.3. Generating Hybrid Models (fig. 10.7)

	Left			Center			Right		
	F + P	F + B	F + BP	P + F	P + B	P + BP	B + F	B + P	B + FP
Constant	0.11	0.06	0.05	0.12	0.09	0.07	0.02	0.04	0.01
	(0.05)	(0.06)	(0.06)	(0.06)	(0.06)	(0.06)	(0.06)	(0.06)	(0.06)
γ	1.23	1.37	1.38	1.18	1.23	1.31	1.35	1.26	1.36
	(0.14)	(0.16)	(0.16)	(0.14)	(0.14)	(0.15)	(0.17)	(0.15)	(0.16)
β	0.97	0.58	0.69	1.05	0.96	0.9	0.93	1.25	0.94
	(0.73)	(0.35)	(0.32)	(0.29)	(0.23)	(0.2)	(0.44)	(0.37)	(0.32)
N	218	218	218	218	218	218	218	218	218

Notes: The dependent variable is observed judicial ideology. See the main text for interpretation of β (γ is also a coefficient). Estimated using 2SLS with year and circuit of appointment as instruments.

Table 10.4. Assessing the Bork "Break" (fig. 10.8)

	OLS			IV		
	M + F	M + P	M + B	M + F	M + P	M + B
Constant	0.25	0.23	0.29	0.17	0.03	0.27
	(0.08)	(0.08)	(0.08)	(0.21)	(0.18)	(0.18)
γ	0.77	0.82	0.69	1.1	1.51	1.41
	(0.15)	(0.15)	(0.15)	(0.53)	(0.54)	(0.55)
β	0.44	0.52	0.12	1.26	2.11	1.28
	(0.25)	(0.19)	(0.21)	(0.91)	(0.63)	(0.82)
Bork	−0.09	0.01	−0.11	−0.23	0.32	−0.34
	(0.11)	(0.1)	(0.11)	(0.3)	(0.24)	(0.28)
γXBork	0.04	−0.25	−0.03	1.11	−0.75	0.13
	(0.23)	(0.19)	(0.21)	(0.91)	(0.78)	(0.92)
βXBork	0.1	0.14	0.08	1.29	0.32	0.23
	(0.35)	(0.43)	(0.27)	(1.42)	(1.5)	(1.28)
	218	218	218	218	218	218
R-Squared	0.21	0.22	0.18			

Notes: The dependent variable is observed judicial ideology. See the main text for interpretation of β (γ is also a coefficient). Left panel estimated with OLS; right panel estimated with 2SLS, using circuit and year of appointment, as well as party of appointing president as instruments.

Notes

I thank David Brady, Josh Chafetz, John Ferejohn, Mo Fiorina, Jonathan Wand, Barry Weingast, and several anonymous reviewers for helpful comments and criticism.

1. On November 21, 2013, Senate Democrats voted to end the filibuster for lower-court nominations; for the moment, the filibuster remains in place for Supreme Court nominations.

2. For a pioneering study, consider Cameron, Cover, and Segal (1990); Epstein et al. (2006) update of Cameron, Cover, and Segal in an insightful study. See also Caldeira and Wright's theory of lobbying in appointment politics (1998).

3. Rohde and Shepsle (2007) also examine the filibuster but do not test their model's predictions.

4. These models, of course, represent only part of the story. As Epstein and Segal (2005) observe, appointee qualifications also matter substantially in appointment politics. My ambition in this study is to test these existing spatial models of advice and consent that center on Senate institutions.

5. The most common utility functions include linear loss and quadratic loss.

6. Krehbiel (2007) is an exception to this trend in that he focuses on how the appointment influences the body median; most scholars focus on the preference of the nominee as the outcome of interest.

7. It is worth noting that Giles, Hettinger, and Peppers (2001) employ this norm as a way to measure judicial ideology. In particular, they assume that any time that a judge hails from a state represented by one senator of the same party as the president, the judge has the same ideal point as that senator; if two senators of the same party as the president represent the state, the judge has an ideal point at the mean of the two senators' ideal points; otherwise, the president appoints a judge with his most preferred ideology. It is important to note that the approach to measurement adopted in this article does not rely on this set of assumptions.

8. For other takes in this partisan line of reasoning, consider, for example, Aldrich and Rohde (1995 and 1998).

9. I do not belabor solutions to these games, as the original papers advancing the various models of appointments generally contained detailed discussions.

10. Limiting the sample to these categories of cases focuses on contentious areas of law in which ideological predisposition is most likely to manifest. Thus, this approach excludes many areas of law, such as contract disputes, that likely carry less information about judicial ideology; including these cases would likely result in a noisier measure of judicial preferences. Opinion data are from a combination of Songer (2008) and Kuersten and Haire (2008).

11. I drop eighteen judges who are represented by fewer than ten relevant cases in the data set; after dropping these—and only these—judges, the data set consists of 218 observations between 1976 and 2001.

12. The fourteen judges and their common-space institutions follow: Buckley (Senate); Coffin (House), Hickey (Senate), Meskill (House), Mikva (House), Russell (Senate), Thornberry (House), Wiggins (House), Blackmun (Supreme Court), Stewart (Supreme Court), Marshall (Supreme Court), Burger (Supreme Court), Stevens (Supreme Court), and Scalia (Supreme Court). Data on judges' professional history from Gryski and Zuk (2008).

13. The intercept shift indicated by this approach is 2.08 (0.63); the slope shift is −6.23 (2.03), where I report standard errors in parentheses. The $R2$ from the bridging regression is .39.

14. Environmentalists, for example, often file suits "against the southwest regional offices of the Forest Service and the Fish and Wildlife Service in Arizona simply to be heard within the Ninth Circuit," which is widely viewed as a left-leaning circuit (Mullins and Mullins 1999, 35). By contrast, the Seventh Circuit has a relatively conservative reputation, and "Plaintiffs will make every effort to avoid filing antitrust cases in district courts located in the Seventh Circuit because the judges of that court are viewed to be pro-defendant in such litigation" (Mullins and Mullins 1999).The fact that right- (left-) leaning cases gravitate toward right (left) circuits suggests that a liberal opinion on a rightist (leftist) court

potentially reflects a more rightist (leftist) ideology than a liberal opinion on a leftist (rightist) circuit. Notice that three-judge panels within circuits tend to be selected randomly, mitigating the concern about comparability within circuits.

15. The current *AFJ* contains entries for 158 judges in my data set; I cannot evaluate judges who have retired.

16. For this fi I include in the circuit medians any judge who served at any time during the Congress. Thus, if a judge left office in 2000, after the start of the 106th Congress, she or he is included in the fi.

17. Notice that the predictions themselves follow from equation. The locations of the president and relevant pivots derive from Bailey (2012); the locations of the status quos reflect the Krehbiel (2007) previous-median approach, using novel scale-consistent measures of judicial ideology as inputs to determine the previous median. Notice that the ideal empirical result for a theoretical model is for both coefficients to be indistinguishable from one.

18. In this context, evaluating the β coefficient is equivalent to conducting an F-test.

19. Notice that although three-judge panels decide most cases, Giles, Hettinger, and Peppers (2001) argue that the circuit median is able to control these panels through en banc review.

20. The previous median is calculated by finding the median of (1) all judges on a given circuit whose first year on the bench was before the appointment of judge X and whose last year on the bench was after the appointment of judge X and, unless the seat is new, (2) the judge who vacated the seat in question.

21. I say "standing alone" but recall that the median is always a potential binding pivot in these models: a majority of senators must support the appointment.

22. Here, I do not consider the median stand-alone model as a baseline. As discussed earlier, adding any institution to the median improves performance.

23. For comparability, I follow Primo, Binder, and Maltzman's (2008) choice of dividing the data on January 1, 1989. Note that Bork's appointment failed in October 1987. See Epstein et al. (2006) for evidence of a systematic break in confirmation voting behavior following Bork's nomination. Notice, however, that Epstein et al.'s study focuses on votes, whereas this study focuses on a measure of appointee ideology. Also, they focus on the Supreme Court, whereas this study focuses on the courts of appeals.

24. For the remainder of the results, which closely resemble those reported in fig. 10.8, contact the author.

25. Here, notice that the influence of the filibuster is distinct from the role of the filibuster described in Krehbiel's pivotal politics (1998). The central point in the appointments context is that the filibuster constrains the ability of a noncentrist president to use his agenda-setting powers to appoint noncentrist judges. By contrast, Krehbiel assumes a median proposer and therefore studies the role of the filibuster in preventing policies from converging to the center. The role of the filibuster in politics very much depends on the identity of the proposer. With respect to judicial appointments, the filibuster thus illustrates a separation-of-powers rationale for the maintenance of internal legislative rules

that endow nonmedian members with formal veto authority (de Figueiredo, Jacobi, and Weingast 2006).

26. Adding the majority-party constraint to these two models does not alter the basic conclusion that removing the filibuster induces a shift from a unimodal to a bimodal distribution of appointee policy preferences.

References

Aldrich, John A., and David W. Rohde. 1995. "Theories of the Party in the Legislature and the Transition to Republican Rule in the House." Presented at the annual meeting of the American Political Science Association, Chicago.

———. 1998. "Measuring Conditional Party Government." Presented at the annual meeting of the American Political Science Association, Chicago.

Bailey, Michael A. 2007. "Comparable Preference Estimates across Time and Institutions for the Court, Congress, and Presidency." *American Journal of Political Science* 51 (3): 433–48.

———. 2012. "Measuring Court Preferences, 1950–2011: Agendas, Polarity and Heterogeneity." Typescript, Georgetown University.

Caldeira, Gregory, and John Wright. 1998. "Lobbying for Justice: Organized Interests, Supreme Court Nominations, and the United States Senate." *American Journal of Political Science* 42 (2): 499–523.

Cameron, Charles, Albert Cover, and Jeffrey Segal. 1990. "Senate Voting on Supreme Court Nominees: A Neoinstitutional Model." *American Political Science Review* 84 (2): 525–34.

Congressional Record. 2003. U.S. Congress, July 30. https://www.congress.gov/congressional -record/2003/07/30.

Cox, Gary, and Mathew D. McCubbins. 2005. *Setting the Agenda: Responsible Party Government in the U.S. House of Representatives.* New York: Cambridge University Press.

de Figueiredo, Rui J. P., Jr., Tonja Jacobi, and Barry Weingast. 2006. "The New Separation of Powers Approach to American Politics." In *Handbook of Political Economy,* edited by Barry R. Weingast and Donald Wittman. New York: Oxford University Press, 220–22.

Epstein, Lee, Rene Lindstadt, Jeffrey A. Segal, and Chad Westerland. 2006. "The Changing Dynamics of Senate Voting on Supreme Court Nominees." *Journal of Politics* 68 (2): 296–307.

Epstein, Lee, Andrew D. Martin, Jeffrey A. Segal, and Chad Westerland. 2007. "The Judicial Common Space." *Journal of Law, Economics, and Organization* 23 (2): 303–25.

Epstein, Lee, and Jeffrey Segal. 2005. *Advice and Consent: The Politics of Judicial Appointments.* New York: Oxford University Press.

Giles, Micheal W., Virginia A. Hettinger, and Todd Peppers. 2001. "Picking Federal Judges: A Note on Policy and Partisan Selection Agendas." *Political Research Quarterly* 54 (3): 623–41.

Gold, Martin, and Dimple Gupta. 2005. "The Constitutional Option to Change Senate Rules and Procedures: A Majoritarian Means to Overcome the Filibuster." *Harvard Journal of Law and Public Policy* 28: 205–72.

Gryski, Gerard S., and Gary Zuk. 2008. "A Multi-User Data Base on the Attributes of U.S. Appeals Court Judges, 1801–2000." http://www.cas.sc.edu/poli/juri/auburndata.htm (accessed June 10, 2008).

Jacobi, Tonja. 2005. "The Senatorial Courtesy Game: Explaining the Norm of Informal Vetoes in Advice and Consent Nominations." *Legislative Studies Quarterly* 30 (2): 193–218.

Jo, Jinhee, David M. Primo, and Yoji Sekiya. 2013. *A Dynamic Model of Judicial Appointments.* Unpublished manuscript, University of Rochester.

Johnson, Timothy R., and Jason M. Roberts. 2005. "Pivotal Politics, Presidential Capital, and Supreme Court Nominations." *Congress and the Presidency* 32 (1): 31–48.

Kagan, Elena. 1995. "Review: Confirmation Messes, Old and New." *University of Chicago Law Review* 62 (2): 919–42.

Krehbiel, Keith. 1998. *Pivotal Politics: A Theory of U.S. Lawmaking.* Chicago, University of Chicago Press.

———. 2007. "Supreme Court Appointments as a Move-the-Median Game." *American Journal of Political Science* 51 (2): 231–40.

Kuersten, Ashlyn K., and Susan B. Haire. 2008. "Update to the Appeals Court Database: 1997–2002." http://www.cas.sc.edu/poli/juri/appctdata.htm (accessed June 10, 2008).

Maltese, John Anthony. 2003. "Confirmation Gridlock: The Federal Judicial Appointments Process under Bill Clinton and George W. Bush." *Journal of Appellate Practice and Process* 5 (1): 1–28.

McGinnis, John O., and Michael B. Rappaport. 2005. "The Judicial Filibuster, The Median Senator, and the Countermajoritarian Difficulty." *Supreme Court Review* 2005 (1): 257–305.

Moraski, Bryon J., and Charles R. Shipan. 1999. "The Politics of Supreme Court Nominations: A Theory of Institutional Constraints and Choices." *American Journal of Political Science* 43 (4): 1069–95.

Mullins, Edward M., and Rima Y. Mullins. 1999. "You Better Shop Around: Appellate Forum Shopping." *Litigation* 25 (4).

Perine, Keith. 2006. "Senate Vote 127: Judge Owen Confirmation." *Congressional Quarterly Weekly,* January 9.

Poole, Keith, and Howard Rosenthal. 1997. *Congress: A Political-Economic History of Roll Call Voting.* New York: Oxford University Press.

Primo, David M., Sarah A. Binder, and Forrest Maltzman. 2008. "Who Consents? Competing Pivots in Federal Judicial Selection." *American Journal of Political Science* 52 (3): 471–89.

Rohde, David, and Kenneth Shepsle. 2007. "Advising and Consenting in the 60-Vote Senate: Strategic Appointments to the Supreme Court." *Journal of Politics* 69: 664–77.

Shor, Boris, Nolan McCarty, and Christopher Berry. 2008. "Methodological Issues in Bridging Ideal Points in Disparate Institutions in a Data Sparse Environment." Working paper, University of Chicago, Harris School of Public Policy.

Snyder, Susan K., and Barry R. Weingast. 2000. "The American System of Shared Powers: The President, Congress, and the NLRB." *Journal of Law, Economics, & Organization* 16 (2): 269–305.

Songer, Donald. 2008. "The United States Courts of Appeals Data Base." http://www.cas.sc .edu/poli/juri/appctdata.htm (accessed June 10, 2008).

Spriggs, James F., II, and Paul J. Wahlbeck. 1995. "Calling It Quits: Strategic Retirement on the Federal Courts of Appeal, 1893–1991." *Political Research Quarterly* 48: 573–97.

Stiglitz, Edward H., and Barry R. Weingast. 2010. "Agenda Control in Congress: Evidence from Cutpoint Estimates and Ideal Point Uncertainty." *Legislative Studies Quarterly* 35 (2): 157–85.

Discussion Questions

1. How does the use or threat of the filibuster affect the composition of the federal judiciary?

2. What does the author mean when he distinguishes between confirmation hearings and the confirmation process? Which is more important?

3. How might expectations about the next presidential election affect the politics of judicial appointments?

PART FOUR

REFLECTIONS ON CONGRESS

11

Reflections on My Career in
the House of Representatives

William Clinger

AT ABOUT 10:30 ON THE NIGHT OF November 7, 1994, my life as a member of Congress was turned downside up. For the preceding sixteen years I had been an anonymous spear-carrying extra in a comic opera written and staged by the Democratic majority in the United States House of Representatives. That night I was in a hotel suite in Erie, Pennsylvania, monitoring the vote for my friend Tom Ridge and his race for governor of Pennsylvania, when my chief of staff, Jim Clarke, rushed in from the next room to announce that Republicans had won a majority of seats in the House. Focused as I was on the Ridge race, I assumed he meant the Pennsylvania House, which I knew would be good news for Governor-Elect Ridge. "No, No," Jim said. "It's the U.S. House."

After more than forty years as the House minority party, Republicans were going to run the place, and I, a powerless backbencher, was in line to become chairman of the Government Reform and Oversight Committee (GROC).

I need to put my rise to the chairmanship in context. Oversight of an administration's performance is considered one of the least attractive career paths for a member of Congress, and most members appointed to an oversight committee try to get off as soon as possible and move on to a more glamorous committee, like Appropriations or Ways and Means. I was either too dense or unambitious to realize this. As a result, as members ahead of me in seniority moved on, I kept rising in the pecking order and was the most senior member of the committee on the night of November 7, 1994.

Early on in our tenure as the majority party we realized that the House had become a very different place, not just because of the switch in control. Certain time-honored traditions were changing or forgotten. Seniority was no longer a sinecure for advancement. Regular order, that is, the orderly progression of legislation from subcommittee to full committee to Rules Committee to the House floor, was weakening. Power was shifting from committee chairs to the leadership, and in some cases from the leadership down Pennsylvania Avenue to the White House. Finally, negotiation and compromise between the majority and the minority were becoming much more difficult.

These developments became apparent during the months-long debates over elements of the "Contract with America." The contract was a laundry list of conservative reforms that Republicans ran on in 1994 and that they pledged to enact into law in the first one hundred days of the new Republican Congress. Several of these items were z to GROC to bring to the floor for passage.

Within a week or so after the House convened in January 1995, it became apparent how much the House culture had changed since I was first sworn in as a member in 1977. For example, at that time freshmen members were welcomed to be seen but not heard and to demonstrate obsequious deference to senior members at all times.

Deference was not something the freshmen Republican members paid much if any attention to in 1995: for example, five of them were assigned to my committee, and I arranged to meet with each of them individually. My stated objective was to find out how the committee could be helpful to them in their reelection campaigns. My unstated objective was to ensure that they would be team players in the battles that lay ahead, that is, to vote the way I directed them to. I explained that our committee would be taking the lead on significant albeit controversial legislation and we might have to negotiate and compromise from time to time in order to carry the day.

To a man, these rookies told me that they had not come to Washington to compromise and they would not compromise with Democrats or even with the Republican leadership, for that matter. The first item on the committee's agenda was to approve a change in the federal employees' pension plan as a cost-saving measure. I was prepared to give two veteran members a pass on voting for the proposal because each represented a district with a high percentage of federal employees who would not look kindly on a prospective reduction of their pensions. That meant I needed all other Republican members to be in favor. Result? I was unable to move the bill out of committee to the floor because my five freshmen wanted much, much deeper cuts than the bill provided, and they accordingly cast nay votes. Further action on the bill was kicked up to the leadership.

This was an early example of the shifting of power from the committee and "regular order" level to the leadership level, and a harbinger of things to come. It was caused less by a usurpation of power by the Speaker but rather by the committee's inability to act. Political scientists, media, and congresspeople themselves decry the collapse of regular order in dealing with legislation and the shifting of power from authorizing committees to party leadership for the initiation, consideration, and passage of legislation.

I, too, would like to see congressional authority restored to a position of prominence in the initiation of policy. I am, however, alarmed by overtures of groups such as the Freedom Caucus seeking more seats for their members on important authorizing committees. The Freedom Caucus is a group of ultraconservative Republicans who are basically against everything Democrats want to do and much of what Republicans want to do as well. Their allegiance is to organizations like the Heritage Foundation, a conservative think tank, or to Citizens United, an ultraconservative political action committee, rather than to the Republican Party. The less Congress does, the better, as far as the Freedom Caucus is concerned. I fear that their objective in seeking more important committee seats is not to facilitate a legislative program but to derail it by blocking passage at the committee level.

Congressional Reform

I am a skeptic when it comes to systemic congressional reform of government entities and practices. Resistance to change is epidemic in Washington and comes not just from the federal bureaucracy but from the private sector and Congress itself, as well. In fact, Congress may be the most serious deterrent to change. For example, the Economic Development Administration (EDA), created by the Johnson administration as part of its war on poverty and situated in the Department of Commerce, is a case in point. I first came to Washington to serve as chief counsel of the EDA in 1972. I did not expect to stay long at the agency, because the Ford administration was determined to abolish it. The EDA's mission was to provide economic assistance and professional advice to businesses in depressed areas of the country in an effort to create new jobs. The Ford administration concluded that the EDA was ill equipped to identify potential winners and sure losers in distributing financial aid and should be terminated.

It didn't happen, and in the following forty-four-plus years every Republican president from Reagan to George W. Bush has tried to get rid of it and failed. The EDA survives because a strong bipartisan majority of both the House and Senate love it. It is one of the few programs for which members are able to announce and take full credit for bringing home the bacon to their districts.

Congressional resistance was also chiefly responsible for foiling Republican plans to eliminate the Department of Commerce and divvy up its many components among the surviving departments. The Government Reform and Oversight Committee (GROC) was charged by Speaker Gingrich to orchestrate its demise. As chairman of the committee I spent hours in the winter and spring of 1995 meeting with my fellow committee chairs, each of whom had jurisdiction over one or more components of Commerce. Each viewed eliminating the department as a threat to his jurisdiction and, hence, power, and together they threw up roadblock after roadblock to thwart the elimination effort, and at the end of the day, they won. Meanwhile the Department of Commerce continues to lumber along with its hodgepodge of unrelated entities ranging from the EDA to patents to foreign trade, weights and measures, and more.

A subtler example of congressional intransigence when it comes to reform arose out of oversight hearings regarding the Branch Davidian disaster in Waco, Texas, in 1993. The conflict was prompted by a standoff between the FBI and the Branch Davidians, a cultlike religious sect, which began after four Alcohol, Tobacco, Firearms and Explosives (ATF) agents were killed by members of the cult when they tried to act on a search warrant. The FBI took over and mounted a siege of the compound. After fifty-one days, they had had enough and tried to bulldoze their way in. The Davidians set a number of fires in the compound, and a firefight developed. Between the fires and the gunfire, seventy-six men, women, and children were killed.

Investigations into what went wrong and why and who was to blame blossomed in the aftermath of the debacle. Among them was a joint investigation conducted by the GROC and the Judiciary Committee. Over a period from April 1995 to May 1996, we interviewed over one hundred witnesses and conducted ten days of hearings. After all that, as far as I was concerned, the whole exercise was a waste of time and an excellent example of how not to conduct oversight.

The initial decision to have a joint investigation involving two standing committees was doomed from the start. The GROC is almost exclusively an oversight committee with very limited legislative authority. Its primary function is to oversee the administration of legislation enacted by others and to make recommendations for reform and change.

The Judiciary Committee, on the other hand, is primarily a legislative committee and has limited oversight authority. It has authorizing jurisdiction over the FBI, among other agencies, and woe betide any other committee that might try to make inroads into its business. In essence, the FBI is a ward of the Judiciary Committee, which tends to be an overprotective guardian.

At some point during our investigation I realized that our friends on the Judiciary Committee were reluctant to criticize the actions taken by the FBI during the siege and the ultimate deadly fire and firefight. The GROC's efforts to strengthen the report and point out areas where the agency had made critical mistakes were consistently rebuffed. The written report had to be watered down and significantly weakened to get Judiciary members to sign off on it. The opportunity to improve and reform the operating protocols of the FBI was lost.

As already noted, the first one hundred days of the first Republican-led Congress in forty years were devoted to passing the Contract with America proposals. The specific items assigned to the GROC were the Unfunded Mandates bill, the Line Item Veto bill, and a proposed constitutional amendment requiring the federal government to operate under a balanced budget, as almost all the states are required to do. All three were relatively popular conservative reform measures.

The Unfunded Mandates bill was first up. This was a bill honoring the Republican pledge to get the federal government off the backs of state and local governments by strictly limiting the mandates it placed on them unless it paid for them. As a reaction to the Democratic procedure when the Democrats were in control of limiting the number and scope of amendments that could be offered, Republicans opted for open rules allowing any and all amendments to be considered.

I managed the bill on the floor and spent between six to ten hours a day for eight days batting down thirty amendments seeking to exempt everything from health care to the environment from the requirement that the federal government pay for any mandates. None of the amendments passed. The bill passed on a party-line vote, and the Republican leadership reverted to closed rules for consideration of the remaining Contract with America bills.

The Line Item Veto bill, which gave the president authorization to veto a limited number of items from appropriations bills he found to be wasteful or ineffective, was next up, followed by the balanced budget amendment. Because few amendments were allowed, both were approved in relatively short order.

Looking back on the measures that came out of the GROC, now decades after their passage in the House, what was accomplished? Not very much, I am afraid. The Senate never took up the balanced budget amendment. The Supreme Court declared the line-item veto unconstitutional on the grounds that it violated the separation of powers, and the Unfunded Mandates bill turned out to be a toothless tiger with no power to compel compliance with the law.

On balance, I think my skepticism about the ability of Congress to bring about reform is well founded. Still, I don't think it should stop trying. More about how it might go about doing so lies ahead.

Private Sector Impediments to Reform

Other resistance to change and reform in government comes from private sector sources. It is no secret that the reason there has been no significant gun-control legislation in decades despite the approval of a large majority of Americans is that the NRA uses both carrot and stick to work its will in Congress to block it. The carrot is in the form of generous campaign contributions to members; the stick is in the form of threats to oppose noncompliant members in their next election as well as to shut off future contributions.

Likewise, action on any attempt at tort reform, also favored by a solid majority of Americans, goes nowhere because the American Trial Lawyers Association (now named the American Association of Justice) uses identical tactics to keep the issue on the very back burner.

In my own experience, outside pressure on members nearly derailed an effort to reform government procurement practices to make them more like those of the private sector. Again, the reform effort was prompted by citizen outrage at the excessive cost the government was paying for almost everything from toilet seats to F-16s, which the GROC revealed in a series of hearings in 1994 and 1995. The basic problem was that Congress over many years had added more and more hoops for prospective suppliers to jump through. A potential bidder had to certify compliance with a host of regulations dealing with things like the environment, safety, fair labor practices, archaeological protection, and on and on. All of this took time and cost money.

As a result, fewer and fewer firms were willing to submit bids. With less competition and the increased cost of compliance for those still willing to compete, the cost for just about everything kept going up and up.

In the beginning we didn't realize how intense the opposition might be to what we were trying to do. *How could anyone be opposed to getting the best bargain for the taxpayer's money?* we thought. We were wrong.

In the first place, the firms still doing business with the government didn't want any change at all. After all, they had an inside track. Any radical changes in procurement threatened them by attracting more competition and would reduce their ability to game the system.

But it wasn't only the powerful private interests that wanted to preserve the status quo. There was substantial opposition from within the federal bureaucracy itself. Many procurement officers also felt threatened by change. The Judiciary Committee was proposing to give them greater authority (and opportunity) to make decisions. We suspected that they feared it would make it more difficult to pass the buck if one of their decisions turned out badly.

We spent some months putting together the bill and lining up support, including from the Clinton administration and most importantly the Armed Services Committee, which procures more goods and services than any other part of government, and from its chairman, Floyd Spence of South Carolina.

Early in the first session of the 104th Congress, Chairman Spence and I introduced our bill with all of the procurement streamlining provisions we hoped to attach to that year's National Defense Authorization bill on the floor. This was a "must pass" bill. After all, who is going to vote against national defense? If we could attach our bill to the National Defense Authorization express train, it was a slam dunk—sure to pass. I offered our bill as an amendment to the defense bill—and it got killed!

It took us some time to discover what had gone wrong. Our enemies were more numerous than we had expected, but our principal and most effective opponents were the lead lobbyists for AT&T and Sprint. These high-powered operatives managed to convince the chairman of the House Small Business Committee as well as a significant number of members that our bill was not just bad, but that it would be disastrous for small businesses.

Talk about chutzpah (also hypocrisy). Here were two Fortune 500 corporations shedding crocodile tears over how small businesses were going to be shut out of doing business with the federal government. What they failed to mention was that at the time, they had exclusive contracts to provide virtually all telecommunication services to the government. The contracts were due to be rebid in three years' time, and these two champions of small business did not want contract bidding procedures changed in any way. They had an inside track and wanted to keep it that way.

This story had a happy ending. Three months after our defeat we brought the measure to the floor as a freestanding bill, which we again planned to attach to the Senate-passed National Defense Authorization bill in conference with the House. This time the gutting amendment that passed earlier was defeated, the bill passed as part of the defense bill, and it became law.

Balance of Power—Congress versus the President

As already noted, the gridlock in Congress seems to get worse and worse. Congress appears unwilling or unable to deal with important issues like health, safety, income disparity, infrastructure, and tax reform. This has led to a growing public contempt for Congress and its acquiescence in the presidential assumption of increasing power. How can Congress go about trying to redress the balance of power between itself and the president? There are at least three areas where Congress could set about reasserting lost power: First, by restoring member discipline. Second, by overhauling the way oversight is conducted. And third, by encouraging members to aggressively solicit campaign contributions from small donors in lieu of large donations from special interests.

Discipline

First and perhaps most important, leaders need to deal with the unruliness of a significant number of their members. The lack of discipline is apparent in both parties, but more noticeable in the majority party.

In part the fraying of discipline in any House majority accelerates the longer it is in power. During its forty years in the minority Republicans came to realize that they needed to be united if they were to have any influence at all. Thus when the party came to power in 1994 its members supported the leadership's agenda almost unanimously, even though the membership was much more politically diverse than it is today, ranging from liberals to moderates to ultra-conservatives.

With each passing year in control, however, seams and cracks began to develop in Republican unanimity, and leaders found it increasingly difficult to marshal enough votes to advance the party's agenda. Now, more than twenty years later, the party having been out of power in the meantime and now back in again, the lack of discipline is immeasurably worse. The Republican party is now really two parties: one that might be called the establishment party, led by Majority Leader Mitch McConnell (R-KY) and his team, and the other a rogue element mostly evident in the House, called the Freedom Caucus, composed of thirty or so members with perhaps two dozen tea party acolytes. As previously noted, their allegiance is devoted to entities other than the party, which often exhort them to vote against even their own leadership (as they did with respect to Speaker Ryan) and the party agenda.

The Freedom Caucus is the principal cause of gridlock and inaction in the House and responsible for much of the contempt and distrust many Americans have for Congress, which is fostered in turn by a concession Speaker Ryan was pressured to make when he assumed the speakership. He agreed to continue enforcing the so-called Hastert Rule, named for former Speaker Dennis Hastert. The rule dictates that no bill can be brought to the floor for a vote unless a majority of the majority in the House is prepared to vote for the measure. Accordingly, the thirty-plus members of the Freedom Caucus kept measures they opposed off the floor by vowing to keep their Speaker from getting a majority of a majority to pass them.

Nancy Pelosi (D-CA), who is the current Speaker of the House and faces her own internal party opposition, could decide not to enforce the rule in all instances. This would free her to seek bipartisan support for passage. The argument against taking such action is that it would undermine the power of the majority and shift significant power for managing the floor to the minority. But, in fact, as hostage to the Freedom Caucus or other caucuses/factions, a Speaker is unable to manage the floor already. Used sparingly, the threat of seeking bipartisan support would be a powerful tool in bargaining with recalcitrant members, leading to passage of legislation, and would refute the perception of many that today's House of Representatives is an ineffectual "do-nothing" institution.

In addition, a practice that has fallen into disuse but which should be reinstated to foster better discipline among the members is to withhold or revoke a member's committee assignments as punishment for persistent defiance of party leadership and its agenda. An individual member's defiance because of strongly held views or principles is one thing and can be tolerated. But when the defiance is part of a persistent group effort to prevent the orderly operation of Congress, a price needs to be paid.

Another concern about the gradual shifting of power from the legislative to executive branch is that Congress should stop voluntarily ceding power to the president, which adds to the perception of many that Congress is gradually becoming an irrelevant institution. Both political parties have been guilty of turning over pieces of congressional authority to the president. The Republican Party did so in 1995 with passage of the line-item veto, authorizing the president to unilaterally veto specific items in appropriation bills. The spending or not spending of money is a responsibility given to Congress and specifically to the House of Representatives under the Constitution. It was startling that Congress would actively seek to abridge its responsibility. It was especially quixotic since in this instance it was a Republican-controlled Congress ceding power to a Democratic president, which President Clinton happily took advantage of in vetoing a number of line-item appropriations. It took the Supreme Court to the save the party from itself by ruling that the measure was an unconstitutional violation of the separation of powers

The Dodd-Frank Wall Street Reform and Consumer Protection Act was a Democratic majority's ceding of power to the executive. The bill created the Consumer Financial Protection Bureau (CFPB), by which Congress ceded power to the bureau to appropriate money for its operations from the Federal Reserve without the consent or approval of Congress. Again it was the Supreme Court that put at least a temporary halt to the provision by declaring this funding practice unconstitutional.

Oversight

As another way to improve the "brand" of Congress as a responsible partner in shaping policy, there is a need to restructure the way it conducts oversight of administration activities as well as itself. As noted earlier, the most effective oversight occurs when Congress is controlled by one party, and the White House by the other. House and Senate oversight committees are then most vigorous in examining and critiquing administration programs and operations, hopefully with its cooperation or by exercising their subpoena powers if not.

Also, effective oversight most often occurs when the overseer has no legislative relationship with the overseen activity. Only then is the resulting report likely to be balanced in reaching conclusions and making recommendations for reform.

Oversight is less thorough or intense when one party controls both Capitol Hill and the White House. In that case the majority is often reluctant to conduct oversight if it is liable to make the administration look bad, and the minority is powerless to do so without the support of the majority. Britain's House of Commons is beset by more scandals than our House of Representatives largely because the majority party controls both itself and 10 Downing Street and there is no incentive for it to conduct zealous oversight.

The weakness of the minority in conducting meaningful oversight where the administration is controlled by the opposite party was brought home to me in 1994 when I wrote White House Counsel Bernard Nussbaum to point out that Hillary Clinton's expansive task forces working on a universal health-care program appeared to be in violation of the Federal Advisory Committee Act (FACA). The act provides that if there are nongovernment employees working on a task force that makes policy recommendations to the president, their names must be made public and meetings they attend must be advertised and open to the public.

In my letter to Mr. Nussbaum I pointed out, very politely I thought, that Mrs. Clinton herself was not a full-time federal employee, and I offered to try to amend FACA to exempt First Ladies from its provisions. Second, I told him, however, that if any members of the task forces were not federal employees, their names needed to be made public together with the time and place of the meetings they attended.

Mr. Nussbaum responded, very snarkily I thought, that the White House deemed that FACA did not apply to the task forces, and, moreover, he did not require any assistance from the minority members of the GROC. I next made him an offer I didn't think he could refuse, unless he wanted to be torn apart by the media and good-government groups, which all favor greater transparency in the way the federal government does business and would take offense at star-chamber task forces shaping health-care policy in secret.

I invited him to come to my office for a chat, and we discussed the matter for about forty-five minutes during which time I retreated to my fallback position that Republicans would not make a big deal out of the fact that Mrs. Clinton was not a full-time federal employee so long as all the names of nonfederal employee members of the task forces were made public in compliance with FACA. Mr. Nussbaum's fallback position was not to fall back. His final words to me with regard to the unidentified task force members were, "Congressman, I don't have to give you those names. I am not going to give them to you and you can't make me give them to you." And of course, he was right. Without the support of the majority chairman and lacking subpoena power, I could not force him to do so.

Fortunately, a court ultimately did compel him to comply, which revealed that the task forces were composed primarily of representatives from left-of-center special-interest groups with no representative from other interests, such as health-care providers or health-insurance companies. As a result there was a groundswell of opposition to the proposal, which became so intense it never even got a vote in either the House or Senate.

An existing rule in the House provides that the chairman of the GROC, or a majority of the majority members on the committee if the chairman is opposed or unavailable, has subpoena power. The rule could be amended to provide the ranking member of the GROC with subpoena power. This would not be as broad a power as the majority's, by not including a majority of the minority, but would ensure that the minority would have the ability to pursue oversight without majority concurrence.

As noted earlier, my experience working on the joint Judiciary Committee–GROC regarding the Branch Davidian debacle convinced me that authorizing committees are unsuitable overseers of administration entities within their legislative jurisdiction. A threat to reduce or eliminate either money or power of an agency under its authority is an attack on the committee itself. This fact seriously tempers a committee's enthusiasm for undertaking any oversight that could end up eroding its power or prestige.

Failure to engage in robust oversight is yet another reason for the distrust of Congress and the public's willingness to accede to presidential aggrandizement. For that reason congressional oversight should be conducted exclusively by an expanded GROC, which has no legislative authority, and the numerous oversight subcommittees should be dissolved.

In addition, an expanded GROC should have the authority to require a response proposing legislative action from the appropriate authorizing committee. Under present practice, such a GROC report is provided to the overseen agency and its authorizing congressional committee. No action or even response is required from either entity, and too often the report is put on the shelf to gather dust.

In the late 1980s, for example, the GROC undertook a series of hearings examining the government's stewardship of Native American tribal trust funds. Sometime in the 1890s, the Department of the Interior undertook the management of moneys earned by tribes and their individuals for timber sales, oil, gas, and mineral royalties, and grazing fees on tribal lands. The Bureau of Indian Affairs was the agency assigned by Interior to oversee the operation and keep track of how much was earned and who earned it. The problem was that the bureau didn't ever actually do it. No tribe or individual Native Americans knew or could find out what they were entitled to. The GROC held its first hearing on the problem in 1992 and issued a critical report with recommendations on how the bureau should proceed to rectify it. When no progress ensued, the committee held another hearing—and then another and yet another. Still no progress cleaning up the mess.

Somewhere along the way a group of Native Americans sued the government, claiming Native Americans collectively were owed millions, if not billions, of dollars. They demanded an accounting followed by payment. In the course of the lawsuit the judge became so furious that he cited two Interior secretaries—a Democrat in the Clinton administration and a Republican in the Bush administration—for contempt of court because of their failure to act.

Subsequently, Native Americans won a judgement in 2004, twelve years after the GROC initiated its oversight of the bureau, but it was not until seventeen years after the GROC's initial hearing that the government finally negotiated a settlement of all claims for about $3 billion. The case is an example of the limitations of the GROC's oversight power. It can expose government ineptitude but it is unable to fix it.

While the GROC does not and should not have the power to mandate compliance with recommendations in its reports, it should, however, be entitled to a response indicating why the recommendations will or will not be adopted. Hopefully this should lead to a dialogue between the GROC and the authorizing committee and to an amended report, which the latter would be willing to act on.

Campaign Funding

Respect for and trust in the U.S. Congress are low, according to Gallup poll-
ing, with just 11 percent of Americans expressing strong confidence in the institution. Congress and its members have never been held in high esteem. Mark
Twain always got a good laugh when he declared that "there is no distinctly native American criminal class except Congress." But what we have today seems
to be a deeper and more profound distrust of what is supposed to be the representative body of a vibrant democracy. According to a 2019 Gallup Poll annual
survey, confidence in the institution has not been above 20 percent since 2005.

The distrust, it can be argued, is misplaced and evokes a line from the old
Pogo cartoon: "We have met the enemy and he is us." As the founders intended, the present-day Congress quite accurately reflects the state of the union
and its people, who are divided almost equally between those on the right of the
political center line and those to the left.

The worrisome thing for citizens is not that the Congress has become a rogue
body unmindful of their concerns. Rather, as referenced throughout this chapter, they should be worried about an ongoing realignment shifting power from
Congress to the president, which is accelerated by their distrust of the former.
Congressional weakness enables the president to assert power. His or her approval rating almost always waxes when Congress's wanes.

Two ways by which presidents try to exercise power in reaction to congressional failure to act or in defiance of congressional action he disapproves of are
executive orders and signing statements. Executive orders are legally binding
orders issued by the president to direct federal agencies in the execution of
congressionally established laws and policies. Signing statements are written
comments issued at the time of signing legislation. Both have been used by presidents to change or ignore congressional intent in the administration of laws.
Controversy over the use of them occurs most often when Congress is controlled by one party, and the executive branch by the other.

In the last months of the Obama administration, with his approval rating in
the mid-fifties, the president took aggressive action by executive orders and
signing statements to address issues that he said Congress had refused to act on
or neglected. He used executive power to commit the United States to the Paris
Agreement on climate change, to institute the Clean Power Plan to reduce emis-
sions, to reduce new energy exploration in the Arctic Ocean and new coal leases

on government lands, to cap many student loan payments, and to tighten rules on gun sales. The administration made it harder for corporations to use so-called inversions to lower their taxes, required retirement-investment advisers to eliminate conflicts of interest, and made more than four million workers eligible for overtime pay.

He was able to seize the high ground with his bully pulpit because he realized that congressional gridlock gave him more room in which to operate and thus to embellish his legacy. During the first weeks of his administration, President Trump followed the same pattern.

As noted previously, in recent years the collapse of regular order in congressional operations and its increasing inability to function have seriously eroded public respect for Congress. Republicans have received much of the blame for the periodic shutdowns that have occurred when they were in control, during the George H. W. Bush administration and most recently in 2018 (ending in 2019).

The empowerment of the executive branch at the expense of the congressional branch is the result. The challenge for congressional leaders is how to restore public confidence in the body so that it regains parity with the president in shaping policy.

Disparity in the source of funding for President Obama's campaigns for president and the campaigns of most members of Congress may have something to do with their respective approval ratings. Much of Obama's campaign funds came from millions of small, average-American donors, while campaign funds for members of Congress come largely from organizations with intense interest in what Congress does or doesn't do—large corporations, trade associations, unions, and other special interests. Whom do you trust more? The president who is supported with money by millions of people just like you, or the congresspersons who get four- or five-figure donations from special interests with issues pending in Congress?

The answer seems pretty obvious, which is why confidence in Congress is at such a low ebb. It has gotten worse since the Supreme Court ruling in its *Citizens United* decision, which concluded that political contributions were exercises in free speech and if limited would violate the First Amendment. Neither a reversed decision by a future court nor a constitutional amendment to do so is likely anytime soon.

This has led to the formation of a bipartisan group of over one hundred former congressmen and -women and governors who are exploring possible ways to limit the seriously ill effects of unlimited amounts of money sloshing around in the political world. One approach would be to provide a robust incentive for individual citizens to make political contributions to candidates of their choice. As President Obama demonstrated in 2008 and 2012, and as Senator Sanders verified in the 2016 primaries, fundraising on the Internet is an inexpensive and effective way to raise money for political campaigns.

Candidates elected in campaigns financed primarily by individual citizens would address the perception problem that presidents are elected by the people but members of Congress are elected by special interests. It could also in time hopefully redress the balance and restore the congressional "brand" as a co-equal and not a subservient branch of government.

Most members are honest and trustworthy and do not sell their votes to the highest bidder. But in politics perception is reality, and for many the perception is that today's members are the "best Congress that money can buy," as American humorist Will Rogers once opined.

The Internet provides the means for people to easily contribute to their preferred candidates. Congress should consider enacting legislation that will provide an incentive for people to contribute to their preferred candidates. And if winning candidates are supported primarily by modest individual contributions rather than by special interests, the perception that Congress is a corrupt institution would hopefully fade.

I hope that these reflections, based upon an eighteen-year career in Congress, will suggest some of the ways that Congress can recapture its constitutional position as the First Branch of American government.

Discussion Questions

1. How did the end of strict seniority rules affect the balance of power between congressional committee chairs and the Speaker?
2. What does the author mean by "regular order?" (See chapter 5 of the 2019 book *Congress: The First Branch.*)
3. What does the author see as the main impediments to congressional reform?

12

The Future of Congress

Tom Manatos

FOR ELEVEN YEARS, I WORKED ON Capitol Hill and had a front-row seat to witness history and the inner workings of Congress. This is the reason I know that Congress matters. I started as Nancy Pelosi's (D-CA) staff assistant in the first year of her being the first woman to assume congressional leadership as minority whip and then to become the first woman Speaker of the House. It was interesting to watch members of Congress react to a female telling them what to do for the first time in history, which was different for the institution. But along with that, we were in the middle of a time when congressional leadership's power and influence seemed to continue to grow. I became a senior advisor and liaison to House Democrats on behalf of Speaker of the House and minority leader Pelosi as well as Democratic National Committee chair Debbie Wasserman Schultz. I continue to work in and around the institution as vice president of government relations at Spotify, and before that as the director of government affairs at the Internet Association, a trade association representing the world's leading Internet companies. During the time I was working on the Hill, the institution passed a number of historic pieces of legislation, including the Patient Protection and Affordable Care Act (popularly known as "Obamacare"), the Wall Street Reform and Consumer Protection Act (popularly known as "Dodd-Frank"), and the American Recovery and Reinvestment Act of 2009. It also dealt with controversial issues such as the Iraq War, immigration, gun control, abortion, and equal rights for the LGBTQ community.

If you look back in history, the committee structure in Congress had much more power than it has today. Traditionally, the leaders in Congress set the schedule for the institution and asked the committees what priorities they had. They negotiated the timing of those priorities but really left it up to the committees as to what types of legislation they would produce. The end result of the committees' work made it to the House or Senate floor, and then those committee leaders managed the floor, including putting together the coalitions to pass the bill, made up of members from both political parties. They also negotiated conference reports and the final legislative product that made it to the president's desk. In those times—and I think this is part of the reason for the shift to a largely powerful leadership, which dictates most of the agenda—there was bipartisanship in Congress. Back then you had committee chairs willing to work with the ranking member and vice versa. You had the minority party willing to work with the majority party to create winning coalitions within the committee that hashed out the final results of that committee legislation.

In today's partisan Congress, most major bills that have committee markups are passed by a straight party-line vote. One of the main reasons for this behavior is that the minority party understands that its most likely path back to the majority is to oppose everything the majority does in order to create a clear contrast. Another reason is that with the growth of gerrymandering, congressional districts are more partisan. Therefore each member of Congress has less incentive to appeal to the other party and has more incentive to appeal to his or her party's base.

Due to the partisan nature of the committee process and these straight party-line votes, the majority leadership has to cobble together support mostly from its own party in order to pass the legislation on the House or Senate floor. Since the responsibility of passing the legislation on the floor lies with majority leadership, those leaders often dictate what the bill looks like, even during the committee process. In contrast to decades of bipartisan coalitions passing bills, today's congressional leadership mostly decides whether to go forward with a bill on the floor based on the Hastert Rule, known as the "majority of the majority." The Hastert Rule operates under the assumption that if a majority of members of the majority party would support the legislation, it is likely to pass with most or all of that party's support. The rule also limits the minority party's influence on the legislative process and does not allow for it to take credit for the passage of legislation since a majority of the majority party always voted for the passed legislation. This also allows for the minority party to vote against most majority-backed legislation since it can claim its ideas weren't considered or included in the legislation.

I saw this scenario play out when I was lucky enough to be a part of Speaker Pelosi's leadership team that helped get legislation passed on the House floor. In the case of health-care reform and the resulting Affordable Care Act, if the Republicans had been willing to participate in the crafting of the legislation and have some of their members vote for passage, the bill would not have had to be shaped so strongly by Speaker Pelosi. In fact, some parts of the eventual Obamacare law were conservative ideas from the 1990s of how to reform the health-care system. But due to the partisan nature of Congress since the mid-1990s, the minority party decided to withhold all of its support from major reform in order to create a clear contrast from the majority party that it could capitalize on in the next election.

Even though Pelosi knew she wouldn't have any Republican support, she had a large, 256-member Democratic majority from which to try to get 218 votes. The difficulty for her was that 40–50 Democratic members represented traditional Republican districts where a majority of their constituents were Republicans or had voted for Republicans in the past. These members had been elected in the 2008 Obama wave, and Speaker Pelosi had to persuade a certain percentage of those moderate members to vote to pass the health-care-reform law. If the Republicans' goal was to take the majority after the next election, they were smart to not allow a single Republican to vote for the bill, since it forced many Democrats representing traditional Republican districts to vote for Obamacare, which was unpopular with Republicans.

Since Pelosi was dealing with such a small margin for final passage without Republican votes, she, along with Senator Reid and the White House, had to micromanage every step of the legislative process to make sure the final product was able to pass. It took some creative legislating, including using reconciliation (the process that directs committees to report legislation-changing spending, revenue, or the debt limit to conform with the budget resolution), but the final bill passed the House with 220 votes and the Senate with 56 votes.

Before the "Republican Revolution" of 1994, which was led by Speaker Newt Gingrich (R-GA), Congress had a much more emboldened committee process. Especially in the House of Representatives, with a longtime Democratic governing majority, the leadership left the power to the committees because there was more bipartisanship and the large majorities created more room for error. When the Republican Revolution happened, there was a venomous view toward the then-minority Democratic Party for having ruled with an iron fist for so long. Due to this perceived abuse, the Republicans decided to railroad their own agenda through the Congress with disregard for the opinions or votes of the Democratic minority. They did not care about bipartisanship; they only cared about passing their agenda with the votes of their party.

The 1994 Republican Revolution and the governing style of Speaker Gingrich set forth the path of partisan-style governing for future Republican and Democratic majorities. These historic levels of partisanship have led to the strengthening of the congressional leadership and especially the Speaker's office—the "follow the leader" aspect of the new order in Congress that Ginsberg and Hill discuss in their book *Congress: The First Branch* (2019)—and the majority or minority leadership. Speaker Gingrich did give some power to the committees, but equally important is how he started controlling Congress more. After his reign, the successive Republican Speakers and Democratic Speakers continued the same thing. Unless there is some breakthrough in bipartisanship, the Speaker, no matter which party is in control, has to worry about getting 218 votes.

Alongside this kind of calculus for passing new legislation—which is necessary due to the lack of bipartisanship and the resulting shifting in power to the leadership office—is the breaking open of the campaign finance system, where you have historic levels of money in politics. With the Citizens United decision that opened the floodgates to even more money and super PACs, there is no end in sight for even more money in politics. What this means within Congress is that because the Speaker's office and the Senate majority leader's office are more powerful with more money in the political process, they also hold the power of who gets reelected or not. These congressional leadership offices raise significant amounts of money for the party and accordingly have a great deal of say on how that money gets doled out to the reelection campaigns for members. This directly translates into some of the power congressional leaders have over members to get their votes on the floor.

At the same time, there has been a dramatic weakening of the power of the leadership's offices on the legislative side of things due to earmark reform (see chapter 5 in this volume). That is one of the leadership's "carrots and sticks" that have largely gone away, and some argue that this has emboldened those minority parts of each of the caucuses, whether it is the Freedom Caucus or Republican Study Committee of the Republican Conference, or the Progressive Caucus, New Dems, or Blue Dogs of the Democratic Caucus. This means there is only the campaign funding left in the carrot-and-stick basket to "hurt" or punish members for not cooperating with the leadership. A case in point is from when Speaker John Boehner (R-OH) tried to remove one of the members of the Freedom Caucus from one of the plum committee assignments as a disciplinary measure, but was pressured by the caucus and eventually had to put him back on that committee. This type of action never would have happened in the Congresses before the mid-1990s.

Within the legislative process the one thing the leadership had in terms of giving and taking away projects due to bad or good behavior in the eyes of the leadership was rewards based on the earmark process, and they have largely lost that. Those tools are gone, so the only two leadership tools left to get members to do what leadership wants are committee assignments and campaign resources. Due to the power of the hundreds of millions of campaign dollars that Boehner, Ryan, Pelosi, Hoyer, and so on have raised over time, a Speaker does still have the ability to hold that over the members' heads, and the power of that cannot be overstated.

All of these changes in the role of leadership and money within Congress mean that there is a changing role for lobbying, too (also see chapter 6). Due to the lack of major pieces of legislation or large-scale reform coming out of Congress, the lobbying industry has had to show the private sector its worth and that it is getting things done. Some of the largest lobbying firms, over the last eight to ten years, have developed public relations (PR) or communications portions of their firms. This is because they have so little action to show their clients on the legislative side that they need to make "noise" in the public sphere, whether it is in op-eds or articles to accentuate their lobbying capabilities or their messaging to bring attention to their clients' interests.

Nevertheless, the lobbying activity represents a correction or a reaction to the lack of movement on Capitol Hill. The partisanship discussed earlier and the resulting lack of producing bills mean lobbyists have to figure out a different way to lobby. Whether someone is an in-house lobbyist or a contract lobbyist or at a trade association, lobbyists in all settings must set their clients' or membership's expectations on a lower level because not much is happening. Lobbyists generally do not turn to a regulatory ruling or an executive-branch action because they don't have the same weight and power of the law, but when those opportunities are there, people definitely go after them. When one talks about real change, however, it really starts with the legislature. There are exceptions, like an investigative agency (for example, the Federal Trade Commission or the Securities and Exchange Commission) going after a certain company or country or individual on a certain action or case that agency has made. Absent that, it all begins with Congress.

Former President Barack Obama (D) said time and time again how shocked he was at how weak the office of the presidency is to make change domestically. In light of so many mass shootings during his presidency, he desperately wanted to do something to address gun control. Due to the growing immigration problem, President Obama wanted to do something on immigration. He tried using executive orders in both cases, and none of those actions made the type of change he sought. Despite having the power of the bully pulpit and executive actions, President Obama was not able to effect real change without action by Congress. President Trump is making heavy use of executive orders so far, but the limits of that strategy were also evident early in his administration with the courts stopping enforcement of his initial executive order on immigration. The genius of our founders was to create this system of government with three branches: two of those initiate or effect a change, and the third rules on it. Yet today and in the future, even with a lack of production of bills and new legislation coming out of the Congress, the heart of our democracy still starts and ends on Capitol Hill.

Discussion Questions

1. What are the chief differences Manatos sees between the contemporary Congress and its predecessors?
2. Does Manatos think there is any chance for a reduction in partisan strife in the Congress?
3. What does Manatos mean by "follow the leader" lawmaking? How does this differ from lawmaking by committees?

WILLIAM CLINGER represented Pennsylvania's Fifth District in the U.S. House of Representatives from 1978 to 1996. He was chairman of the House Government Reform and Oversight Committee, vice chairman of the Transportation and Infrastructure Committee, and chairman of the House Wednesday Group. Prior to his congressional service, Mr. Clinger was the chief counsel to the U.S. Department of Commerce, Economic Development Administration. He currently serves as a senior fellow at the Johns Hopkins University Center for Advanced Governmental Studies.

RICHARD DOYLE joined the faculty of the Naval Postgraduate School in 1990 as associate professor of Public Budgeting, retiring in 2012. Between 1987 and 1990, Dr. Doyle was senior analyst for defense on the staff of the Committee on the Budget, United States Senate. The focus of Doyle's teaching, research, and writing is the congressional budget process, budget policy and national security. He received his MA and PhD in political science from the University of Washington and a BS in international affairs from the United States Air Force Academy. He was awarded the National Defense Service Medal, the Vietnam Service Medal, and the Republic of Vietnam Campaign Medal.

LEE DRUTMAN is a senior fellow in the program on political reform at the New America Foundation and a visiting fellow at GuideStar USA. An expert on lobbying, influence, and money in politics, he has been quoted and/or cited in the *New York Times,* the *Washington Post, The Economist, Slate, Mother*

Jones, Vox, Politico, and many other publications, and on *Morning Edition, All Things Considered, Planet Money, This American Life, Marketplace, Washington Journal,* and *The Colbert Report,* among other programs. His book *The Business of America Is Lobbying* won the Robert A. Dahl Award in 2015. Drutman was previously a senior fellow at the Sunlight Foundation. He has also worked in the U.S. Senate and at the Brookings Institution. He holds a PhD in political science from the University of California–Berkeley, and a BA from Brown University.

TOM MANATOS is currently the vice president of government relations for Spotify, the world leader in music streaming. Prior to his position at Spotify, Tom was the vice president of government affairs at the Internet Association, a trade association representing over forty of the world's leading Internet companies. Before joining the tech world, Manatos was a senior advisor to both the Speaker of the House and the chair of the Democratic National Committee as a liaison to members of Congress, senators, local elected officials, and outside stakeholders. Tom has also spent time working on two presidential campaigns, a presidential inauguration, four Democratic conventions, and numerous congressional campaigns. He is founder of tommanatosjobs.com, the top jobs-and-internships list on Capitol Hill in Washington, DC, and in the political and policy world. He holds an MA in government from Johns Hopkins University and a BA from Cornell University.

JOHN RAY is a political science PhD candidate at the University of California–Los Angeles. His research focuses on informal processes in Congress, and the interaction between Congress and the Federal bureaucracy. Find out more about his latest research at jloganray.com.

EDWARD H. STIGLITZ, known as "Jed," is an assistant professor of law and the Jia Jonathan Zhu and Ruyin Ruby Ye Sesquicentennial Fellow at Cornell Law School. His research focuses on administrative law, with an emphasis on the relationship between judicial review and the values of trust and accountability in the administrative state. He also studies legislation and other areas of public law. His work has appeared or is forthcoming in the *Cornell Law Review, Southern California Law Review, Journal of Legal Analysis, Theoretical Inquiries in Law, the Oxford Handbook of Law and Economics, Legislative Studies Quarterly,* and the *NYU Journal of Legislation and Public Policy,* among other journals. His coauthored book on American elections was published by Princeton University Press in 2012.

PAUL WEINSTEIN JR. is the director of the MA in Public Management Program at Johns Hopkins University. A veteran of two presidential administrations, he was senior advisor to the National Commission on Fiscal Responsibility and Reform (Simpson-Bowles). From 2001 to 2008, Weinstein was chief operating officer and senior fellow at the Progressive Policy Institute, and chief analyst at Promontory Interfinancial Network. He is coauthor of the textbook *The Art of Policy Making*. His writing has also appeared in the *Boston Globe,* the *Baltimore Sun, New York Newsday, Forbes, Investor's Business Daily,* and *Politico,* among others.

DANIEL WIRLS is a professor of politics at the University of California–Santa Cruz. He received his PhD in government from Cornell University. His research spans American political history, from the debates at the Constitutional Convention and the evolution of the Senate to the latest developments in military policy. His most recent book is *The Federalist Papers and Institutional Power in American Political Development* (Palgrave Macmillan, 2015). He is also author of *Irrational Security: The Politics of Defense from Reagan to Obama* (Johns Hopkins University Press, 2010) and coauthor of *The Invention of the United States Senate* (Johns Hopkins University Press, 2004).

DONALD R. WOLFENSBERGER is a fellow with the Bipartisan Policy Center, a congressional fellow at the Woodrow Wilson Center, and former staff director of the House Rules Committee. During his twenty-eight years in Congress he assisted the Republican leadership in developing congressional reform proposals to be offered at the beginning of each Congress. He is author of *Congress and the People: Deliberative Democracy on Trial* (2000). His chapter in this volume is adapted from *A Brief History of Congressional Reform Efforts* (February 22, 2013), a background report prepared for use by the Bipartisan Policy Center's Commission on Political Reform.

CREDITS

Chapter 2 is a condensed version of the article by Daniel Wirls, "Staggered Terms for the U.S. Senate: Origins and Irony," *Legislative Studies Quarterly* 40 (2015): 471–97, and is included with the author's permission.

Chapter 3 is from the report *Super PACs in Federal Elections: Overview and Issues for Congress,* by R. Sam Garrett, published in 2013 by the Congressional Research Service of the U.S. Library of Congress, which allows this without granting formal permission. Please note that an updated version of this report was issued in full and can be found at: https://fas.org/sgp/crs/misc/R42042.PDF.

Chapter 4 is based on the report *A Brief History of Congressional Reform Efforts* originally prepared by the author Donald R. Wolfensberger for the Bipartisan Policy Center in 2013 and is included with permission.

Chapter 6 appears by permission of Oxford University Press (www.oup.com), where it was published as chapter 10, "The Business of America Is Lobbying," in Lee Drutman's book *The Business of America Is Lobbying: How Corporations Became Politicized and Politics Became More Corporate* (2015).

Chapter 10 appears with permission of the author, Edward H. Stiglitz, from his article "Appointment Politics and the Ideological Composition of the Judiciary," *Legislative Studies Quarterly* 39 (2014): 27–54.

INDEX

Figures and tables are indicated by f and t following page numbers.